W9-BLW-706

Praise For Value Investing For Dummies

"*Value Investing For Dummies* will educate you, entertain you, and enhance your portfolio and your life!"

> — Scott McKain, Vice Chairman, Obsidian Capital Corporation

"This book has much to offer — fundamentals, useful tools, and practical advice. A useful primer for experienced and novice investors alike."

> — Thomas A. Meyers, CFA, Executive Vice President, Phoenix Investment Partners

"True investing is logical. Speculation is gambling. If you want to profitably invest, let *Value Investing For Dummies* be your guide."

> — Jack Everett, CFP, AIMC

"This book is a must read! What a valuable aid it can be throughout your investing career. Excellent, clear, and insightful!"

> — Tim McCabe, CFP, Atlanta, GA

"Peter Sander and Janet Haley have distilled the reference books and current practice of value investing and present a comprehensive, informative, and, thankfully, entertaining book for the everyday investor seeking insight into the tried and true methods of value investing. Whether one is a novice or an accomplished investor, this book is written to put you in a value investing frame of mind."

> — Linda Wenker Boutin, Vice President of Investments and Financial Advisor, major, multinational brokerage firm

TM

References for the Rest of Us!®

BESTSELLING BOOK SERIES

Do you find that traditional reference books are overloaded with technical details and advice you'll never use? Do you postpone important life decisions because you just don't want to deal with them? Then our *For Dummies*® business and general reference book series is for you.

For Dummies business and general reference books are written for those frustrated and hard-working souls who know they aren't dumb, but find that the myriad of personal and business issues and the accompanying horror stories make them feel helpless. *For Dummies* books use a lighthearted approach, a down-to-earth style, and even cartoons and humorous icons to dispel fears and build confidence. Lighthearted but not lightweight, these books are perfect survival guides to solve your everyday personal and business problems.

Already, millions of satisfied readers agree. They have made For Dummies the #1 introductory level computer book series and a best-selling business book series. They have written asking for more. So, if you're looking for the best and easiest way to learn about business and other general reference topics, look to For Dummies to give you a helping hand.

Wiley Publishing, Inc.

5/09

Value Investing

FOR

DUMMIES®

by Peter J. Sander and Janet Haley

WILEY

Wiley Publishing, Inc.

Value Investing For Dummies®

Published by
Wiley Publishing, Inc.
111 River Street
Hoboken, NJ 07030
www.wiley.com

Copyright © 2002 by Wiley Publishing, Inc., Indianapolis, Indiana

Published by Wiley Publishing, Inc., Indianapolis, Indiana

Published simultaneously in Canada

For general information on our other products and services or to obtain technical support, please contact our Customer Care Department within the U.S. at 800-762-2974, outside the U.S. at 317-572-3993, or fax 317-572-4002.

Wiley also publishes its books in a variety of electronic formats. Some content that appears in print may not be available in electronic books.

Library of Congress Cataloging-in-Publication Data:

Library of Congress Control Number: 2001097471

ISBN: 0-7645-5410-7

Manufactured in the United States of America

10 9 8 7 6 5 4 3

3B/SR/QX/QU/IN

About the Authors

Peter J. Sander is a professional investor and writer living in Granite Bay, California. Peter has been successfully investing and trading stocks for 32 of his 44 years. A native of Ohio with an MBA from Indiana University, Peter previously worked for 20 years as a marketing specialist for a Fortune 50 technology firm. This is his fourth book on personal finance and investing.

Janet Haley is a securities industry professional, currently employed as a regional sales director for a large mutual fund company servicing a broad broker-dealer clientele. Previously she was a regional vice president for the Calvert Group. She has a bachelor's degree in international business and political science from Marymount College in New York and is a Chartered Mutual Fund Counselor with NASD Series 6, 7, and 63 licenses. She is currently working on her MBA and CFP certification.

Publisher's Acknowledgments

We're proud of this book; please send us your comments through our Online Registration Form located at www.dummies.com/register.

Some of the people who helped bring this book to market include the following:

Acquisitions, Editorial, and Media Development

Senior Project Editor: Tim Gallan

Senior Acquisitions Editor: Mark Butler

Copy Editors: Tere Drenth, Ben Nussbaum,

Technical Editors: Bill Urban, Jennifer Ellison

Editorial Manager: Pamela Mourouzis

Editorial Assistant: Carol Strickland

Cover Photos: © Arthur Holeman/ International Stock

Composition

Project Coordinator: Dale White

Layout and Graphics: LeAndra Johnson, Jackie Nicholas, Jill Piscitelli, Jeremey Unger, Mary Virgin, Erin Zeltner

Proofreaders: TECHBOOKS Production Services

Indexer: TECHBOOKS Production Services

Publishing and Editorial for Consumer Dummies

Diane Graves Steele, Vice President and Publisher, Consumer Dummies
Joyce Pepple, Acquisitions Director, Consumer Dummies
Kristin A. Cocks, Product Development Director, Consumer Dummies
Michael Spring, Vice President and Publisher, Travel
Brice Gosnell, Associate Publisher, Travel
Suzanne Jannetta, Editorial Director, Travel

Publishing for Technology Dummies

Richard Swadley, Vice President and Executive Group Publisher
Andy Cummings, Vice President and Publisher

Composition Services

Gerry Fahey, Vice President of Production Services
Debbie Stailey, Director of Composition Services

Contents at a Glance

Cartoons at a Glance

By Rich Tennant

"IT HASN'T HELPED ME SELL MORE HOT DOGS, BUT I'VE HAD SEVERAL INQUIRIES FOR INVESTMENT ADVICE."

page 5

"OUR GOAL IS TO MAXIMIZE YOUR UPSIDE AND MINIMIZE YOUR DOWNSIDE WHILE WE PROTECT OUR OWN BACKSIDE."

page 47

"What made you think you were the one to own and operate a china shop, I'll never know."

page 179

"All right, ready everyone! We've got some clown out here who looks interested."

page 281

"In the interest of a future stock issuance, I highly recommend you NOT use your family name as part of your corporate identity, Mr. Defunct."

page 325

Cartoon Information:
Fax: 978-546-7747
E-Mail: richtennant@the5thwave.com
World Wide Web: www.the5thwave.com

Table of Contents

Introduction

· ·

*B*eautiful early spring day. You stare out the window as the radio drones
in background:

> The Dow finished the day at 9392, down 212 points for the day and six
> points off bear market territory, or down 20% from its high. The NASDAQ
> is down 118 points or 5.2% for the day and 62% from the high set just a
> year ago. The S&P 500 is down 32 points, 3% for the day and almost 30%
> from the high. . . .

Sigh. What happened? Did the value of corporate America just drop 62%? Bricks
and mortar, machines, inventories, human capital, intellectual property — all
left out in last weekend's rain to rust?

No. The assets of corporate America, while perhaps slightly tarnished, did
indeed not corrode into fine black dust. What happened, as most are realizing
post mortem, is that during the final stages of the great 1999-2000 investing
boom, is simple. *Asset prices* — known to most of us as stock prices — simply
got away from *asset value.*

Which leads us to where we're going with this book. *Value Investing For
Dummies* takes you on a journey back to the tried-and-true principles of
valuing a stock as one would value a business. (After all, how can one discon-
nect the two, as a share of stock is a share of a business?) When the price, or
value, of a stock matches the value of a business, the value investor *considers*
buying it. When the price of a stock is *less* than the value of the business, the
value investor warms and may *get excited* about buying it. It may be a true
buying opportunity. And when the price of the stock skyrockets past value of
the company, yes, the value investor *sells* it.

It's good old-fashioned investing. Believe it or not, markets do undervalue
businesses, and do it frequently. For a variety of reasons markets are far
from perfect in valuing companies. And furthermore, because there is no
one secret magic formula for valuing a business, the true value of a stock is a
matter of difference of opinion anyway. All of which serves to make investing
more fun — and profitable — for the prudent and diligent investor who sorts
through available information to best understand a company's value.

A value investor who applies the principles brought forth in this book is
essentially betting with the house. The odds, especially in the long term, are
in your favor. Value investing is an *approach* to investing, an investing *discipline;* it is not a specific formula or set of technologies applied to investing.
It is art and science. It is patience and discipline. Done right, it increases the

odds but doesn't guarantee victory. For you active and day traders, it's a slower ride. But the value approach lets you share in the growth of the American (and world) economy, while also letting you sleep at night.

How to Use This Book

In this book, we present to you the principles and practices of value investing. As with all investing books, you probably shouldn't follow this material to the letter, but rather incorporate it into your own personal investing style. Even if you don't adopt most of the principles and techniques described here, we think your awareness of them will make you a better investor.

Our coverage of value investing visits tools that all but the most inexperienced investors have heard of: annual reports, income statements, balance sheets, P/E ratios, and the like. *Value Investing For Dummies* uses these tools to create a complete, holistic investing approach. We tell you *why* annual reports and information contained therein are important, and *how to use* that information to improve your investing. And it's hardly just annual reports. There are myriad sources of other information, both online and offline, that can greatly enhance your knowledge of a company's prospects and your proficiency as a value investor. We take you through these, too.

What We Assume About You

Value Investing For Dummies assumes some level of familiarity and experience with investments and the world of investing. We assume you understand what stocks are, what the markets are and have already bought and sold some stocks. If you are starting completely from scratch, you may want to refer to Eric Tyson's *Investing For Dummies* (Hungry Minds, Inc.) or a similar introductory treatment of the investing world. Not that what we present here will be "hard" or scary, it will just flow more smoothly with a base level of knowledge.

How This Book Is Organized

Like all *For Dummies* books, this book is a reference, not a tutorial, which means that the topics we cover are organized in self-contained chapters. So you don't have to read the book from cover to cover if you don't want to (but we hope you do, of course). Just pick out the topics that interest you from the Table of Contents or Index and go from there. What follows is a breakdown of what the book covers.

Part I: The What and Why of Value Investing

In Part I, we explain what value investing is (and what it isn't) to give a clear picture to the reader and provide a framework for the rest of the book. We put value investing in context with a discussion of markets, market history, and overall performance, with an emphasis on *market nature* — key market behaviors and quirks that repeatedly, through history, provide opportunities for the value investor. We explore the history of the value investing approach and the fantastic success of some who practice it, notably the master himself, Warren Buffett.

Part II: Fundamentals for Fundamentalists

In Part II, we open the value investor toolbox. First, painful for some but necessary, we engage in a short exploration of investing mathematics and show how a few simple math principles can make you a better investor. Next up is a discussion of information and information sources key to the value investor. Then we dig in further with a tour of the financial statement landscape, including balance sheets, income statements, and cash flow statements. Ratios and ratio analysis are explored as a way to make more sense of these numbers. Finally, we help you to find and interpret non-numeric influences in the value equation.

Part III: So You Wanna Buy a Business?

Out of the frying pan and into the fire. Now we apply the tools as a business buyer would (or should!) to assess or *appraise* the value of a company and relate that value to the stock price. We examine some of the proven methods of business value assessment, including intrinsic value, book value, discounted cash flow, and the strategic profit formula. Then we sprinkle in a dash of intangibles (investors shouldn't live by numbers alone) and discuss buy and sell decisions. To bring these tools and techniques together into a system, we use none other than the full example of the master, Warren Buffett. Finally, to provide practice and reinforcement we provide case studies of value, and for further reinforcement we resort to the age-old technique of showing opposites: examples of *un*value.

Part IV: Becoming a Value Investor

This part offers information on setting goals and developing your own value investing style. We provide some commentary on how to figure out what works best for you. As value investment choices go far beyond common stock, we present chapters describing mutual funds, bonds and convertible securities, real estate and real estate investment trusts, and other specialty investments.

Part V: The Part of Tens

Finally, we give you short lists reviewing characteristics of a good value stock, indications of an overvalued stock, and the habits of successful investors.

Icons Used in This Book

Throughout the book, we flag bits of text with little pictures called *icons*. Here's what they look like and what they mean:

Just as the name suggests: a piece of advice.

The dark side of tip: advice on what to avoid or watch for.

Deeper explanation of a topic or idea. You can usually skip text flagged with this icon if you want to.

Not a must-read but fun, relevant facts to enjoy as you drill through this 300-page book.

If all else fails, and you forget everything else you read, keep this information in mind.

Part I
The What and Why of Value Investing

In this part . . .

We hope to give a clear picture of what value investing is and isn't and also provide a framework for the rest of the book. We put value investing in context with a discussion of markets, market history, and overall performance, with an emphasis on *market nature* — key market behaviors and quirks that repeatedly, through history, provide opportunities for the value investor. We explore the history of the value investing approach and the fantastic success of some who practice it, notably the master himself, Warren Buffett.

Chapter 1

An Investor's Guide to Value Investing

I will tell you we have embraced the 21st century by entering such cutting edge industries as carpet, insulation, and paint.

—Warren Buffett, 2001 annual letter to Berkshire Hathaway shareholders

So you wonder . . . what happened? You look at the numbers, the charts, the graphs. The euphoria of the '90s bull market appears to be at an end. You were once flying high, checking your portfolio daily to see what had grown that day and by how much. JDSU +5, CMRC +6½, EXDS +2½, EMC +3. You totaled everything up monthly, quarterly, and yearly. You could rattle off the doubles, triples, homeruns, and 10-baggers. You bragged to your friends about how your stocks made more money last year than you did. You had a can't-miss attitude towards your stock selections, and you couldn't wait to tell your friends at the water cooler (well, the espresso machine) about your latest stock, your latest success.

But now you're just hanging on. Hoping, as if in an airplane in steep descent, that the pilot indeed has control of the plane and that eventually you will level off and perhaps even climb to a comfortable cruising altitude once again. Wouldn't it be great just to be flying level, not caring about the altitude? You wonder if maybe, blinded by success and the euphoria of the moment, you missed something obvious in your investing practices. You wonder . . .

"Did I get caught up in a frenzy, like so many others have in history? Am I another Dutch tulip bulb trader? Another Florida land speculator? Another 1929 stock speculator? Was I really better than everyone else, a breed apart, or was I just part of the frenzy, part of the times?

"Were my stocks, my portfolio, my investing strategy really a breed apart? Should I have paid $225 for Ariba, $175 for Yahoo, $85 for Amazon, $300 for Microstrategy, $75 for Gadzoox Networks? With no earnings and little-to-no assets (except the cash already invested by others 'in the know')? Should I have believed those who were touting the New Economy in every newspaper and magazine, on every TV show, on Wall Street Week, pontificating that earnings don't matter, interest rates don't matter, that seemingly all the old investing yardsticks had been thrown in the trash heap, and that things 'really are different' this time?

"Did prices get away from value? Should I have been thinking about my investments differently?"

If this sounds like you, you may be an ideal candidate to take up value investing. Or at least learn a little more about it. You're hardly alone — thousands of investors are discussing their investing style with themselves, and many more-experienced investors have gone through this ritual before. If you've seldom or never invested before, you are also an ideal candidate, for a value investing approach will make you less likely to experience the opening scenario. You know what they say about an ounce of prevention.

So what is value investing? It's the subject we take up in depth in this book (which you knew from the title!). In this chapter, we define value investing, explain the value investing approach, and compare the value approach to other investing styles. We also write a little about the traits of a good value investor. This chapter alone won't make you an expert, but it will at least enable you to know what others in the office are talking about when the topic of value investing comes up. The rest of the book is designed to get you to know *more* than the others.

What Is Value Investing?

You were hoping for a simple, straightforward answer to this one. Learn a couple of formulas and go beat the markets once again. Well, partly right. Value investing goes beyond formulas. It's an approach, a style of investing. It doesn't provide a panacea or quick fix to all of your investing problems. Rather, as an approach or style it provides the basis for you, the prudent investor, to apply your skills towards selecting better investments in a more rational, less speculative market.

Buying a business

Here's a definition:

> Value investing is buying stocks as if you were buying the business itself. Value investors emphasize the intrinsic value of assets and current and future profits and pay a price equal to or less than that value.

Okay, sounds good so far. That's what you always did, right? Looked at the profile, looked at the industry, industry position growth rates, analyst ratings, yadda, yadda, yadda. But how closely did you look at the balance sheet? Income statement? Cash flows? Did you compare what you saw to other companies in the industry? Did you try to evaluate what the company was worth? Or did you merely rely on analyst projections of sales growth and income growth rates? Something else? How did you pick that company, anyway?

Moreover, what about the price? If you tried to value the company, did you *then* check to see whether the price was below that value? Anywhere near it? Or did you look at the price first, noting the trend, relative strength over the last 3 months, volume, and it's steady up-and-to-the-right pattern? Did that pattern excite you? Did it cause you to jump on board, hoping that the train wouldn't leave the station without you? If you're in this latter camp, you weren't taking a value approach. And if you were listening to chat rooms and investment "advice" from your room-service personnel, you were far removed from the confines of the value investing world. Not that these habits are necessarily wrong; they simply indicate something other than a value approach.

Take this advice from Warren Buffett: "For some reason, people take their cues from price action rather than from values. What doesn't work is when you start doing things that you don't understand or because they worked last week for somebody else. The dumbest reason in the world to buy a stock is because it is going up."

Making a conscious appraisal

If you were interested in buying a business for yourself, and thought the corner hardware store looked attractive, how much would you be willing to pay for it? You would likely be influenced by the sale price of other hardware stores and by opinions shared by neighbors and other customers. But you would still center your attention on the intrinsic economic value — the worth and profit-generation potential — of that business, and a determination of whether that worth and profit justified the price, before you committed your hard-earned dough.

We value investors like to refer to this as an *appraisal* of the business. We appraise it just as one would appraise a piece of property or a prized antique. In fact, a business appraisal is deeper and more systematic than either of those two examples, as value is assigned to property or antiques mainly by looking at the market and seeing what other houses or vases of similar quality sold for. In the investing arena, there's so much more to go on. There are real facts and figures, all publicly available, upon which the investor can base a true numbers appraisal, an appraisal of *intrinsic* value.

Appraising the value, relating the value to the price, and looking for a good bargain capture the essence of the value approach.

Putting on the pinstripes?

You've heard of the analysts. Those guys (and gals) who raise and lower earnings estimates and offer buy, hold, and sell recommendations. Those guys and gals who occasionally dress their recommendations up as NT neutral, LT accumulate, market outperform, or some other clever euphemism meaning buy, hold, or sell. They often get it right, but you would be surprised at the number of times the experts get it wrong, either making calls on horses already out of the barn or just blindly following the herd wherever it might wander. Our point here is not to flog the analysts, but to point out that, in some sense, at least in normal times, they perform a task akin to value investing. They take a close look at the numbers and the company in their analysis process, but often they're influenced by their peers, their firms, and investor sentiment when making their calls. Whether or not you use or leverage their work is entirely up to you.

The point: Adopting the value investing approach means you'll *become your own investment analyst*. The pay can be good, but isn't guaranteed. One thing for certain: You'll never have to buy or dry clean a Brooks Brothers suit!

Ignoring the market

How can you spot the value investor at a cocktail party? Easy. He's the only one talking about an actual company while all others stand around discussing the stock market.

The bird of a value-investing feather is easily spotted. Focusing on the company itself, *not* on the market is a consistent value investing attribute. As a general rule, value investors ignore the market and could care less what the Dow or NASDAQ do on a particular day. They tune out the analysts, brokers, commentators, chat-roomers, and friends (insofar as their investment advice is concerned, anyway).

Value investors have a long-term focus. And if they've done their homework right, what the market does to their stocks on a daily basis is irrelevant. If the company has value but the stock went down on Tuesday, a value investor feels that it's probably a result of the market misreading the company's value.

Now, to be sure, extrinsic factors can affect stock prices. Interest rates, in particular, can affect not only stock prices but also the true intrinsic value of companies, as the cost of capital rises and falls and the value of alternative investments increases (we explore the details on these later). So while it makes sense to pay some attention to the markets, especially in the long term, daily fluctuations, particularly when they are *just* that, should be ignored. The value investor waits a few years to forever for their investments to mature (bet *that's* a concept some of you haven't thought about in awhile.) The value investor looks for a good price with respect to value, but doesn't try to time the market. If the value is there and the price is right, it will probably be right tomorrow too.

AGAP: Assets and Growth at a Price

To help you remember what value investing is all about (and with so much to remember these days, a little help is probably a good thing), we would like to furnish you with an acronymic handle for the value investing approach: AGAP. Sort of a rule of thumb, or in this case, a rule of mind.

That is to say, the value investing approach is to apply AGAP principles. When examining a company for the first time (or when examining one of those dogs or puppies already lurking in your portfolio), you want to look through the AGAP lens.

- ✔ **Assets.** Does this company have the assets or the worth (deducting liabilities) to prosper in its business?
- ✔ **Growth.** Are there profits, and are profits on a growth path?
- ✔ **At a price.** Finally, considering both assets and growth, is the price right? Is it a *bargain?*

The rest of this book centers around making you a good AGAP investor. You will be able to recognize and value assets and growth, and will gain the ability to assess whether the price is right. Think AGAP as you make all of your investing decisions going forward, and you may save yourself some mouse-finger mistakes in the form of impulsive price- or market-driven investments.

Figuring out what should determine a stock price

Nobody knows what really does determine a stock price. If anyone did, you'd be reading his or her book, not ours. It makes sense at this juncture to add a little financial theory, but only a very little. You see, financial theory, with all its fancy equations and statistical constructs, hasn't really explained much. But we think it's useful to at least be aware of the fundamental basis of a stock price.

Financial scholars suggest that a stock price should be equal to the sum of all cash flows likely to be returned from that investment over the indefinite future, translated to an equivalent present value (A dollar 30 years from now is worth less than a dollar today, but we'll get to that in Chapter 4).

In the short term, this cash flow usually occurs in the form of dividends. In the long term, this cash flow is made up of dividends, but also includes proceeds from divesting assets to shareholders or proceeds if the company is acquired for cash or securities by another company. These cash flows are virtually impossible to estimate precisely, as they not only depend on the company's performance over a long time but also on management's policy towards payout. Nevertheless, this long-term view of value should be kept in the back of our minds. Enough theory for now.

Evaluating your values

Value can be defined in many, many ways. Kind of like *pleasure*, the term probably means something different to each one of us. Investors of all feathers attach different meanings — a day trader can look at a small uptick and call a stock a value at a current price. Even among value investors, the definition of the word might vary. Not to settle the issue here (we can't), but we thought additional perspective might be in order. Timothy Vick, in his book *Wall Street on Sale* (McGraw-Hill, 1999) provides a few definitions of value that are recognized by U.S. civil law:

✔ *Fair market value* is whatever someone will be willing to pay for a similar asset — a.k.a. market value.

✔ *Book value* is a company's net worth on an *accounting* basis, which may differ from true financial value because of accounting rules, timing, and so on.

✔ *Liquidation value* (which is very subjective and hard to predict) is what a company would be worth if all the assets were sold

✔ *Intrinsic value* is "what an appraiser could conclude a business is worth after undertaking an analysis of the company's financial position," based on assets, income, and potential growth. The value investor looks to establish intrinsic value. Only in some situations will the value investor take book or liquidation value into account.

Going beyond AGAP

We're going to go just a bit deeper, beyond AGAP, to add a little context. In our experience, relying on the numbers alone is a bit dangerous. If you were a Lucent Technologies investor (and as widely held as Lucent was, that's somewhat likely) back in 1999, you probably felt pretty good about things. Strong brand, strong income growth, balance sheet looked okay, everyone was saying positive things about Lucent. But here was a company that started to miss forecasts, was admittedly behind the curve on the latest optical technology, and whose biggest customer was AT&T, which was already in trouble and slipping daily. The point is, it's important to examine the fundamentals, to examine the basics, but it's also important to understand the business context in which a company operates.

Expanding on AGAP, a company that has the "right stuff" will also perform *consistently* and possess the right *intangibles*.

Consistency

How steady is the business, how steady is the market that the business is in, how steady are the profits, and how steady is the growth? Going back to the hardware store example from earlier in the chapter, before agreeing to buy the store you would want to know that the customer base is stable and that income flows are steady *or at least predictable*. If that's not the case, you would need to have a certain amount of additional capital to absorb the variations and perhaps a reserve for more advertising or promotion to bolster the customer base.

In short, there would be a certain uncertainty (oops, sorry about that!) in the business, which, from the owner's point of view, translates to *risk*. The presence of risk requires additional capital and causes greater doubt about the success of the investment for you or any other investors in the business. As a result, the potential return required to accept this risk and make you, the investor, look the other way is greater.

The value investor looks for consistency in an attempt to minimize risk and provide a margin of safety for his or her investment. This is not to say the value investor *won't* invest in a risky enterprise; it's just to say that the price paid for earnings potential must correctly reflect the risk. Consistency need not be absolute, but predictable performance is important.

Intangibles

We devote an entire chapter to intangibles (see Chapter 14). Here, we just give the basics. To be a good value investor or any kind of investor who looks beyond ticker symbols, you must see behind the pure numbers. Looking at the market or markets in which the company operates is important. Looking at products, market position, brand, public perception, customers and customer perception, leadership, opinions and actions of the investment community, and a host of others factors is important.

So now back to the Lucent example. The statements looked okay, but there were problems with intangibles: saturated market, older technology, customer problems. Problems were also emerging with consistency that, as it turns out, the company went to great lengths — making bad decisions — to try to overcome. There was a lingering concern about price, which at 50 to 60 times earnings was rich and certainly demanded perfection. From a value standpoint, were investors in for a fall? You bet.

The Value Investing Style, Compared To Others

Throughout market history, much has been made of the different approaches to investing. We hear about fundamental and technical analysis, momentum investing, trading, day trading, growth investing, income investing, and speculating. And there's story or concept investing, where the investor goes with whatever fad or technology is popular or *sounds* popular, without regard to intrinsic value *or* price. Add to these the academic treatments of security valuation and portfolio theory that may make it as far as institutional trading desks but seldom find their way to individual's bookshelves.

Aside from the academic treatments, an assortment of practical schools of investing, or investing *styles,* exist. In words that Abraham Lincoln might have used, all styles make money some of the time, but no one style makes money all of the time. Each style suggests a different approach to markets, the valuation of companies, and the valuation of stocks. As a teaching tool, explaining other investing styles is one of the best ways to illustrate what value investing is and is not.

Table 1-1 summarizes the differences among various investing styles. The following sections cover each style in more detail.

Table 1-1	Comparing Investing Styles			
Investing Style	**Stock Price Driven By**	**Relationship between Price and Value**	**Buy Based On**	**Is It Value Investing?**
Fundamental	Financials, earnings, dividends	Price will *eventually* equal value	Positive or improving fundamentals	Yes. Value investors look at fundamentals, then price.
Technical	Patterns, trends, market psychology	Not related	Buy signals	No

Investing Style	Stock Price Driven By	Relationship between Price and Value	Buy Based On	Is It Value Investing?
Story	Company story, market psychology	Not related	Timeliness	Can be part of intangibles of value investing.
Momentum	Price trend, trend strength	Not related	Trend strength, relative strength	No
Growth	Earnings growth, growth prospects	Value will eventually equal price	Sustained or improving growth prospects	Yes. Growth is part of the value equation.
Income	Cash yield vs. alternatives	Price should equal value	Yield vs. alternatives, risk profile	Sometimes. Income can be part of the value equation.
Speculation	Events, probability of occurrence	Usually none	Reward vs. risk	No
Value	Intrinsic value	Price should be at or below value	Value obtained for price	Of course

Bible-totin' fundamentalists

Fundamentalists look at the fundamentals of a business — assets, revenue, expenses, growth, earnings, dividends, cash flows, productivity, profit margins, products, markets, company news, and the like. They assess the quality of the business based on numbers, goals, and execution against those goals. A fundamentalist is looking at the intrinsic value of the business and the value that the business is likely to deliver to the shareholder. And fundamentalists live by the rules and live by the book. No funny business, like chasing the glamour stock of the day. The term "fundamentalist" has been around for decades, maybe longer, to describe a school of investing. Such classics as *Security Analysis* by Benjamin Graham and David Dodd (more about Graham later) and *How to Buy Stocks* by Louis Engel have been creating fame for the fundamentalist since the 1930s and 1950s, respectively. You guessed it: A fundamentalist largely fits the definition of a value investor, except that a value investor also *looks for a bargain price.*

Technicians: Head and shoulders above the rest

At the other end of the spectrum is the technician. The technician, like the fundamentalist, deals in a world of numbers. But beyond that — way beyond — the technician attempts to apply statistical models and patterns to the stock price with little to no regard for the performance or characteristics of the underlying company. For the technician, a company's stock price is completely detached from the underlying value of the company.

The technician studies price charts and statistically calculated buy and sell signals all day long. In a sense, the technician is a student of market behavior rather than company performance. The price patterns observed are really the collective decisions, attitudes, behaviors, and psyche of the public at large. The technician studies the price behavior that results from these collective decisions and believes that market behavior can be predicted.

As an example, one popular pattern is the *head and shoulders*. In this pattern, a stock will peak, and then sell off as the first wave of profit takers emerges. Then it peaks again at a higher level, and then sells off more sharply. Finally, it peaks at a third and lower level as those missing the first two peaks try to capitalize, then reverses lower as the whole thing runs out of steam. Then there is a *cup and handle* formation, where a slowly turning and rising stock price movement is followed by a short sell-off and then further short upward movement, creating the chart pattern that bears the name. As we're all human, certain behavior patterns do repeat themselves. Markets aren't driven by random number generators. Therefore, there is merit to the technical approach (and there's merit in the myriad software packages and books that support it). But technical investing is a far cry from value investing.

A storied approach

Fundamental and technical approaches to investing can be considered rational and based on factual evidence and a clear understanding of facts. Moving afield from these rational approaches, we approach story (also known as concept) investing. This one isn't hard to describe. Did you, or anyone you know, ever get excited about a company because it's name ended in *dot.com*? Or *Networks*? *Communications*? These stocks all had a story, and it invariably sounded good. Going with the story are the numerous press releases and narcissistic ramblings about "excellence" emerging from the company itself, adding credibility to the story.

Blue chips and glamour stocks

You may have heard the term *blue chip* to describe certain kinds of stocks. The poker table from which the term emerged is long since forgotten, but the term has been used for years to refer to the large, steady, relatively safe companies. These are the types of companies traditionally found in the Dow Jones Industrials, Fortune 50, Fortune 100, and so forth.

Blue chip is really a popular definition, not a technical definition. As is its counterpart: *glamour.*

In the '60s, if you owned Avon, Polaroid, or Xerox you owned a glamour stock. In the late '90s, almost any Internet stock fit. Interesting territory is the crossover, where Microsoft and Intel are now part of the Dow Jones Industrial Average. Are they blue chips? Or glamour stocks? Depends on your perspective.

To be sure, there are tamer forms of story investing. Former Fidelity guru Peter Lynch is fond of telling people to invest in what they know about and what seems successful as they encounter it in daily life. Starbucks could be considered a story stock , capitalizing on changes in social patterns that have taken people away from the corner bar. If you look at the story as *part* of the value picture (under the intangibles category) it can benefit the value investor.

Mighty mo'

Momentum investing is really a combination of technical investing and story investing. The momentum investor piles on to stocks that are already making a directional move (and it can be either direction, buying stocks that are going up and short-selling stocks that are going down). The theory is that success begets success, and attracts attention from still more investors (greater fools?), which will in turn drive the stock price up. If a stock's momentum is the fire, then the story is the gasoline. Cool, sexy stocks with a driven chart pattern and numerous press releases, analyst attention, and the like can go from warm to blazing hot almost instantaneously. There was certainly a lot of this behind the 1999-2000 boom, and an almost equal fervor to the downside as the whole thing unwound in 2000 and 2001. Momentum investing is great when it works for those who are agile market players. It's no place for the value investor. Remember, value investors invest without regard to price except as it relates to value. Value investors don't invest *because* of price.

Trading places

Some would define value investing as true investing, where the investor looks at the business and its fundamentals, then makes a long-term investment in the business to achieve long-term returns. If that's an *investor*, then what's a *trader*?

A trader makes his living by buying and selling stocks back and forth, hoping to profit on a long series of individual transactions. The trader can be compared to an antique dealer who buys things at apparently attractive prices with the exclusive intention of selling them later at a higher price, thus resulting in a profit. Sure, the antique dealer is interested in and quite knowledgeable about antiques, but the purpose of acquiring them is to resell them advantageously later on.

The stock trader is similar, except that, unlike the antiques dealer, he or she often trades with the intent to profit on a downward move — a *short sale*. The stock trader acquires with the intent to sell, not — and we emphasize that word — the intent to hold for the future.

The day trader is a special stock-trading species. The objective of the day trader is to make trades, sometimes hundreds in a day, to profit on tiny spreads (markups) and fluctuations in the stock price. The day trader takes all his or her money off the table by the end of the day. The day trading "profession" has been greatly enhanced by the availability of real-time online trading tools and information that was unavailable even to professionals just a few short years ago.

Contrary to a degree of popular belief, traders do serve a useful role in the market and the investing world. They provide *liquidity,* which is the ability for others to buy and sell in real time and at a true market price. They keep the dealers honest, reducing undue price influence that can occur in a market dominated by gorilla market makers such as Merrill, Morgan, Goldman, and the like. But again, traders are anything but value investors. Most pure traders scarcely look at company fundamentals, if they do so at all. They deal strictly in the world of ticker symbols, price levels, and short-term price movements.

Growth and income

The terms "growth" and "income" pop up frequently when discussing investing styles. These terms are also used to classify mutual funds. Growth investing is what the name implies: Investors seek stock price growth through growth in underlying earnings, usually retained in the business. Income investors, on the other hand, look for high rates of return paid out as dividends.

If growth were the *only* thing a value investor looked for, growth and value investing would be one and the same. When growth investing is done with the discipline of the value investor, looking for growth but also for underlying business fundamentals supporting growth , always at the right price, it would be considered value investing. The value investor would regard growth investing done without business assessment and bargain price focus as speculation.

Income investing, on the other hand, is investing for the highest possible yield in the form of cash paid back to the investor. This can take the form of dividends from stocks or interest from bonds and fixed-income investments. The income investor looks for the amount of yield and factors in consistency and risk. Income investors are for the most part value investors, but they're only looking at part of the value equation. But value investors may not necessarily be income investors. Many value investors are content to have a company leave its earnings in the business.

Speculation

The speculator is the antithesis of the value investor. Speculators come in all stripes, but what they really do is buy on chance: the chance that a company will strike gold, the chance that a company will be acquired, the chance that a company will turn around a bleak earnings picture, the chance that a story turns into fantastic profits. Speculation is not necessarily bad — it serves to provide risk capital to risky ventures that would probably have difficulty sourcing it otherwise. The speculator may do some research, but he or she isn't looking for the same things as the value investor. It's often the speculator who causes prices to separate from a firm's intrinsic value.

The Value Investing Style

We've stated it before: Value investing is a style of investing. It's an approach to investing. You, as an investor, will adopt some of the principles presented here, but not all of them. You will develop a style and system that works for you, and the knowledge available in the rest of this book will contribute to your style.

Are dividends important?

The role and value of dividends is an ongoing debate among value investors and commentators. Is it better for companies to keep it all or return some or all of it to you? The keep-it-all school maintains that the company has better ways to invest it than you do (after all, if this weren't the case the company probably isn't a good value investment in the first place). The give-it-back school wants some of their returns back as cash to keep management honest, and because they're confident that they themselves, as talented value investors, will find good ways to invest the return.

Take stock or not: Types of value investments

You probably think first of stocks when you think about investments. Not a bad place to start, and for sure there are literally hundreds, probably thousands, of stocks that could be considered as value stocks. This book focuses primarily on assessing value in companies and investing in their stocks.

But other valid and occasionally exotic ways exist to play the value game. Most bonds are considered value investments for the income-oriented value investor. There are convertible bonds (bonds that offer a base income level with the added benefit of growth participation, as they are convertible to common stocks at a certain price). Value-oriented mutual funds are everywhere. And if true value can only be represented to you by something you can stand on and that they ain't making any more of, there's real estate and real estate investment trust (REIT) vehicles that can land you in value territory. We cover these alternatives in Part IV and stick, for now, to companies and their stocks.

Don't look for a magic formula

Some people buy and read investing books looking for a magic formula that guarantees success. Buy when a stock crosses its 50-day moving average and you'll profit every time, or buy when the PEG is less than 1.0 (we cover this later). Value investing isn't quite that simple. There are so many elements and nuances that go into a company's business that you can't know them all, let alone figure out how to weight them in your model. So rather than a recipe for success, you will instead have a list of ingredients that should be in every dish. But the art of cooking it up into a suitable value investment is up to you.

Like all other investing approaches, value investing is both art and science. It is more scientific and methodical than some approaches, but it is by no means completely formulaic. Why, if it were, everyone would use the same formula, and there would be no reason for a market! Stock prices would simply equal formulaic value. Wouldn't that be boring?

Do due diligence

We can't say it enough: The value investor must do the numbers and work to understand a company's value. Although, as we explore in Chapter 5, there are information sources and services that do some of the number crunching, you're not relieved of the duty of looking at, interpreting, and understanding the results. Diligent value investors review the facts and don't act until they're confident in their understanding of the company, its value, and the relation between value and price.

Nipping closely at the heels of diligence is *discipline*. The value investor does the work, applies sound judgment, and patiently waits for the right price. That is what has separated the masters like Buffett from the rest.

Investing is no more than the allocation of capital for use by an enterprise with the idea of achieving a suitable return. He or she who allocates capital best wins!

A surprise: Don't diversify

You probably have heard that the key to investing success is to diversify. It's on every talk show and it's in every investing magazine. Diversification provides safety in numbers and avoids the eggs-in-one-basket syndrome, so it protects the value of a portfolio.

Well, yes, there's a certain truth to that. But again, borrowing from the masters we find that diversification only serves to dilute returns. If you're doing the value investing thing right, *you are picking the right stocks at the right price*, so there's no need to provide this artificial insurance. Well, maybe diversification isn't a bad idea until you prove yourself a *good* value investor. But remember, diversification per se is not a value investing technique. We write more about this in Chapter 4.

Remember that it's not all or nothing

If you decide that you like the value investing approach, it doesn't have to be an all-or-nothing commitment. The value investing approach should serve you well if you use it for, say, 80 percent or 90 percent of your portfolio. Be diligent, select the stocks, and sock them away for the long term as a portfolio foundation. But that shouldn't exclude the possibility of trying to hit a few home runs through more aggressive short-term tactics. These tactics can make you a lot of money a lot faster than traditional value investments, which may require years for the fruits to ripen. Of course, this doesn't mean taking unnecessary or silly risks; rather, it means that sometimes investments can perform well based on something other than intrinsic value. It doesn't hurt to try to capitalize on that, so long as you understand the risks and are willing to face losses.

You don't have to use the value investing approach for *all* of your investments. Depending on your goals, it's okay to mix investing styles.

Are You a Value Investor?

By now, you've probably asked yourself this question a few times. "Am I patient enough?" "Can I do the numbers stuff?" Here are seven character traits we find in ourselves and other value investors we know:

- ✔ **Bargain hunter.** Do you check the price of the hotel across the street before you check into your chosen hotel? Do you study detailed automobile specifications and prices before you buy? Do you look at different boxes of detergent to see how much better the deal is on the 67-ounce size versus the 43-ounce size? You have a key trait of a value investor, although we continue to be surprised at otherwise frugal folks who are willing to throw investment dollars at almost anything.

- ✔ **Do it yourselfer.** Value investors want to check the numbers themselves and build their own assessments. By doing so, they develop a better understanding of the company and its fundamentals. Who can trust an analyst anyway?

- ✔ **Like margins of safety.** People who actually slow down when it rains are more likely better value investors.

- ✔ **Long-term focus.** Value investors would rather make a lot of money slowly than a little money in one day. Sort of like going for marriage instead of one-night stands.

- ✔ **Business, not price oriented.** The value investor focuses on the underlying business, not the price or superficial image. They look under the hood instead of at the trim. Value investing is sometimes called inside-out investing.

- ✔ **Numbers oriented.** Not advanced mathematics, mind you, but you can't get completely away from the numbers. Value investors are concerned about company business fundamentals and performance. For those who don't like numbers, fortunately there are software packages that do much of the computation and preparation for you. And there are screeners to semi-automate company selection. Find out more in Chapter 5.

- ✔ **Contrarian.** Value investors are not crowd followers! Value investors stay away from what's exciting and hip quite purposefully. By definition, popular stocks aren't normally bargains.

Value investors are given to making lists of selection criteria and then choosing companies that match the greatest number of them. You can do the same here. To be a good value investor, you certainly don't need to excel in every trait! But five or six out of the seven would be a big help.

Chapter 2

A Value Investor's Guide to the Markets

In This Chapter

▶ Understanding markets and market performance

▶ The tortoise and the hare: looking at value investing in today's markets

> *The stock market is the only institution in the world where people feel more secure buying an expensive item than one reasonably valued.*
>
> —Timothy Vick, *Wall Street On Sale*

*I*t's become a familiar story. Five trillion in investment value or "market cap" wiped out in the 2000–2001 bear market. Is this a big deal? You bet — for all of us.

And for value investors — and potential value investors — it signified an important change and an important turning point in the history of investing. Clearly, investing, investors, and investment practice had moved away from analysis of value and the business fundamentals that support it. As the percentage of stock-owning households moved from the teens in the early 1970s to almost 50 percent, a growing portion of the investing public knew little about reading financial statements — or perhaps even where to find one!

People bought stocks based on stories they heard from colleagues at the office, friends at cocktail parties, and neighbors over the backyard fence. And the retail brokerage industry got into the game, too, offering investment analysis that seemingly supported almost anything. Add to that the proliferation of online brokerages and the reinvention of do-it-yourself investing as online *trading,* not independent investment analysis.

This chapter doesn't dwell on that already-familiar story. But it does furnish a contextual canvas onto which we can paint the value investing picture.

Markets and Market Performance

The story of markets and market performance, particularly over the last two years, could fill many books (and has). We won't go there — all the way. We also won't belabor the different markets, how trades are executed, or the myriad performance indicators. There are plenty of other places to pick up this information. But, more to the point:

Value investors don't care. Now *that's* a bold statement, starting out the second chapter of what we hope to be a significant work on value investing. Does it sound like value investors have an attitude problem?

Nope. The point is that value investors aren't that concerned about markets, trading process and behavior, and the like. The market is simply a place to buy a portion of a business — and perhaps not sell it for a long, long time. Value investors care little about whether an order is executed on the bid or ask price, nor do they care what regional market, ECN, or execution system was used. The transaction is an investment, a long-term investment. The market simply provides a place to acquire the investment. So the NYSE (New York Stock Exchange) or NASDAQ, market or limit order, SOES or SuperDot, and other jargon from the world of active trading really don't matter.

So in a departure from most investing books, we don't talk much about markets. And if you're really a value investor (or want to become one), you yourself don't care about markets . . . *except when they undervalue businesses.*

Despite the academic rumblings of the "efficient market theory" (which holds that with good information and a sufficient number of players, markets will find the right price for a business), markets aren't perfect. There are *always* bargains. Stocks may be undervalued because of lack of knowledge or lack of visibility, or perhaps they're part of a group that's out of favor altogether. These stocks are selling for less than might be indicated by the value of the business or the potential of the business. So in this sense, value investors love the markets. The markets, through their imperfections, provide value investors their opportunity. As Warren Buffett says, if markets were perfect, he'd be "standing on the corner holding a tin cup."

Where the Markets Have Been: An Overview

A stock market represents the sum total of the public's perception of the business value of the companies trading in that market. True business value, which we explore in great depth in this book, is the sum total of productive assets and, in particular, what companies produce in the form of current and future earnings. As long as companies produce more, it makes sense that their values rise, and that the public perception of their values rises in tandem.

You can and should expect, in aggregate, that the total value of all businesses would rise roughly in line with the increase in the size of the economy, as represented by GDP, or gross domestic product. This is true, and it can be argued that business value grows further through increases in *productivity*. And further, the value of market-traded businesses could rise still more if they grew their *share* of the total economy — as Borders Group and Barnes and Noble have grown their share of the total bookselling business. If you look closely at long-term *stock market* growth (by most measures, 10 to 11 percent) you see how the long-term GDP growth of the 3 to 5 percent, productivity growth of 1 to 2 percent, and long-term inflation in the 3 to 6 percent range, *added together*, provide an explanation for the long-term market growth rate. In the short term, depending on the value of alternative investments, such as bonds, real estate, and so on, market value may actually rise faster or slower than business value. And inflation also tampers with market valuations. So can markets grow at 20 percent per year? Not for long.

This story is well illustrated by looking at Figure 2-1.

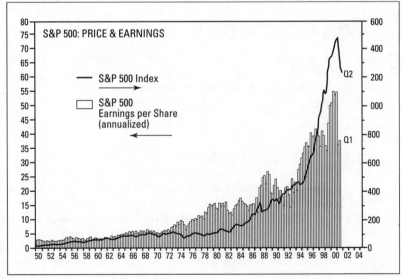

Figure 2-1:
S&P 500
Price and
Earnings
over 50
years.

Source: yardeni.com

Before going into the explanation, it's worth pointing out the usefulness of Ed Yardeni's Web site (www.yardeni.com), the source of Figure 2-1. Yardeni is chief economist and investment strategist for Deutsche Bank Alex Brown Inc. and a perennial market sage with a strong focus on macro economic and market trends (as opposed to individual stocks). Economic and market data, market sector data, and graphs are easily accessed at the site for free (a feature that value investors like).

Now, back to Figure 2-1. The line represents the Standard & Poor's 500 index, a weighted market index or "basket" of 500 chosen, and generally leading, companies in the economy. The S&P 500 has been viewed by most intermediate and advanced investors as the best overall indicator of the market, although it has been criticized for being too heavily weighted — up to 40 percent — in technology stocks because of recent overemphasis on the "new economy."

No pain, no gain

Anyway, Figure 2-1 clearly shows the gains and acceleration of those gains in the markets. (Markets? Yes, S&P indexes contain stocks traded on both the NYSE and NASDAQ.) And were those gains justified? Up through 1997, probably so. Why? Earnings and earnings growth tracked the growth in stock prices.

Pain with no gain

For a few periods (1976–1981, 1986–1988, and 1993–1994), earnings even outpaced the S&P. Why? Interest rates and inflation put a damper on stock prices, as alternative investments and reduced "real" value of future earnings, respectively, came into play.

Gain with no pain

The markets "broke out" starting in 1998. The 1997–1998 Asian recession took a piece out of earnings growth, but stock prices largely ignored this as a temporary blip (save for a few painful days in late October 1997). Favorable interest and inflation rates helped, and prices were on a roll. True, companies were churning out good earnings reports, having finally figured out how to improve asset productivity and utilization by outsourcing, just-in-time production, and other techniques, and how to sell goods into firm markets at premium prices through effective marketing and branding. Acquisitions delivered improved economies of scale and filled-out product lines, further strengthening brands. So earnings grew, but as you can see from Figure 2-1, prices grew faster.

And so, the 2001 odyssey

Starting in 2000, the economy became overheated by an overestimation of the impact of the Internet and related overspending on capital goods particularly related to the Internet. The overspending was a double-whammy as (1) demand for capital goods, especially computers and telecom equipment, dried up, and (2) the previously freewheeling venture capital funding went away. It remains to be seen how much of this "tech wreck" filters through to the rest of the economy, as layoffs and negative perceptions about the economic future take hold.

Putting the story in numbers

The price to earnings ratio, or *P/E ratio,* is probably the most published and familiar beacon of market (and individual stock) value. We take apart P/E in Chapter 16. For now, P/E is the ratio of stock price to earnings (different ways to calculate earnings exist, but we defer that). And the inverse of P/E, earnings-to-price or *earnings yield,* tells us how much an equity returns a percentage, similar to a bond yield. So a P/E of 15 implies an earnings yield of about 7 percent. A P/E of 25 implies an earnings yield of 4 percent.

Where are we going with this? Here are a few points of interest along this scenic highway of investing:

✔ The P/E ratio for the S&P was fairly steady and less than 15 for most of time before 1997. Implied earnings yield: 7 percent or more. Then, with the spike in stock prices and the greater weighting of technology stocks, the P/E went to almost 30 before settling back to about 23. The jury is still out on whether that number makes sense.

✔ The P/E ratio for the tech-heavy NASDAQ was much higher than the P/E ratio for the S&P. For the NASDAQ 100, a basket of the leading NASDAQ stocks — mostly tech stocks — the P/E went to almost 100 (earnings yield: 1 percent) before settling back to the 60s. True, this indicator is a bit harsh, because it includes companies losing money and doesn't factor in growth. But still, earnings yield less than 2 percent.

✔ And what about growth? True, earnings growth, finally evident and supported by technology-driven productivity and a low interest rate and inflation climate, was firmly in place. But how much and for how long? It's hard to grow things as much as everyone expects (or hopes for) as the numbers get bigger and bigger. Large numbers, diminishing returns, competition, and the finite nature of customer markets all work against very high, sustained growth rates. Yet, growth rates required to support valuations of companies such as Yahoo! and Cisco implied each would become a significant portion of gross domestic product (GDP) — 5 percent to 10 percent — if continued for 20 years. No company has ever become a significant portion of GDP, not even 1 percent.

✔ The P/E ratio, even for the venerable Dow Jones 30 Industrials, rose over 23 from a historical norm in the to 17 range. True, as shown in Figure 2-1, growth rates increased, and Microsoft and Intel replaced older, stodgier industrial counterparts such as Goodyear. But still, people were paying higher prices for earnings and growth, even for these more traditional, big-name stocks. As Table 2-1 shows, higher prices for earnings and growth can be in part justified by the interest rate and inflation climate, but it's easy to take this too far. Climate improvements lead to short-term adjustments, not long-term marches beyond the outer reaches beyond what makes sense.

✔ And what about value stocks? As all of this happened, traditional value stocks were left in the dust. This bifurcated market placed heavy emphasis on just a few stocks. Although the averages broke record after record, more stocks were actually down than up in 1999–2000. If a company had growth and a story, especially a tech or dot-com story, its price ran towards what anyone would pay for it. Meanwhile, the market landscape was littered with companies selling at P/Es of 10 or 12, ripe for regained interest. Some called this a *barbell market* with groups of stocks in two polar extremes. In hindsight, *dumbbell market* may have been a better term.

Table 2-1	Return, P/E, Growth and Climate for Dow Industrials through 2000					
	Total Return (Appreciation + Dividends)	P/E	Earnings Growth	Earnings/ Price (Earnings Yield)	Inflation Rate	Aaa Corporate Bond Yield
1 year	27.2%	23.2	13.9%	4.3%	2.7%	7.1%
3 years	23.3%	20.6	6.0%	4.8%	2.0%	6.9%
5 years	27.0%	17.4	11.4%	5.8%	2.4%	7.2%
10 years	18.3%	17.4	6.8%	5.7%	3.0%	7.7%
20 years	18.1%	13.4	6.7%	7.5%	4.3%	9.5%
50 years	12.9%	12.7	6.1%	7.9%	4.0%	7.1%

And we could go on. Some of the facts and figures of the markets, and particularly the "bubble" boom and bust of 1998–2001, are astounding. But the time would be better spent focused on the "value" portion of the market.

And Now, What About Value?

This is a value investing book, and you're correct to presume that there will be something in this chapter, in every chapter, about value and value investing. This chapter is no exception.

Rather than engage in a long, drawn-out history of value investing and value performance, the rest of this chapter is more like a highlight reel.

The tortoise and the hare

The proverbial hare runs fast, but often and unpredictably, stops along the way to feed, gaze, and may even turn around and head back a few steps here and there. Meanwhile, the tortoise plods steadily along and wins the race.

In the late 1990's, technology stock "hares" ran well ahead of value stocks, to the extent that the financial press and almost everyone else was busily voicing the epitaph for value. But the hare did stop and look around, and in fact, ran several steps — maybe 60 percent of the way backward in 2001. The "new economy" didn't happen or at least didn't turn out to be the high-octane rabbit food everyone expected.

Value stocks, meanwhile, continued on. That tortoise, as it turns out, may have found some pretty cool lettuce himself. Consider these facts:

- Since the 1920s, for any five-year period, value stocks have outperformed traditional "growth" stocks by an average of 10 percent.

- In the 2000–2001 market, value stocks are up 15 percent, while big-cap growth declined 45 percent.

- Many value funds have returned between 10 percent and 20 percent to their investors in 2001, and a few, such as the Oakmark Funds, have returned north of 30 percent. (For a map of value fund returns, see Morningstar at www.morningstar.com. It maps returns by type and market cap. Value has the distinct advantage.)

- During the tech boom of the late 1990's and especially in 1999–2000, value really did almost bite the dust. Over 200 value funds went under, including the Julian Robertson iconic Tiger Fund. Warren Buffett's Berkshire Hathaway dropped almost 50 percent as his portfolio eked out a paltry gain of less than 1 percent. Buffett and his investing style were declared dead on numerous occasions.

Where is value investing now?

Is value overvalued? Money coming out of tech had to go somewhere, and although much of it is on the sidelines, there has also been a value renaissance. Result? Arguably, value may be overvalued! Such value icons as Coke, Gillette, and Caterpillar are selling well in excess of a P/E of 20, with growth stories that hardly justify those valuations. Most professionals agree today that the true value opportunities lie in the small (less than $1 billion market capitalization) and midcap ($1 billion to $5 billion) area. They're harder to find, but certainly there are plenty for everyone.

So some parts of the traditional value universe may not be value anymore. But in any market, there is always value somewhere. Even in tech stocks. You just have to find it.

The enduring goal of this book is to help you understand value and incorporate a value philosophy and approach into your investing style. So long as there are markets, there will always be value opportunities. The trick is to recognize them and act on them. Reading this book should help your dependable investing "tortoise" win most investing races.

Chapter 3

The Value Investing Story

> *It mystifies (Warren) Buffett that the majority of investors pursue and adopt one Wall Street fad after another when the secret to safety and high returns is right under their noses and has been for decades.*
>
> —Janet Lowe, *Value Investing Made Easy,* 1996

*V*alue investing has been around since the beginning of the market. Yet, especially until recently, it has had relatively low visibility. Many investors are excited more by the go-go world of trading and aggressive growth investing. Many are more intrigued by companies that make 2GB fabric- and fiber-channel storage-area network routers and switches than they are by companies that sell paint and insurance. Many investors stay glued to *Wall Street Week* when some New Horizons fund manager is the guest, but doze off or head for the fridge when a major value fund manager appears.

While boring to some, the value investing approach has earned strong returns for its faithful followers, often double the market average. Value investing has allowed investors to prosper in healthy markets and survive the numerous downturns throughout the century.

Value investing often deals in boring industries and requires patient examination of the nitty-gritty details of financial statements. Value investing analysis comes slowly, as does value investing *success*. Because that may be discouraging to some investors, we decided to share the journey and thoughts of the most successful value investors, Benjamin Graham and Warren Buffett. Value investing got its beginnings and developed into a serious investing discipline based on their teachings and experience.

The Patriarch: Benjamin Graham

The beginnings of value investing as a documented discipline go back to Benjamin Graham. Graham was a self-made financial analyst and investor who went on to become a very successful investor through some very trying investing times (as in the Great Depression). Graham was born in 1894, excelled in academics, started with a Wall Street firm at age 20, and was managing other people's money before he was 30. He went on to found Graham Newman, a New York investment firm, and to build a substantial investment portfolio for his clients.

Graham left a legacy for the rest of us when he went on to write the original bibles of value investing and to teach the art of value investing at Columbia University. One of his many famous students is Warren Buffett. To this day, Mr. Buffett and other Graham disciples pay the utmost respect to his pioneering leadership.

The good books of value investing

During the Depression (1934, to be exact), Graham teamed up with one of his junior Columbia colleagues, who took notes during his lectures, to write *Security Analysis*. The most recent edition of the book (McGraw-Hill, 1996) is 725 pages and is hardly an easy read. Aimed largely at the professional investment community, the book takes apart businesses and financial statements brick by brick. The book has been in print, in several editions, since 1934, and probably has the longest legs of any investing book.

Now here's a value investment: A 3rd edition, 9th 1951 printing of Graham's *Security Analysis* was recently quoted on vintage bookseller Alibris (www.alibris.com) for $938. An original 1934 first hardcover edition of the book was listed at $30,000!

Although *Security Analysis* is targeted at investment professionals, it is useful to all types of investors. In the words of writer/biographer Janet Lowe, the early editions are worth reading "because they show how much things change and how much they don't." Truly, Graham's recognition of the importance of fundamental business basics (assets, earnings, cash flow, risk, cost of capital, and interest rates) is timeless. Also interesting are the observations on the speculation and shady investment schemes that happen today just as they did back then. Graham was quite outspoken and cynical about the motives and methods of the speculator, stating that when a stock purchase is "motivated by speculative greed" the investor "desires to conceal this unlovely impulse behind a screen of apparent logic and good sense."

Graham was among the first to separate market movement and timing from investing. For Graham, the market was an emotional animal, and trying to time its moves was guesswork that amounted to speculation. He described the market as an "emotionally disturbed business partner." To Graham, investing required a focus on the company. The student of Graham learned a few specific mathematical formulas and relationships, but went on to learn the reasoning processes and investing philosophy that drive the value investing style. Graham specifically taught people to calculate intrinsic value to look for the margin of safety, and to avoid speculative impulses.

In 1949, Graham came out with another classic book, *The Intelligent Investor*. It's available today, priced at $30.00. Because it's a normal-sized book, you might initially question its price versus its intrinsic value. But if you weigh in the intangibles of having one of the classics of investing history — and the fact that the book may help you make a good investment — the rather high per pound price is justified!

The Intelligent Investor is mainly a repackaging of *Security Analysis* for the nonprofessional investor, although the language and formulas are still a bit intimidating for some. Unless you're really into this, the more contemporary books on value investing (such as this one) are easier to digest.

The foundation

Benjamin Graham and those value investors who followed him relied on the balance sheet for the first indication of a company's status and value. The balance sheet is basically a snapshot of what the company *owns* and what it *owes*. If it owns more than it owes, the company scores points with the value investor. If what it owns is productive and has marketable value, the company scores more points. Graham and some value investors place more emphasis on the balance sheet, while others, notably Buffett, take a closer look at the income and cash flow statements. The reality is that you have to look at all three statements; they are inextricably linked. None of the three alone can tell the whole story.

Graham believed that the balance sheet revealed the foundation, the value below which a company would never go. The balance sheet also reveals the *degree of safety,* in the form of liquid assets and assets in excess of debt.

A brief word about assets and asset quality. Assets come in all shapes and sizes. *Liquid* assets are those that can be quickly and easily sold or converted at or near their reported value. Cash, most accounts receivable, and marketable securities owned by the firm are liquid. Certain inventories may be liquid, but many are not. For example, a stock of Intel 486 processors is likely obsolete.

Fixed assets, such as plant and equipment, are usually considered *illiquid*. True, they can be sold, often for prices meeting or exceeding their reported value. But the selling process may take a long time and the cash will not be available for use in emergencies. Likewise, *hard* assets — those that you can see, feel, and touch, or that show up on a bank statement — have more value than *soft* items, such as patents, business agreements, and other items of goodwill. Assets not only come in different shapes and sizes but also have different degrees of quality. A warehouse full of rotary dial phones is certainly less valuable than the latest state-of-the-art semiconductor manufacturing machine.

Nets and net net

Graham liked to take a close look at assets and particularly current assets. Then he compared per share asset values with stock prices. When a stock was selling at a discount to asset value, particularly current asset value, it was a bargain.

Net current asset value

Graham used two key measures: *net current asset value* and *net net asset value per share.* Net current asset value is defined today by most financial analysts as *working capital.* Working capital is the asset base that recirculates through the business as cash, receivables, and inventory and is used to acquire raw materials and to produce and sell products.

A company with a strong working capital position can expand its business, try new things, and produce new revenue and earnings streams. A company short on working capital struggles to produce and market its products, can't capitalize on new business opportunities, and is vulnerable to downturns. Working capital is analogous to a household checking and savings account. High balances and low debt afford the household more opportunity and safety — the same is true of a company with good working capital.

What we just said about working capital — the more, the better — is generally true. However, modern corporate finance as practiced by some companies, notably retailers and some high-efficiency manufacturers such as Dell, uses very low or even negative levels of working capital. In effect, these companies run the business on someone else's money or on very short-term cash receipts through sales. Increased profitability results from high asset turnover and asset productivity and reducing exposure to obsolete inventory. For such a company, Graham's formula wouldn't make much sense: Return on assets or return on equity are better yardsticks.

Graham would typically look for companies selling at prices lower than net current asset value. A stock selling at less than two-thirds of working capital was considered a bargain. In today's world, with more efficient use of capital and a focus on reducing asset efficiency and exposure, stocks meeting this criterion are hard to find.

Net net asset value

Net net asset value per share is an even more conservative view of liquidity and company health. Net net asset value is current assets less not only current but also long-term liabilities. For Graham, a company whose current assets were one-third greater than both current and long-term liabilities was in great financial health, and if the share price was less than the net net asset value per share, it was a bargain.

Net net asset value per share:

> (Current assets – Current liabilities – Long-term debt) ÷ Shares outstanding

By the book: book value

Another of Graham's focal points is *book value*. Book value represents the accounting value of owners' equity in the business. Book value is a fairly subjective look at company valuation and one on which there is considerable debate. Per share book value is defined as

> (Total assets – Intangible assets – Liabilities – Preferred Stock value common) ÷ Shares outstanding

From an accounting viewpoint, book value can become theoretical because of the way companies manage and depreciate fixed assets and how they account for intangibles (goodwill, patents, value of research and development, and the like). For manufacturing and technology companies especially, book value can be misleading. For banks and other financial institutions where most assets and liabilities are in cash or cash equivalents, book value is more relevant.

Book value is, at least in theory, what a person buying a business would want to look at first. It is the bottom-line net value of the company. But because of the accounting complexities, Graham and others did not compare it directly to share price. A number of value investors, including Buffett, like to observe whether book value is *growing* and is at least within reasonable range of the share price. In fact, Buffett uses book value as the key yardstick to measure the success of Berkshire Hathaway.

Up and to the right: Earnings and growth

Graham started with the balance sheet, but he certainly did not stop there. Earnings, more specifically, earnings *growth*, is the engine that moves a stock price upward. Indeed, unless a payout of company assets is imminent, it is the combination of earnings and earnings growth that defines the *intrinsic value* of a business, and thus a stock price. Since we're talking future earnings growth, company value defined by earnings and earnings growth represents the upper end of the value range, while the asset base represents the lower end.

Our first trip to the P/E counter

We've come to the most basic and well known of all the stock-valuation tools: *Price to Earning ratio,* or *P/E ratio.* If you have heard or read any investment analysis at all, you've heard of this one. It's listed in most daily paper stock listings. Football players ask one another about P/Es in brokerage house TV commercials. It's everywhere.

Graham probably didn't invent P/E, but it was a key part of his investing philosophy. Naturally, he recommended looking for stocks with a low P/E relative to the market. Although he didn't specifically mention a more contemporary measure, the Price/Earnings to Growth, or PEG ratio, which attempts to scale the P/E according to underlying growth, he did recognize that different stocks should have different P/Es. Growth stocks could have a P/E in the 20s, while other stocks probably should be lower. Moreover, Graham recognized that good bargain stocks have a P/E lower than past P/Es for that stock. Graham's advice to investors generally was to avoid stocks with a P/E higher than 20.

Intrinsic value . . . and beyond

Although Graham didn't invent P/E, he did create an intrinsic value formula. This formula is about as close to a comprehensive value investing formula as you'll ever get. Graham was trying to establish a stock's value based on earnings and earnings growth with an eye on available bond yields as an alternative. This, by the way, is a common and recurring theme in value investing. The diligent and skeptical value investor is always looking to compare and adjust valuation according to bond yields. Higher bond yields suggest a stock must return relatively more to be a choice investment, and further high bond yields suggest high cost of capital and inflation that depreciate future earnings and cash flows, thus driving down valuation. Bond yields are an important valuation and pricing factor for value investors.

Ensure that a stock's return is reasonably higher than that of a boring bond, reasonable considering the risk taken. If not, just buy the bond, sleep at night, and be done with it!

Back to Graham's formula: You take current earnings, apply a base P/E ratio, add a growth factor if there is growth, and adjust according to current bond yield. The result is an intrinsic value that the stock can be expected to achieve in the real world if growth targets are met.

PEG

You may be familiar with the popular valuation metric known as *PEG,* or Price Earnings/ Growth. PEG is the price to earnings ratio divided by the earnings growth rate. The lower the PEG, the better.

PEG's message is that high P/E ratios are justified by high growth rates. If the P/E outstrips the growth rate, the resulting PEG is high. The reason we bring it up here: A closer look at Ben Graham's intrinsic value formula reveals a relatively high implied PEG, consistently over 2.0. Then when added to the base no-growth 8.5 P/E multiplier, the resulting calculated PEG consistently exceeds 2.0 at all growth rates — at least until interest rates are factored in (an important "until"). Still, given many investors' reluctance to buy stocks today with PEG exceeding 2.0, Graham's formula is less conservative than you may expect.

Formula: Intrinsic value = $E(2r + 8.5) \times 4.4/Y$

E is the current annual earnings per share.

r is the annual growth rate. (Graham would have suggested using a conservative number for growth.)

8.5 is the base P/E ratio for a stock with no growth.

Y is the current interest rate, represented as the average rate on high-grade corporate bonds. Note that lower bond rates make the intrinsic value higher, as future earnings streams are worth more in a lower interest rate environment.

Take Hewlett-Packard as an example. With current earnings projected at $1.50 per share, a growth rate of 10 percent, and a corporate bond interest rate of 6 percent, the intrinsic value is

$\$1.50 \times ((2 \times 10) + 8.5) \times (4.4/6)$

or $31.35 per share

This value matches the price at the time that these assumptions were made almost exactly, suggesting little potential price appreciation in the stock.

You shouldn't go out and buy or sell stock based on this formula alone, of course, but it illustrates Graham's viewpoint on earnings and intrinsic value. It may be somewhat out of date, as government bonds are more often used as today's bond benchmark, and the 4.4 factor may not truly reflect today's growth, interest, and inflation climate. But it's one of many tests for rational pricing of a security.

Before takeoff: A checklist

In addition to identifying and quantifying important value components, Graham left us with some general rules for selecting stocks. He created a number of checklists at different times in his career to serve different investment objectives and portfolio strategies. The checklists review different aspects of a company's financial strength, intrinsic value, and the relationship with price. Table 3-1 can help you identify undervalued stocks.

Table 3-1	**A Ben Graham checklist for finding undervalued stocks**	
Number	*Criteria*	*Measures*
1	Earnings to price (the inverse of P/E) is double the high-grade corporate bond yield. If the high-grade bond yields 7%, then earnings to price should be 14%.	Risk
2	P/E ratio that is 0.4 times the highest average P/E achieved in the last five years	Risk
3	Dividend yield is ⅔ the high-grade bond yield	Risk
4	Stock price of ⅔ the tangible book value per share	Risk
5	Stock price of ⅔ the net current asset value	Risk
6	Total debt lower than tangible book value	Financial strength
7	Current ratio (current assets ÷ current liabilities) greater than 2	Financial strength
8	Total debt no more than liquidation value	Financial strength
9	Earnings doubled in most recent ten years	Earnings stability
10	Earnings have declined no more than 5% in two of the past ten years	Earnings stability

If a stock meets seven of the ten criteria, it is probably a good value, according to Graham. If you're income oriented, Graham recommended paying special attention to items 1 through 7. If you're concerned about growth and safety, items 1 through 5 and 9 and 10 are important. If you're concerned with aggressive growth, ignore item 3, reduce the emphasis on 4 through 6, and weigh 9 and 10 heavily.

Again, these checklists are a guideline and example, not a cookbook recipe. Don't log on and restructure your portfolio just this minute! They are a way of thinking and an example of how you might construct your own value investing system.

The criteria in Table 3-1 are probably more focused on dividends and safety than even today's value investors choose to be. But today's value investing practice owes an immense debt to this type of financial and investment analysis.

The Master

It seems that about once a century the English-speaking world is blessed with a gifted leader and philosopher of unique and extraordinary talent. These special people have an incredible gift for understanding and doing complex things. But the gift goes further into how they explain their thoughts and pursuits to others with a remarkably effective use of humor. Benjamin Franklin, Abraham Lincoln, and Winston Churchill all qualify easily, and we submit that Warren Buffett also belongs in this elite group.

Warren Buffett arrived on the scene on September 30, 1930 and has turned his steady devotion to value investing principles into about $30 billion. He is the second wealthiest person in the world (depending on the price of Microsoft stock). We like to refer to Buffett as the Michael Jordan of value investing. His on-court record cannot be touched. It is simply the greatest. A good part of this book describes elements of his game. And it would be a disservice not to mention Buffett's off-court demeanor, where his candor, clairvoyance, and wit combine with his own enviably humble lifestyle to create a model for investors to emulate — if only they would emulate it!

In the beginning

The early stages of Buffett's career and lifestyle suggested investing success, although hardly on the scale he actually went on to achieve. Warren grew up in an investing environment. His father, Howard, ran an Omaha brokerage house in the 1930s that was known as Buffett, Sklenicka & Co. In his late teens, Warren worked in the house posting stock quotes and doing odd jobs, providing exposure to the trade. He learned about business through this experience and through a series of small business ventures in his high school days.

Like many other financial prodigies, Warren's aptitude did not go unnoticed by his parents, who urged him to attend the revered Wharton School at the University of Pennsylvania. This didn't work out too well. Warren soon became bored and dissatisfied, feeling that he knew as much or more than Penn's vaunted faculty. Perhaps he was homesick, perhaps he had a more practical view of matters than the pages and pages of portfolio theory he was likely exposed to. Anyway, he retreated to more familiar territory at age 19 to finish his degree at the University of Nebraska.

Benjamin Graham's *Intelligent Investor* hit the shelves, and legend has it that Warren, with a newly rekindled interest in investing and the business world, decided to put the finishing touches on his business education by attending Harvard Business School. Again, a poor match. Warren was rejected, as the story goes, after a 10-minute interview. Perhaps the admissions department had already reached its quota of Nebraskans.

Warren bounced back quickly from this setback and applied to Columbia Business School. There, Buffett hooked up with Benjamin Graham. Warren took to Graham's preachings like a pig takes to mud. The two bantered in engaging dialogue from the opening bell to the end of class. Warren graduated in a year with a master's in economics. More importantly, he left with a philosophy of investing based on valuing companies and finding under valuation in the marketplace.

Buffett returned to work in his father's brokerage firm and later went to work for Graham at Graham's brokerage firm, Graham Newman. There, he learned to manage investment portfolios and use insurance company assets as an effective investing vehicle. From these beginnings Buffett started his own investment fund (with contributed capital from neighbors, relatives, coworkers, and the like) and later built the Taj Mahal of investment companies, Berkshire Hathaway.

Taking charge

Like most investors, Buffett evolved his investing style, trying different things along the way. Often, Buffett would simply buy shares, hold them, and wait for growth prospects to materialize. Sometimes his objective was a little more short term in nature, buying to capture arbitrage — small differences between price and value that often emerge in merger, acquisition, and liquidation situations. (Capturing arbitrage is value investing too, but you had better be good, as you're going up against other professionals who have access to a lot of information and are betting for something different to happen, hence the price difference.)

Sometimes Buffett would buy a large stake in an undervalued company, large enough to be noticed and reported to the SEC, usually 5 percent or more. He then would get himself installed on the company's board of directors. Many of these companies were having financial problems or problems translating company value into shareholder value. Many welcomed his presence. Buffett would help right these problems and, if necessary, assist in selling or finding a merger partner for the company. Of course, most ordinary investors can't do this, but the thought process is important.

The start of Berkshire Hathaway

Buffett spied a faltering Massachusetts textile company known as Berkshire Hathaway. He saw potential value in a very depressed stock and began buying shares cheap for his partnership. These shares traded at less than one-half of working capital (remember Ben Graham's *net current asset value* model). If the stock price would just grow to reflect the balance sheet value, a 100 percent gain was in store, at the very least. Buffett continued to accumulate shares until the partnership owned 49 percent of the company by 1965. He effectively controlled the company.

Originally, Buffett planned to right some of the wrongs and capture quick gains by selling or merging the company. But he saw a tempting opportunity to use Berkshire as an investment conduit to build worth by buying other businesses. The opportunity owes its origin to favorable tax treatments for companies owning other companies The ability to defer taxes is very important in value investing as a way to keep capital deployed and continuously earning returns. For the specifics, see Chapter 4.

When Buffett distributed the partnership in 1969, he offered a choice of cash or Berkshire shares as part of the distribution. For his portion, Buffett took shares. He offered to buy the shares of other partners for himself. Suppose you had invested with Buffett. Your modest investment in the partnership results in getting offered 200 shares of Berkshire Hathaway or $8,400 cash (equivalent to two new cars, or maybe a third of a new house in 1969). What would you have done? We all know the answer *now:* At a current share price of $65,500, your investment would be worth over $13 million! A small group of wealthy folks made the choice to stick with Buffett. Many of them make the annual pilgrimage to Omaha to enjoy those juicy steaks and count their blessings.

To insurance and beyond

Neither Berkshire nor Buffett made it very far in the textile business. There is no Buff It with Buffett line of designer towels on the shelves at Nordstrom's. Instead, Berkshire is now the world's largest investing pool. The Berkshire formula:

Employ cash flows from businesses owned within the holding company.

Buy stocks and bonds in the open market.

Use the cash flow to buy businesses outright — preferably cash rich and cash generating — to build the investment pool and increase book value.

Acquire solid insurance companies to provide cash flow and further build investing float and to insulate from downturns.

In short, Berkshire as a combined insurer and investment holding company is a fabulous investment ship and capital allocator — especially when you have someone of Buffett's investing prowess at the helm.

From socks to stocks

Gradually, Buffett shifted his emphasis from small, opportunistic, turnaround situations, often of a short-term nature, to longer-term large cap investments and even acquired whole companies when the numbers were right. He did this with a clear eye on tapping the growth potential of the major companies and major brands that are abundant in American life. No more buying "cigar butts with one puff left in them," as he often did in the mid-1950s. No more trading-stamp companies and the like. Berkshire Hathaway was off to the races with a winning portfolio of value investments, a world-class pit crew, and high-octane fuel, provided by the insurance companies.

Things go better with Coke

Berkshire put together a world-class portfolio of high visibility blue chip growth stocks, including such household names as Coca-Cola, Gillette, American Express, and Wells Fargo. Buffett could not resist the low price of Coca-Cola in the mid-1980s as the company seemed to struggle for reinvention with new Coke and other twists and turns in corporate strategy (most of which turned out to be unnecessary). Coca-Cola had the balance sheet and certainly the stability of earnings that one would expect of the world's leading purveyor of sugar water. Buffett saw not only the intrinsic value but also the franchise or marketplace value. Coke is arguably the world's most recognized brand, and that brand was and still is the closest thing to a guarantee against dips and significant competitive inroads. It's what Buffett calls a moat around the business.

Intrinsic value on the balance sheet, solid earnings with at least some growth and growth potential, and solid value in the franchise are what Buffett looked for in all his investments. And always — repeat, always — at a good price. Berkshire Hathaway acquired 200 *million* shares of Coke in the mid-1980s at around $6 to $6.50 per share (split adjusted). Coke generally sells at over $50 today. The Berkshire before-tax profit is in the $10 *billion* range.

Wanna know what Berkshire buys? It isn't easy. Berkshire keeps its purchases a secret (to avoid market overreaction, among other things). But as much as it tries to avoid disclosure, investments of certain size and that constitute a certain proportion of ownership must be disclosed. SEC 13F filings contain the disclosures as statements of change of ownership. You can watch these directly or just watch the news. Any time a 13F surfaces, the financial news media is quick to pounce. Not that quickness really helps. The filing uncovered in April 2001 revealed Berkshire made large purchases in the third and fourth quarter of 2000 of The Gap, Wells Fargo, Costco, Nucor (a steel company), and GPU (a utility holding company). We know now, but hardly soon enough to have made a market killing from the knowledge!

Shares? Why not the whole company?

Acquiring shares certainly works over time and is what we ordinary value investors should be focused on. But Berkshire went beyond this strategy — way beyond — to buy whole companies for its portfolio. Why? Two reasons, mainly. If you own the whole company you're entitled to its cash and cash flow and can reinvest it as you wish, and you don't have to compete with other interests in the company or in the market.

So Berkshire Hathaway has made many whole enchilada investments (see Table 3-2). The Insurance group consists of seven companies (including GEICO, originally bought by Ben Graham in the 1950s). The companies play in different insurance arenas, and combined to produce $22.1 billion in revenue in 2000, with $92.1 billion in asset value and millions in cash flow despite an off year. This money fuels other investments.

The manufacturing, retail, and service group now consists of 44 companies, large and small, all successful in their own arena. An obvious favorite is Borsheim's, a chain of high-end jewelry stores. Dairy Queen, Dexter Shoe, Kirby (vacuum cleaners), and See's Candies are strong consumer names. Campbell Hausfeld (air compressors and tools), Executive Jet (company jet leasing), FlightSafety International, and Western Enterprises (gas fittings and appliances) are for the business-to-business world. Some companies are large and others are small, including the Nebraska Furniture Mart, which Buffett bought one morning as a $60 million birthday present to himself.

Table 3-2	Berkshire Hathaway Manufacturing, Retail, and Service Subsidiaries
Subsidiary Name	*Subsidiary Business*
Acme Building	Face brick and other building materials
Adalet	Electric enclosure systems and cable accessories
Ben Bridge Jeweler	Retail fine jewelry
Benjamin Moore	Architectural and industrial coatings — paint
Blue Chip Stamps	Marketing motivational services
Borsheim's	Retail fine jewelry
Buffalo News	Newspaper
Campbell Hausfeld	Air compressors and air tools
Carefree	Comfort and convenience products for the RV industry

(continued)

Table 3-2 *(continued)*

Subsidiary Name	Subsidiary Business
Cleveland Wood Products	Vacuum cleaner brushes and bags
CORT Business Services	Rental furniture
Dexter Shoe Company	Casual, dress, athletic shoes
Douglas Products	Specialty and cordless vacuum cleaners
Executive Jet	Fractional ownership programs for aircraft
Fechheimer Bros. Co.	Uniforms and accessories
FlightSafety International	Training for aircraft and ship operators
France	Sign transformers, components
H.H Brown Shoe Co.	Work shoes, boots, casual footwear
Halex	Zinc conduit fittings, other electrical materials
Helzberg's Diamond Shops	Retail fine jewelry
International Dairy Queen	Licensing and servicing D.Q. stores
Jordan's Furniture	Retail home furnishings
Justin Brands	Western boots, hats
Kingston	Appliance controls
Kirby	Vacuum cleaners
Lowell Shoe, Inc.	Women's and nurses shoes
Meriam	Pressure and flow measurement devices
MidAmerican Energy	Production, supply, distribution of energy
Nebraska Furniture Mart	Retail home furnishings
Northland	Fractional horsepower electric motors
Powerwinch	Marine and general purpose winches
Precision Steel Products	Steel service center
Quikut	Cutlery
ScottCare	Cardiopulminary rehab and monitoring equipment
Scot Labs	Cleaning compounds and solutions

Subsidiary Name	Subsidiary Business
See's Candies	Boxed candies, confectionary
Stahl	Truck equipment
Star Furniture Company	Retail home furnishings
Wayne Combustion Systems	Oil and gas burners
Wayne Water Systems	Sump, utility, well pumps
Western Enterprises	Compressed gas fittings
Western Plastics	Molded plastic components
R.C. Wiley Home Furnishings	Retail home furnishings
World Book	Encyclopedias, other educational material

What do all Berkshire Hathaway companies have in common?

✔ They are profitable, safe, and solid.

✔ They are easy to understand with simple business models.

✔ They produce plenty of cash flow to reinvest.

✔ They are unique businesses with strong market positions and franchises.

✔ They have solid, trustworthy management.

✔ They were bought at reasonable prices.

We ordinary value investors can't assemble this kind of portfolio, but we can learn from what makes Berkshire Hathaway and its master tick. That's ground we cover in the rest of this book.

For more on Buffett

Whole books can be — and have been — written on Buffett, his personality, humor, lifestyle, experiences, and teachings. We cannot begin to approach the rich material available in other books more devoted to him as a topic. Another interesting, though plain and simple to the extreme, place to get information from and about Buffett and Berkshire Hathaway is the corporate Web site, www.berkshirehathaway.com. Buffett's letters to shareholders are particularly interesting and exemplify his deep understanding and sense of humor.

Warren's worth

Of the 1,342,950 shares of Berkshire Hathaway, Warren Buffett owns almost 34 percent, or about 450,000 shares. The shares were recently priced at $68,800 each, so that's over $31 *billion*. Still more remarkable, that holding represents 99 percent of his net worth — a true vote of confidence in his own value investing! Buffett has never sold a share and never intends to, and he seldom gives shares away. His lean charitable giving has been criticized, but considering his growth record, charities are better off to wait and receive more later. And that, of course, is his strategy.

Part II

Fundamentals for Fundamentalists

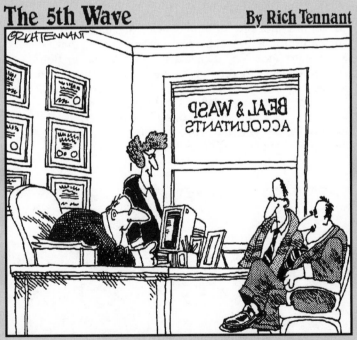

The 5th Wave — By Rich Tennant

"OUR GOAL IS TO MAXIMIZE YOUR UPSIDE AND MINIMIZE YOUR DOWNSIDE WHILE WE PROTECT OUR OWN BACKSIDE."

In this part . . .

We open the value investor toolbox by first engaging in a short exploration of investing mathematics and show how a few simple math principles can make you a better investor. Next up is a discussion of information and information sources key to the value investor. Then we dig in further with a tour of the financial statement landscape, including balance sheets, income statements, and cash flow statements. Ratios and ratio analysis are explored as a way to make more sense of these numbers. Finally, we help you to find and interpret non-numeric influences in the value equation.

Chapter 4

A Painless Course in Value Investing Math

If calculus were required, I'd have to go back to delivering papers.

—Warren Buffett, 1994 securities analyst meeting

*I*f you're like many people, you can't imagine *painless* and *math* being used in the same phrase. In this chapter, we attempt to prove that math can be painless — even when it involves value investing. We present a handful of math concepts that are fundamental to value investing, but we keep it simple and practical and focus on application.

You won't find any statistics, stochastics, or oscillators — just a little algebra and arithmetic. You won't see any fuzzy math, just basic principles that value investors employ daily. You won't encounter the fancy Ivy League portfolio-theory higher-math stuff that you may have heard about, or seen, or even studied in school at one time or another. Generally, that stuff doesn't apply to value investing. And you won't come across formulas with little Greek symbols popping up like dandelions to spoil what might otherwise be a pretty good read. We promise to give you only the basics you need for value investing.

The tools that we cover in this chapter, as well as the underlying principles, are thoroughly understood and employed by value investing masters. After you understand them, these concepts should become part of your investing vocabulary, just as knowing the taste and strength of garlic is part of your cooking vocabulary. Knowing the chemical makeup and concentration of the allyl propyl disulfide that is in garlic is hardly important for cooking. Likewise, we don't get into esoteric levels of investing math. In fact, we pondered whether to use the word *math* at all in this chapter.

Lesson 1: Time Value of Money

In this section, we explore a cornerstone principle in all of business and finance: A dollar today isn't worth the same amount as a dollar yesterday. Nor is it worth the same amount as a dollar tomorrow. In a nutshell, invested money appreciates with time. Here we explore how and how much.

As we explore the how much part, we warn you in advance that there will be exponents, meaning that we raise a mathematical expression to a power. Keep the faith: The calculations are easy, and today's calculators easily automate them.

If you're already familiar with the basics of time value of money you can probably skip Lessons 1 through 3 in this chapter.

Money and time: An interesting story

Suppose that you have a $10 bill in your pocket. What's it worth today? Ten bucks. If you got this right, hang on. Don't skip to Chapter 5 just yet.

Now suppose that the $10 is in a bank account or some other investment vehicle that pays a return. This return can be a fixed payment for the financial institution's use of the money, known as *interest*. Or it can be a return in some other form, say, a profit generated through the use of the $10 in a business, increasing the value of the business.

Either way, if you leave these dividends alone and don't withdraw them, they become part of the investment. At a 10 percent rate of return, the $10 becomes $11 in the first year, and $11 is invested in the interest or profit-generating asset for the second year. With $11 invested, assuming that the interest or profitability stays the same, you reap the greater rewards due an $11 investment. In this case, the reward is now $1.10, not $1. The investment is now worth $12.10 ($10 + $1 + $1.10). Now $12.10 is invested, and the return is $1.21. And so forth. Both the investment and the incremental dollar return grow over time. Each year's golden eggs become part of the next year's goose, which in turn lays still more golden eggs.

Present and future value

So what is the investment worth? It depends. (You hate that answer, we know, but it's the right answer anyway.) The investment is worth $10 today, as we said earlier. That ten bucks is known as the *present value.* Not too difficult so far, huh? Now we want to talk about the future. If the investment grows over time, then the investment will have a total value of the initial $10 plus all returns generated in that time. This is known as *future value.*

Money invested grows and compounds. In other words, there is growth on the original investment, plus return and growth on returns already earned. A snowball rolling downhill is a good analogy. As the ball gets bigger, it picks up ever-larger amounts of snow. How much? We get to that when we talk about compounding just ahead. Suffice to say for now that the growth drivers — or time value drivers — are the rate of return and the amount of time. Understanding time value effects and the concept of future value is important to investors.

Investment returns in the future: When it isn't yours yet

Suppose that someone promises to pay you $10 five years from now. Can you look at yourself and say that you're $10 wealthier? In five years you can, but what about now? Well, the truth is, if you look in the mirror today, you can't say that you're worth $10 more. The reality is this: To have $10 in the future, you only need to drop some fraction of that $10 in the bank today. How much? Again, it depends. It depends on the same factors that drive future value: rate of return and time. At 10 percent, you would need to deposit only $6.21 today to have $10 five years from now. Same formula, but this time, approach it from the opposite direction. Instead of asking, "What is my $10 worth in five years?" you ask, "What would I need today to have $10 in five years?"

The magic compounding formula

We say in Chapter 1 that there are no magic value investing formulas. We lied a little, but just a little, for what we introduce here isn't a stock-picking formula. It is the fundamental time-value-of-money, or *compounding,* formula that provides an indispensable foundation for value investors. A word of advice: What's important here is to understand the formula, the dynamics, and the factors that drive or have the most influence on the result — not to memorize the formula so that you can do lots of math problems. Furthermore, you need a lot more than this formula to select stocks and be successful — just as it takes more than garlic to cook. But it is a vital piece of working knowledge. Here's the formula:

$$FV = PV \times (1 + i)^n$$

where . . .

FV is future value

PV is present value

i is the interest rate, or rate of return

n is the number of years invested

What's happening in this formula? Well, it's really fairly simple (and because simplicity is our theme, that's a good thing). The formula says that the future value is a function of the present value, expanded or compounded by the interest rate over time. To calculate a return for one year, simply take PV and multiply by 1 (to preserve the original value) plus i (to increment by the interest rate or rate of return). The result is future value.

To calculate the return for more than one year, it gets more interesting. Multiply PV by $(1 + i)$ factored by the number of years, so 5 years is $(PV) \times (1 + i) \times (1 + i) \times (1 + i) \times (1 + i) \times (1 + i)$. Each $(1 + i)$ indicates another year of *compounding* interest. Mathematical shorthand for sequential multiplications by the same value is the exponent symbol.

The FV of $10 invested at 10 percent over 5 years is

$$FV = \$10 \times (1 + .10)^5$$

or

$10 \times (1.61)$, or $16.10

12C your way clearly

If the formulas in Lesson 1 appear cumbersome, there is help in the form of a $50 device from Hewlett-Packard The device happens to be the oldest product in its catalog: the HP 12C Financial Calculator. Other financial calculators work fine, too. These calculators have a built-in set of easy-to-use financial formulas. They also do some of the more complex things, such as calculate FV if you contribute $10 more every year. Regardless, we recommend that a 12C or the more modern 17B or something similar be in every investor's tool kit. Heck, you can even use it to figure out your next car payment. It's the best bucks any investor can invest.

Fine, we can calculate future value. But what about present value? What if you want to figure out what interest rate would give you $16.10 on a $10 investment if held for five years? In other words, what if you want to work backwards? You can transpose the formula algebraically to calculate PV, *i*, and even *n:*

1) $PV = FV \div (1 + i)^n$

2) $i = ((FV \div PV)^{(1/n)} - 1$ or the nth *root* of (FV/PV)

3) **n** — we won't go there. It involves logarithms!

Why Lesson 1 is important

Time value of money helps you estimate or determine the future value of an investment held over time. The importance of time value of money calculations doesn't stop there. Some value investing techniques call for *discounting*, or calculating the present value of future income streams. Time value calculations are an important ingredient in measuring the value of investments and comparing them to alternatives. And you see later in this chapter and in those that follow how compounding becomes a main engine powering the value investing concept.

Lesson 2: Compound It! The Amazing Power of Compounding

The greatest and most powerful investment principle of all is compounding. We suspect that if not for the convenient number of ten, "Thou shalt compound your returns" would have been handed down to Moses on those tablets.

Why? Examine Table 4-1.

Table 4-1		Compounded Return on $1,000 Invested						
	1 year	*2 years*	*5 years*	*10 years*	*15 years*	*20 years*	*30 years*	*40 years*
4%	1,040	1,082	1,217	1,480	1,801	2,191	3,243	4,801
5%	1,050	1,103	1,276	1,629	2,079	2,653	4,322	7,040
6%	1,060	1,124	1,338	1,791	2,397	3,207	5,743	10,286
7%	1,070	1,145	1,403	1,967	2,759	3,870	7,612	14,974

(continued)

Table 4-1 *(continued)*

	1 year	2 years	5 years	10 years	15 years	20 years	30 years	40 years
8%	1,080	1,166	1,469	2,159	3,172	4,661	10,063	21,725
9%	1,090	1,188	1,539	2,367	3,642	5,604	13,268	31,409
10%	1,100	1,210	1,611	2,594	4,177	6,727	17,149	45,259
11%	1,110	1,232	1,685	2,839	4,785	8,062	22,892	65,001
12%	1,120	1,254	1,762	3,106	5,474	9,646	29,960	93,051
13%	1,130	1,277	1,842	3,395	6,254	11,523	39,116	132,782
14%	1,140	1,300	1,925	3,707	7,138	13,743	50,950	188,884
15%	1,150	1,323	2,011	4,046	8,137	16,367	66,212	267,864
16%	1,160	1,346	2,100	4,411	9,266	19,461	85,850	378,721
17%	1,170	1,369	2,192	4,807	10,539	23,106	111,065	533,869
18%	1,180	1,392	2,288	5,234	11,974	27,393	143,371	750,378
19%	1,190	1,416	2,386	5,695	13,590	32,429	184,675	1,051,668
20%	1,200	1,440	2,488	6,192	15,407	38,338	237,376	1,469,772
21%	1,210	1,464	2,594	6,727	17,449	45,259	304,482	2,048400
22%	1,220	1,488	2,703	7,305	19,742	53,358	389,758	2,847,038
23%	1,230	1,513	2,815	7,962	22,314	62,821	497,913	3,946,430
24%	1,240	1,538	2,932	8,594	25,196	73,864	634,820	5,455,913
25%	1,250	1,563	3,052	9,313	28,422	86,736	807,794	7,523,164

Sometimes a picture is worth a thousand words. The picture in Table 4-1 is a picture of the effects of compounding. It shows what happens to $1,000 invested at the beginning of a period of time, defined on the horizontal axis, at a rate of return, defined on the vertical axis. The formula to calculate these values is, you guessed it, the time value of money formula presented in Lesson 1, earlier in this chapter.

And you're right. That is $7 million and change in the lower-right corner, on a $1,000 investment. If you *really* do well and capture consistent 25 percent returns on your investments, in 40 years that's what you'd have. If you invested $20,000, you would have $140 million, assuming no taxes. Easy, right? You just need to know how to achieve consistent 25 percent annual returns!

How to make 8 trillion dollars (in 500 years)

One can go to extremes when applying the principles of compounding. If the Spanish royalty had invested the estimated $30,000 stake it placed in Christopher Columbus at 7 percent, that $30,000 would be worth over $8.5 *trillion* today. Spain would be a major world power (which is, of course, what the country was trying to achieve in 1492!). The trouble is that the Columbus expedition produced immediate results on the world stage, while the compounding approach would have required 500 years. So Ferdinand and Isabella probably made a good decision. Success depends on your time horizon — and what you do with your winnings.

Before you dismiss 25 percent annual returns as out of the question, know that until 1999 Berkshire Hathaway achieved over 30 percent annual *compounded* return for over 30 years. Things flattened a bit in 1999 and 2000, but the compounded annual rate of return is still better than 23 percent. (Nothing can go on forever, right?) Don't assume that high rates of return are impossible. Later in this chapter, we provide a closer look at the dramatic power of beating the market.

The power of i and n

The point isn't necessarily to turn $1,000 into $7 million. The point is to show that the farther you go down and to the right on Table 4-1, the larger the resulting future value gets. In fact, it increases at a faster rate the farther down and to the right you go.

The nature of the $(1 + i)^n$ expression in our formula produces this fascinating result. If i is small, no matter how large the n, the end product doesn't really get that big. (Recall from seventh grade math that 1 raised to any power is still 1.) Likewise, if you have a small n, it doesn't matter so much what the i is. If n is 1, then there is little or no power. The result is a single $1 + i$ multiple of your investment.

Why Lesson 2 is important

The power of compounding assumes its full glory (and your investments reach their full girth) as i, or the rate of return, gets larger and the n, or length of time, gets longer. The *and* is important! Value investors look for a few more i points of return *and* to hold the productive investment for as many n years as possible.

Because *n* is an exponent, it exerts the greatest power and influence on your investing portfolio. Time is an investor's best friend. As Warren Buffett says, "Time is the friend of the good business, and the enemy of the poor one." No wonder value investors tend to be long-term investors! Find the best possible *i* and then let *n* happen.

Lesson 3: The Amazing Rule of 72

No investor in the history of the world understands, or has applied, the principle of compounding to a greater degree and with more success than Warren Buffett. Yet he reportedly does most investing math without a calculator. Does he possess a 1,000-megahertz mind that's able to grind out multiple power and exponential calculations faster than you can say Coca-Cola? Hardly. Not to say that being the gifted individual that he is, he *couldn't* perform so many rapid-fire calculations in his head. But he *doesn't*. Instead, he uses one of the most useful general rules in investing, maybe in all mathematics, as a computational shortcut. It's known as the Rule of 72.

How the Rule of 72 works

The Rule of 72 is based on the mathematics of the compounding formula. The Rule of 72 enables you to quickly estimate the rate of return or time period you need to double a sum of money with compounding. If you know the rate of return, you can compute the approximate time period. If you know the time period, you can compute the approximate rate of return. Here it is:

Number of years to double an investment at a given interest rate:

= 72 divided by the rate of return (as an integer: the rate × 100)

Rate of return required to double an investment over a given number of years:

= 72 divided by the number of years

Here are some examples of the use of the Rule of 72:

- ✔ At 12 percent, it takes six years to double your money (72/12).

- ✔ To double your money in eight years, you must earn a 9 percent rate of return (72/8).

- ✔ At 10 percent, how many years does it take to quadruple your money? Answer: It doubles in 7.2 years (72/10), so quadrupling would take twice that long, or 14.4 years.

✔ If your best friend brags about having bought a house for $150,000 that's now worth $600,000 and he's had it for ten years, what is the rate of return? Answer: It doubled twice ($150K to $300K to $600K) in ten years, or once every five years. So (72/5) gives you 14.4 percent. Not bad, but you could very well have beaten your friend in the stock market! In addition, you can really impress him by doing this calculation in your head!

Rates done right

Just what is the rate of return on an investment? It depends: Often on just how you calculate it. Take a look at the example we just presented under the Rule of 72. Your friend brags about buying a house for $150,000 and selling it ten years later for $600,000. He might call that a 300 percent return and, because it occurred over ten years, come out with an average of 30 percent per year. On the surface, he is correct. But when evaluating the home purchase as an investment (compared to other investments), one must include the compounding effect to have an accurate, apples-to-apples comparison. If that $150,000 were invested ten years ago and that investment were allowed to compound, what rate of return would have given you $600,000? As approximated using the Rule of 72, the compounded rate of return is only 14.4 percent. Although this return is perhaps good enough for bragging rights, it may not win the investment club trophy.

The compounded rate of return is sometimes called the *geometric* rate of return — as opposed to the straight average approach of simply dividing the total return by the number of years (as in 300 percent divided by 10 equals 30 percent per year) So, how do you calculate true compounded, or geometric, rates of return? There is a formula:

Geometric rate of return = [(Ending value/Beginning value)$^{(1/n)}$] – 1

where *n* equals the number of years.

For our example, we have $600,000/$150,000, or 4. Take 4 to the $1/10$th power (use your calculator) and get 1.149. Subtract 1, and get 14.9 percent, not exactly equal to the Rule of 72 result, but remember that the Rule of 72 is an approximation. You'll have a lot of fun at cocktail parties telling people what they *really* made on their investments.

Why Lesson 3 is important

The Rule of 72 gives you tremendous power to make fast calculations and decisions. It helps you to quickly compare investing alternatives and to speed up investing decisions Not only that, it gives you a tool to impress your friends and to figure out how long it will take for you to become a millionaire.

Lesson 4: The Frugal Investor: How Being Cheap Really Pays

What investor hasn't heard the advice "buy low and sell high"? The principle behind this glittering epigram is so obvious that one can hardly write about it. But in the irrationally exuberant markets of 1999 and 2000, this old standard gradually seemed to subside to "buy high, sell higher." Traders (and novice investors experiencing the markets for the first time) bought stocks because they were going up, in defiance of value investing logic.

What's the problem? Well, to put it simply, the higher a price you pay for a stock, the *less likely* it is to achieve a high rate of return. Suppose that a stock has an intrinsic value of $75. If you pay $100 for it, you're essentially betting that something good will happen to dramatically increase intrinsic value — or that some greater fool is out there to pay $110. True, it might happen, and it seemed to happen with regularity in the late 1990s bull run. You may get a 10 percent or 20 percent return on the investment.

But suppose that you were to buy the same stock at $50 as a *value play,* meaning that you think it's an undervalued stock. The chance for a 50 percent return — getting back to intrinsic value — is much higher than with the at-value or overvalued $100 stock. By the way, this has nothing to do with the actual price level, whether $10 or $100. It is the price *relative to value* that counts.

Keep your i on the ball

Value investors always look for that opportunity to achieve superior *i* (think back to the formula in Lesson 1). You achieve superior *i* by buying a stock with good fundamentals, *including* growth. So you get the growth rate — perhaps 6 percent, maybe 8 percent, or even 10 percent. But as a bonus, you also get the return to intrinsic value, which can turn 6 percent, 8 percent, and 10 percent returns effectively into 12 percent, 14 percent, 16 percent, and higher returns. The lower the price paid, the higher the likelihood of above-average returns. This comes straight from the teachings of Ben Graham and the practice of Warren Buffett.

Buffett always tries to find a pricing situation leading to an extra 2 percent or 3 percent or more for his investing return, or *i*. Remember Table 4-1? This is a good, good thing.

Investment gravity

Central tendency, statistical mechanics, or whatever scientific name you want to apply — random numbers tend to move toward means, just as spinning space objects form perfect spheres and choppy water eventually becomes smooth. (Don't worry. We're not going to step off the edge into *physics* now.) This investment "gravity" (not really a function of math and physics but of aggregate investor *behavior*) causes short-term high and low prices to move back towards long-term averages. Similarly, and more important for value investors, asset prices over the long run rise or fall to meet corresponding asset values. Several studies have confirmed this. It doesn't always happen, but taking this perspective is like betting with the house.

How much does buying cheap help?

Take a look at Table 4-2. Note how long-term profits jump as the rate of return grows beyond the market average and time has an opportunity to work its magic. An investor consistently beating the market by 2 percent would achieve 20 percent greater return in 10 years ($9,646/$6,727), 43 percent in 20 years, and 72 percent in 30 years. An investor beating the market by 6 percent would get 71 percent more in 10 years, 189 percent in 20 years, and 492 percent, or almost 5 times as much profitable return, in 30 years.

Table 4-2	Compounded Effects of Increased Annual Returns							
	1 year	2 years	5 years	10 years	15 years	20 years	30 years	40 years
Market Return 10%	1,100	1,270	1,611	2,094	4,177	6,727	17,449	45,259
Beat the Market by 2%	1,120	1,254	1,762	3,106	5,474	9,646	29,960	93,051
Beat the Market by 4%	1,140	1,300	1,925	3,707	7,138	13,743	50,950	188,884
Beat the Market by 6%	1,160	1,346	2,100	4,411	9,266	19,461	85,850	378,721
Beat the Market by 8%	1,180	1,392	2,288	5,234	11,974	27,393	143,371	750,378
Beat the Market by 10%	1,200	1,440	2,488	6,192	15,407	38,338	237,376	1,469,772

Ben Graham bought stocks cheap mostly to provide a margin of safety. Warren Buffett and other more growth-oriented investors might buy cheap to increase the margin of growth; that is, to beat market returns if underlying asset growth develops as expected.

Why Lesson 4 is important

The mathematical power of compounding makes a small increase in investing return, or *i*, very compelling. To increase the chances of achieving a higher *i*, buy cheap. Buy expensive, and you'll be lucky to match market returns.

Lesson 5: Opportunity Lost

By the time you finish this lesson, you may regard it as an extension of the last one. In Lesson 4, we show you how beating the market with even slightly higher rates of return is a shorter path to wealth. This is *especially* true if the investments are left on the table to perform, and perform consistently, over time. This lesson, as the title indicates, is about lost opportunity. What about investments achieving *less* than market average return? What happens when you cling to these investments? Are they like a bad marriage, not only producing inferior returns but also consuming valuable time that you could put to work elsewhere? From an investment perspective, you bet.

Pruning the dead branches

Table 4-3 illustrates that it isn't hard to show what happens when you hang on to the losers, or even the inferior "winners."

Table 4-3	Compounded Effects of Market Underperformance							
	1 year	2 years	5 years	10 years	15 years	20 years	30 years	40 years
Market Return 10%	1,100	1,270	1,611	2,094	4,177	6,727	17,449	45,259
Underperform the Market by 2%	1,080	1,166	1,469	2,159	3,172	4,661	10,063	21,725
Underperform the Market by 4%	1,060	1,124	1,338	1,791	2,397	3,207	5,743	10,286

	1 year	2 years	5 years	10 years	15 years	20 years	30 years	40 years
Underperform the Market by 6%	1,040	1,082	1,217	1,480	1,801	2,191	3,243	4,801
Underperform the Market by 8%	1,020	1,040	1,104	1,219	1,346	1,486	1,811	2,208
Underperform the Market by 10%	1,000	1,000	1,000	1,000	1,000	1,000	1,000	1,000

Compared to market returns, an investor underperforming the market by 2 percent (in other words, achieving an 8 percent return) falls 17 percent behind a market performer after 10 years, 31 percent behind over 20 years, and 43 percent behind over 30 years. An investor underperforming by 6 percent loses 43 percent, 67 percent, and 82 percent to the market performing investor over 10, 20, and 30 years, respectively. That's quite a price to pay for underperformance. Now, if your investments are producing *negative* returns, the results can be an ugly sight.

Don't hang on to the losers! Not only do you lose, but you also lose out on opportunities to gain. If it's broke, fix it!

The $3 million sports car

You can see where this discussion is headed from the heading. You're a successful value investor who can achieve consistent 12 percent, 15 percent, or greater returns, and you have the discipline and fortitude to hang on to investments. Now, you probably know that even successful value investors can have fun, right? They can splurge on a new car, a vacation, a really nice outdoor barbecue. But savvy value investors also know how much they're costing themselves in the long run.

Suppose that you're a modestly successful 12 percent value investor. You spend $1,000 on that new barbecue today. From Table 4-1, you can see that you would have had $3,106 in 10 years, $9,646 in 20 years, $29,960 in 30 years, and $93,051 in 40 years. Spend $30,000 on a new car today, and forgo $289,380 20 years from now, $898,800 in 30 years, and $2.8 million in 40 years, at 12 percent! And, if you're a better investor (an investor normally capable of 12 percent returns or better), the "losses" quickly mount!

Why Lesson 5 is important

A savvy value investor's mind operates in a continuous buzz, deciding whether an investment is achieving its best possible returns or whether it should be replaced. Value investors like cheap stocks, but if the stocks get cheap on their watch, investors should consider a serious reappraisal of a company's prospects. Value investors continuously check for dead branches and aren't afraid to get out the pruning shears. Value investors know the cost of dead wood. Likewise, value investors, like frugal citizens, avoid squandering money that could be put to better use, and they're always thinking of the best use for the money. For Warren Buffett, a penny found on a sidewalk is "the start of the next billion."

Lesson 6: Discounting

In Lesson 1, under "Investment returns in the future: When it isn't yours yet," we discuss the notion that money acquired tomorrow isn't worth as much as money acquired today. This notion becomes very important for value investors, who face the decision of whether to buy a stock today. That decision is almost always based on some future expectation of growth in earnings and cash flow that a company will generate. In fact, a pure value investor *defines* a stock price as the sum of all future cash flows generated per share. Nothing more, nothing less. Well, as a practical matter, it *is* less because of the time value of money. You must discount the earnings or cash flow to achieve an equivalent present value.

How to discount earnings

If an investment returns a dollar today, a dollar next year, a dollar two years from now, and so forth, each dollar should be discounted for time at a reasonable interest rate. The formula is derived from the benchmark formula in Lesson 1, $FV = PV \times (1 + i)^n$. Essentially, each year's cash flow is divided by $(1 + i)$ raised to the power represented by that year, and then the resulting figures are added to arrive at a single figure representing the sum total present value, or PV.

If the cash flows are even, or unchanged each year, then you can use Table 4-4 to estimate the present value at a given discount rate and for a number of years. Thus, $1 returned on an investment for the next 15 years has a present value of $7.60 (not $15, as would be the case if *not* discounted).

Table 4-4	Present Value of $1 Received Each Year							
	1 year	2 years	5 years	10 years	15 years	20 years	30 years	40 years
4% Discount Rate	1.0	1.9	4.5	8.1	11.1	13.6	17.3	19.8
6% Discount Rate	0.9	1.8	4.2	7.4	9.7	11.5	13.8	15.0
8% Discount Rate	0.9	1.8	4.0	6.7	8.6	9.8	11.3	11.9
10% Discount Rate	0.9	1.7	3.8	6.1	7.6	8.5	9.4	9.8
12% Discount Rate	0.9	1.7	3.6	5.7	6.8	7.5	8.1	8.2
15% Discount Rate	0.9	1.6	3.4	5.0	5.8	6.3	6.6	6.6
20% Discount Rate	0.8	1.5	3.0	4.2	4.7	4.9	5.0	5.0

How to discount earnings when cash flows aren't even

Applying the formula gets trickier when the cash flows aren't even. You have to estimate each cash flow, discount it according to which year you are in, and then add up all the value to arrive at a single PV. The example in Table 4-5 shows the PV of a series of per-share cash flows over ten years, starting with $1 in the first year and increasing by 20 percent for the first five years, then by 10 percent for the next five years. Note the total present-value figures in the second column from the left and how they differ according to the discount rate. How do you know what discount rate to choose? We cover that next.

Use spreadsheets, such as those available in Microsoft Excel or Lotus 1-2-3, to make complicated PV calculations much easier.

Residual value

Uh-oh, residual value *sounds* pretty technical, and really, it approaches pretty technical. Some value investors assign company value as the sum of *all* future cash flows, discounted back to the present. In fact, many finance experts consider this the true value of a security. The tricky part is figuring what *all* means. Theoretically, *all* refers to infinity, if a company is assumed to last forever. Even if you reduce the relevant *all* to 50 or 100 years, you end up with a challenging discounting problem, especially if cash flows and growth rates vary over that time period (and they will). Imagine a spreadsheet constructed to discount irregular cash flows expanded to cover 50 or 100 years!

Many numbers-oriented financiers and value investors assign a *residual value* or *continuing value* to all cash flows beyond, say, 10 years. Forecasting growth rates and appropriate discount rates that far out into the future is difficult. Moreover, because of the nature of the discounting formula, individual years don't count for as much. We introduce a computational formula for residual values in Chapter 12. We also share another approach known as the *acquisition approach* in Chapter 12. In this approach, instead of estimating and discounting cash flows far out into the future, we try to predict the value of the business as an acquisition target at the 10 year cutoff. This technique helps to avoid the calculation of residual value altogether.

Table 4-5	Present Value of Uneven Per-Share Cash Flows over Ten Years									
	1 year	2 years	3 years	4 years	5 years	6 years	7 years	8 years	9 years	10 years
Cash Flow	1.00	1.20	1.44	1.73	2.07	2.28	2.51	2.76	3.04	3.34
Present Value										
4% Discount Rate 16.65	0.96	1.11	1.28	1.48	1.70	1.80	1.91	2.02	2.13	2.26
6% Discount Rate 14.81	0.94	1.07	1.21	1.37	1.55	1.61	1.67	1.73	1.80	1.86
10% Discount Rate 11.89	0.91	0.99	1.08	1.18	1.29	1.29	1.29	1.29	1.29	1.29
12% Discount Rate 10.72	0.89	0.96	1.02	1.10	1.18	1.16	1.13	1.11	1.09	1.08
15% Discount Rate 9.26	0.87	0.91	0.95	0.99	1.03	.99	.94	.90	.86	.83

The great discount rate debate

So what discount rate should be used? This is undeniably one of the favorite topics of debate in financial circles. More business school professors have gained tenure writing articles on this subject than on any others (this is undocumented speculation, not a researched fact!). Regardless, the discount rate chosen is an important factor. Here's what it comes down to. The discount rate should reflect the following:

- ✔ What it costs to acquire money to invest (which is in turn driven by interest rates)
- ✔ What the possible returns are from alternative investments (opportunity cost, also driven by interest rates)
- ✔ Some compensation for business risk, inflation risk, and financial risk

Unfortunately, calculating these values just isn't that simple. That's why the whole issue is so much fun to argue about. One thing that is for certain: The conservative approach is to set a higher discount rate, which places a smaller value on future cash flows.

Once again, we like the Buffett approach. Rather than burn energy striving for a precise discount rate ("it's better to be approximately right than precisely wrong," he quips), Buffett suggests using a minimum of 10 percent, and 15 percent if you want to stay conservative. Fifteen percent should cover the range of possibilities — higher inflation, tax law changes, business declines, and so forth. If a stock still looks to be selling at an attractive price, even after you've discounted its cash flows at 15 percent, then it probably has the margin of safety that value investors seek.

The artificially high discount rate that Buffett and other value investors use is sometimes called the *hurdle rate*. As the name implies, it is a rate of return that your investment or company must exceed to be viable.

Why Lesson 6 is important

Making a fair and honest evaluation of a company's value often requires understanding the value of its future cash flows. To understand the real value of these cash flows and their relation to today's price, you must discount the cash flows back to the present. You see more about how this concept is applied in later chapters, in particular Chapter 12.

Lesson 7: Beware of Large Numbers

What?! And here you thought the whole idea of investing was to *produce* large numbers. Now we're telling you to be wary of them? What gives? In investing, like life, some numbers are too good to be true and thus can't go on forever.

The 30 percent beanstalk

Your high-tech company (or mutual fund, for that matter) brags in each report of a continuous 30 percent growth in sales and profits. The stock is priced at a lofty 60 times earnings because it's the norm for stocks in that industry to have price-earnings-to-growth ratios of 2 (that is, P/E can be twice the growth rate, a topic we discuss later). So what's the problem? *Sustainability.*

Suppose that your company has $100 million in sales today. To achieve a 30 percent growth rate, it has to achieve $130 million in sales next year. So far, no problem. But to maintain this rate, what does the company have to achieve in the second year? If you grasp the compounding thing, you know that 30 percent growth in the second year is $130 million plus 30 percent of *that* figure. So 30 percent growth would require $169 million in sales. Still not too bad. But what about in 10 years?

You see the formula coming together. $FV = PV \times (1 + i)^{(n-1)}$. Only this time you don't calculate the future value of an investment. You calculate the future value of sales required to sustain a 30 percent growth bragging right. So for our example,

Future sales in 10 years = $100M \times (1 + 0.30)^9$

Or $1.06 *billion*

In 20 years, that becomes $14.2 *billion,* with an incremental growth of $2.4 *billion* annually.

Now, if you're the sales manager for XYZ Corporation, assigned the glorious task of meeting shareholder expectations for growth, where are you going to find the incremental sales? Your company has conquered the world, but Earth is a small planet. Extraterrestrial markets are still pre-emergent. FedEx and UPS have yet to deliver to Mars or beyond. So what happens? Growth rates likely start to decline. Maintaining the growth rate requires greater and greater acquisition of incremental dollars, which becomes increasingly difficult as the market becomes saturated.

Smart value investors recognize the increasing difficulty in maintaining high growth rates and project lower rates beyond a reasonable number of years.

The $20 billion wall

Over the years, there has been a noticeable trend towards diminished growth when a company hits the $20 billion, and then again the $40 billion, sales mark. IBM, HP, GE, Home Depot, and even big oil companies have experienced the wall. Companies with $20 billion in sales and 20 percent growth rates suddenly see growth rates fall off the table and must buy growth through potentially harmful acquisitions. It seems to happen again at $40 billion. Why? Markets become saturated, and large incremental sales in core businesses become more difficult to find. Additionally, these companies, because of their sheer size, have more difficulty organizing themselves to execute dynamic and aggressive sales plans. The meaning for value investors: Conservative or even zero growth estimates are in order, especially beyond the 5- to 10-year horizon.

The diversification paradox

All TV and radio programs and magazine and newspaper articles on investing start with the same inviolate, unassailable principle. It's presented as if it were etched on God's tablets: Diversify. That principle goes something like this: "The prudent investor will always look for ways to diversify his portfolio by buying multiple stocks or funds in different industries. That way, risk is minimized, and there is a greater chance of achieving market rates of return."

Okay, not bad. Most investors are satisfied with something at least close to market rates of return, and most of them want to sleep at night. The part about "a greater chance of achieving market rates of return" is actually true. But the sheer mathematical fact is that the more stocks you put into your portfolio, the less the odds of *beating* the market.

Think of the old probability models you studied in high school. If you toss a penny into the air, it comes down heads or tails. Fifty-fifty probability. Toss a few more pennies in the air, say six total, and the odds are you'll get three heads and three tails, maybe two and four, maybe one and five, maybe even all six heads. Probabilities decrease as you go to the extremes, but these outcomes are all plausible. Now throw 100,000 pennies into the air. What are the chances of all 100,000 coming up heads? Desperately small. This is an extreme case, but the point remains: The more stocks you have, the more likely your winners and losers will cancel each other out.

Additionally, suppose that you hit a home run and score a 50 percent gain on a stock. If it's one of four stocks in your portfolio and all others break even, the portfolio gains on average 12.5 percent. If it's one of ten stocks, with all the others breaking even, the gain is only 5 percent. Holding too many stocks dilutes the gains of the winners. Combined with transaction costs and management fees, this phenomenon helps explain why 91 percent of mutual funds *underperformed* the market during the 1990s.

But what about reducing risk? True, the more pennies you throw, the lower the odds that they will all come up tails. If the performance of your stocks is really random, then owning more stocks reduces the chance of beating market returns. The converse is also true: Owning many stocks reduces the chance of achieving less than the market return.

Value investors aren't random stock pickers! They take the risk out by understanding the companies and their intrinsic value, not by spreading the risk across more companies. Value investors are *focus investors* — driving towards deep understanding of their investments without diluting possible returns through diversification. They see danger in owning too many investments. Instead of reducing risk through diversification, risk may actually *increase* as it becomes harder to follow the fortunes of so many businesses. Therefore, Warren Buffett and most other value investors reject diversification per se as an investment strategy. They prefer to reduce risk by watching a few companies — companies that they thoroughly understand — more closely.

Why Lesson 7 is important

As a value investor, you need to be aware that large numbers can work against you. Large numbers imply diminishing returns. Companies can't grow at the same rate forever. Further, successful value investors reduce risk through focus and by selecting the right companies, not by adding more companies to the portfolio.

Lesson 8: Inflation, Taxes, Interest Rates, and Risk

How do you factor inflation, taxes, and interest — insidious, largely unavoidable forces — into the world of value investing? You've heard about the wonders of compounding and seen all those seven-figure possibilities on the long-term compounding table. Are you going to let these forces take those gains away?

The answer (again): It depends.

You can imagine these forces acting on your value investments much as the wind acts on a bicyclist. Think of inflation as a persistent head wind, always blowing against you, the issue being how hard. Taxes always blow in your face, too. But as we show you in a minute, you can put up shields to protect yourself from these head winds.

Interest rates are, well, interesting. They can act as a head wind or a tail wind. High interest rates are definitely a head wind, as investment capital becomes more expensive (hence higher discount rates) and safe investments, such as bonds, have relatively more attractive returns. Low interest rates, on the other hand, act as a welcome tail wind, stimulating market performance and helping stocks become relatively more attractive as investments. You can't do anything about interest rates, but you need to watch them for shifts and *signs* of shift out there on the open prairie. Finally, you get to risk, which can act like turbulent gusts of wind coming from all directions. You can manager risk by riding your bicycle slower. Just knowing that risk exists also helps. So now pedal on to an explanation of how these factors affect your investments and investment calculations.

Inflation

Inflation is a bad word for all investors. In this book, we largely ignore it. Although inflation provides a light head wind that reduces the future purchasing power of your investments, it has the same effect regardless of how you have invested your money. Thus, it doesn't materially influence investing decisions or practice, and you could go silly adjusting all prices and future cash flows for inflation. Furthermore, inflation isn't a cash transaction. You don't write checks to the Consumer Price Index gods. And when you discount future cash flows, the discount rate nominally covers some of its effects anyway. Keep in mind, however, that increases in inflation often lead to increases in interest rates, which can alter your interest in buying stocks.

Taxes

You can't avoid taxes completely, but you can defer them. We're not talking IRAs and 401Ks here — those are entirely different matters. You have a secret to expanding value and reducing taxes: Don't sell stocks; hold them for the long term. Why? Once again, the power of compounding. If your investment grows each year but you *sell* it each year and reinvest it, you're liable for taxes on your gain. Why is that so bad? Because that chunk is forever denied the opportunity to compound.

Table 4-6 is a rather extreme but illustrative example of the tax and profitability differences between holding investment gains and cashing out frequently.

Table 4-6	Deferring Taxes: Effect of Hold versus Sell-and-Reinvest Strategy		
	No Sell	*Sell, Reinvest*	
	Value of Investment	*Value of Investment*	*Tax Paid*
1	2.00	1.64	0.36
2	4.00	2.89	0.59
3	8.00	4.41	0.97
4	16.00	7.23	1.59
5	32.00	11.86	2.60
6	64.00	19.46	4.27
7	128.00	31.91	7.00
8	256.00	52.33	11.49
9	512.00	85.82	18.84
10	1,024.00	140.75	30.90
11	2,048.00	230.82	50.67
12	4,096.00	378.55	83.10
13	8,192.00	620.83	136.28
14	16,384.00	1,018.15	223.50
15	32,768.00	1,669.77	366.54
16	65,536.00	2,738.43	601.12
17	131,072.00	4,491.02	958.83
18	262,144.00	7,365.28	1,616.77
19	524,288.00	12,079.06	2,651.50
20	1,048,576.00	19,809.66	4,348.46
Total Tax	**377,487.00**		**11,142.00**
Net Profit	**671,088.00**	**19,809.00**	

Admittedly, Table 4-6 is extreme, as we assume a doubling of your investment every year. Intuitively, you may expect taxes to be a wash, thinking that if you fork over 36 percent, it doesn't matter in the long run whether you do it as a lump sum at the end or a bit at a time, year after year.

But it does matter. The difference is compounding. Every dollar, every doubled dollar, and so on are left untouched in the no-sell strategy, while in the sell-and-reinvest strategy, 36 percent of the golden eggs are sent to Uncle Sam and his statehouse brethren each year. The result: $671,000 in net profit for the hold strategy versus $19,809 for the sell-and-reinvest strategy, even though under the hold strategy, you pay more than 30 times as much total tax! Both you and Uncle Sam win! Why? One hundred percent — not 64 percent — of the golden eggs are allowed to hatch into geese. This result speaks volumes for the value investor's buy-and-hold approach.

Of course, you don't want to buy-and-hold yourself down the drain! If a company's fortunes and prospects change, selling and finding a new investment, regardless of tax consequences, make sense. If your goose isn't laying golden eggs, you'd better find another goose!

Interest rates

As we state earlier in this chapter, interest rates can act as a head wind or tail wind. Higher interest rates tend to diminish perceived investment returns, and hence stock prices, while lower interest rates stimulate economic and profit growth while making stock investments look relatively attractive. So what do you use as your investment weather vane to determine interest rate direction and effect?

Like so many investing issues, much has been written on this topic. For illustration, we'll use the Ben Graham intrinsic value formula from Chapter 3:

Intrinsic value = $E (2r + 8.5) \times (4.4/y)$

where . . .

E = annual earnings

r = average growth rate

y = the interest rate

The second expression, $(4.4/y)$, is what's important here. The interpretation is clear: If the interest rate is greater than 4.4, the expression will calculate to less than 1, dragging down the intrinsic value. Similarly, interest rates less than 4.4 result in a positive influence and a tail wind for intrinsic value.

Is 4.4 still the right number? Conceptually, Graham's approach is good for value investing calculations. The baseline interest rate, which Graham derived from studying long-term corporate bond rates, is probably a little low by today's standards. Considerable debate exists on what kind of interest rate to use and whether it is a long-term or a short-term rate. Until recently, the 30-year Treasury rate was the standard, but the emergence of government surpluses resulted in fewer of these bonds being issued and traded. Some investors watch 10-year Treasury securities, while others watch the Fed Funds and discount rates set by Alan Greenspan and the Federal Reserve Committee. From our experience, anything greater than 5.5 percent probably represents a head wind, and anything less than 5 percent for these key rates probably represents a tail wind. These factors change over time, depending on inflation and investor expectations.

Apart from Ben Graham's intrinsic value formula, interest rates are also a factor in discounted cash flow approaches (introduced earlier in this chapter). Current interest rates affect the discount rate. The higher the current interest rates, the higher the discount rate, resulting in a lower total investment value using the present value formula. Conversely, lower interest rates turn into lower discount rates, which act as a tail wind, and relatively high valuations. Again, there is more theory than fact on how to quantify the effect of interest rates on discount rates, so we like the Buffett approach, calling for simple, conservative, generally inclusive assumptions devoid of heavy quantitative analysis. Buffett would likely set the discount rate at 10 percent in a tail wind environment and closer to 15 percent in a head wind environment.

Risk

Risk is perhaps the most debated, theoretical, difficult-to-quantify element of all. Many types of risk in the business and investing world are beyond the scope of this book. The theorists who have tried to quantify risk as a component of investment analysis have generally circled around the notion of *beta* — a simpler-than-most Greek letter formula that assesses a stock's price movements versus the market and versus other stocks. Essentially, a beta greater than 1.0 means that the stock tends to fluctuate *farther* in the same direction than the base market index or portfolio of stocks it's being compared with. A beta less than 1.0 means that the stock price moves less in the same direction, or even in a different direction. If you've read any investing books, you've probably encountered beta somewhere in the discussion and been told that high beta stocks are riskier and low beta stocks are safer.

What's wrong with this picture? It turns out that beta is relatively meaningless for value investors. Why? Because it measures the fluctuation of stock *prices*. As a value investor, you aren't concerned with stock price fluctuation, only whether the stock price is a bargain compared to long-term value. Value investors ignore the type of risk measured by beta. Beta is useful only in the sense that higher price volatility for an issue may reflect underlying uncertainty in the company itself, such as with many of the higher flying tech stocks in 2000 and 2001. But the risks associated with these stocks become apparent long before you examine beta.

If you reflect again on Buffett's approach, you realize that the risk isn't inherent in the stock's price, but rather on the clarity and consistency of a company's future prospects. The more unpredictable (hard to understand) the company and its future, the greater the risk. There is no way to easily quantify this sort of risk. Generally, business risks are taken into account in the discount rate by making a conservative assumption to provide a margin of safety.

Why Lesson 8 is important

Inflation, taxes, interest rates, and risk all affect your investments and investment decisions. Inflation can be left alone as a decision factor, but watch out for possible influence on interest rates. Taxes affect how investments should be managed. The more taxes can be deferred, the higher the long-run total return. Taxes don't generally influence the *buy* decision, only the *sell* decision for a stock. Interest rates can increase or decrease the valuation of a company as an investment. Risk for the value investor is defined in terms of the company and its prospects, not the volatility of its stock price. Where more risk is perceived, you seek a greater margin of safety, or discount, between price and value. Quantifying these effects is difficult at best; you can do it by adjusting discount rates in valuation formulas or by requiring higher rates of return before committing investing dollars.

Chapter 5

A Value Treasure Map: Knowing Where to Dig

. . . .

In This Chapter

▶ Figuring out what information a value investor needs

▶ Looking at investor resources: what's available and where to get it

▶ Exploring best-in-class investing resources

. . . .

> *Unless facts are placed in a framework that provides meaning, they can be confusing, contradictory chunks of white noise.*
>
> —Randy Befumo, analyst, *The Motley Fool*

*W*ithout a doubt, the fuel that drives all forms of investing today is information. This is especially true for the do-it-yourself investing styles that have emerged since the 1980s with the advent of the computer and the Internet. Whether you're a long-term value investor or a minute-by-minute day trader, you consume some form of financial information in making investing and trading decisions.

This chapter is designed to provide an overview of the types of investing information available to the value investor. We examine their sources, the quality of those sources, and their cost to you. By no means is this a complete list, but we share our favorites and emphasize low cost and simplicity in our selections. We suspect that your approach to acquiring information and other tools is similar to your investing approach: It's a value-based approach. In some ways, this chapter puts the cart before the proverbial horse because we haven't begun to explore value investing practice in depth. You may not know what to look for. We don't think that's an issue. Our advice: Read this chapter once as an introduction and then return to it as your understanding of value investing develops. In fact, you may return again and again as you refine your value investing system.

We assume that most of you are connected to the Internet. The Web has made research and information gathering so easy, cost-effective, and straight-forward that, in our opinion, no investor should do without it. True, value investing is a long-term endeavor, making the real-time nature of Web-based information relatively less important compared to other investing styles. But it's so much easier and often cheaper on the Web. That said, published information available by mail or even at your local library can be quite sufficient. Most of the information presented here, however, is available on the Web.

X Marks the Spot: Deciding What to Look For

No two investors are alike. That's one of the fundamental principles of investing and investors. Investing is a combination of art and science. Quantifiable and unquantifiable facts are mixed together in a stewpot, requiring interpretation according to taste. The "science" part is using numbers, facts and formulas to *measure* business value. The "art" part is taking all the facts and measurements together and weighing them according to intuition and experience to judge a most likely outcome or set of outcomes. This intertwining of art and science is, in fact, what makes markets work. The difference of opinion and judgment coming from thousands of investing "stewpots," combined with differing investing objectives, is what makes markets go up and down. The point: Just as there is no single value investing formula, there is no one set of investing resources guaranteed to make *you* a successful value investor. We can provide only the ingredients.

Further, we should note that, like so many other things in life, the law of diminishing returns applies. Too much information is, indeed, too much information. As all bargain hunters know from experience, driving by every gas station in town in search of a slightly better deal doesn't make sense. Similarly, using too many information sources will probably just confuse you. Our advice: Pick a couple information sources, learn all you can from them, and use them consistently. In other words, keep things simple.

Just the facts, ma'am

Fundamentally, a value investor looks for facts about a company's financial performance. These facts, and there are lots of them, provide the base or foundation for value analysis. Value investors look for current or most recent performance and also trends and changes that can help paint a picture of the future. These facts are available from the company itself as financial statements or from one of many information sources that repackage company-provided data for investor use.

Financial results

Information from financial statements provides a picture of company assets, liabilities, earnings, and growth. The *balance sheet* presents a snapshot of assets, liabilities, and net worth. The *income statement* shows revenues, expenses, and earnings for a defined period of time. The *statement of cash flows* follows the income statement, showing where cash is obtained and used in the business. Each of these documents usually has supporting tables and information conveying other key aspects of business fundamentals and performance. In Chapters 6 through 8, we explore these statements further.

Ratios

From the raw data the value investor will construct ratios — relationships between facts that offer clues to financial safety, quality, profitability, and efficiency, thus providing a clearer picture of company value. Ratios also serve to normalize data so that companies can be compared to other companies or whole industries. Many information resources calculate and provide these ratios in addition to the raw data. Price/earnings, price/book, price/sales, and debt/equity are examples, and there are many others. Doubtless you've used a few in your investing career. We explain more about ratios in Chapter 10.

Percentages

Percentages are the first cousin of ratios. Like ratios, percentages help paint a clearer picture of company performance and normalize data for comparison. Examples include return on equity (ROE), return on assets (ROA), and gross and net profit margin. ROE, ROA, and margins are explored in depth in Chapter 13.

The soft stuff

In addition to financial information, the value investor wants to get a sense of a company's management effectiveness and market position. This is where a lot of the "art" comes in. Understanding a company's products and markets is an exercise in judgment helped by looking at Web sites, advertising and marketing campaigns, the company's own description of its products, and what you see, hear, and experience on the street. You can gauge management effectiveness by looking at a company's financials and financial ratios, previous marketplace and financial decisions, business execution, acquisitions and mergers, and other "track record" items. Many value investors look at management commitment to the enterprise in the form of management ownership. Market position refers to a company's approach to the marketplace and the resulting success — or failure — of that approach. We take a closer look at these "intangibles" in Chapter 14.

Treasure maps come in all shapes and sizes

Have you ever done a Web search on "personal finance" or "investing"? If so, you know that you get thousands of results. For that matter, when you open your mailbox, hit the newsstand, or visit the average Web site, chances are pretty good that some kind of financial information is there. Most of that information consists of ads, articles about the market's recent performance, and even stock quotes. It's amazing how many Web sites carry stock quotes and market tickers. Financial information is everywhere. The tricky part: sorting through it all to find what works for value investing. Value investors are looking for business fundamentals, not information on the latest initial public offering (IPO), market correction, or short squeeze. They want information that's not considered real sexy stuff and isn't very interesting to write about, publish, or display. Can you imagine a section on marthastewart.com showing return-on-equity figures for the last five years for major U.S. firms?

Starting with the "Digging In: Examining Investor Resources" section later in this chapter, we take a closer look at different kinds of available information. We go on to suggest where you can find the most useful or best-in-class material.

Data, research, analysis

The real hard-core value investor — the financial analyst type — may want to start with detailed company-furnished financial results to develop his own picture of company value. We suspect that this approach may not be for most of you. More and more, third-party publishers and Web sites provide packaged information — that is, data plus value-add in the form of analysis. This information includes ratios, percentages, trends, and graphs along with the raw data. The information sometimes contains a company history. Lack of history can be a hindrance for the value investor. Finally, many sites provide research done by their own or other analysts. Sometimes this research includes in-depth review and discussion of financials. More often it includes analysts' projections of earnings for the next year or two. The latter, while creating a lot of cocktail party buzz, is relatively less useful for the value investor.

Online versus offline

In years past, the curious investor sent a postcard requesting a company's annual report, and — voilà — two or three weeks later, the annual report showed up in your mailbox. That was good enough, and with the value investor's long-term approach, it may still be good enough. But today, online tools provide immediate gratification if you want annual reports and are the source of the most useful packaged information that we discuss.

You don't have to use the Web, and many value investors don't. But doing so makes things quicker, easier, and sometimes cheaper.

Fee versus free

You wouldn't be a value investor if the cost of value investing information wasn't important! Fortunately, at least for now, much of the information you need is free or quasi-free. You may need to register on a Web site or view seemingly endless ads on a site. But as with life in general, the quality and utility of information go up with the price you're willing to pay. "Paid for" investing resources (those available for a fee) can provide much greater depth, analysis, and history. They can provide recommendations and can be more timely or current. We believe that you can accomplish value investing by using only the freebies, but fee-based resources are worth a close look for the more serious investor.

Sharpening the saw

This chapter mainly focuses on finding information to make value investing decisions. What if you want to sharpen your value investing skills? We have enough humility to realize that you may not get it all from this book. Many good books on value investing (and a few not-so-good ones) are available. Some of the more value-oriented investing Web sites, such as The Motley Fool (www.fool.com), offer quality educational resource sections within the site.

We can't leave out the master, Warren Buffett, and the huge repository of material that he and his vice chairman and investing buddy Charlie Munger have created on their own. This material is readily available and free — squarely aimed at the value investor. Buffett is uniquely gifted in his manner of speaking and writing about business and investing. And he personifies value investing. Each year he publishes a long letter to Berkshire Hathaway shareholders made readily available on the company Web site (www.berkshirehathaway.com). Letters are available on the site for each year since 1977. The Berkshire Hathaway Owner's Manual, also available on the site, is worthy far beyond the needs of a Berkshire shareholder, providing a broader window into Buffett's investing approach. And as an entertaining way to learn value investing, *Warren Buffett Speaks* by Janet Lowe (John Wiley & Sons) is really a hoot and full of useful facts and gems for the value investor. Other books detailing Buffett's life, philosophy, investing approach, and experience (and there are many of them) would be recommended "reads" for the value investor.

Digging In: Examining Investor Resources

In this section, we provide a glance at some of the sites, tools, and offline resources that we've used and evaluated. Here are some of the things we look for in each resource:

- ✔ **Company performance and results data:** Sources of raw financial information about companies and company performance.

- ✔ **Research and analysis:** Sources of packaged analysis, such as ratios, percentages, and other processed and information. Also includes narratives and opinions on companies or aspects of their performance. The goal of most of these tools is to paint a complete picture of company performance. The better tools relate performance to that of other companies, industry groups, and the price of the stock.

- ✔ **Stock screeners:** These are action tools. Instead of looking at the numbers yourself to evaluate and select companies, you enter broad characteristics or specific numbers that *you want,* and the stock screener returns companies that meet your criteria. The selection criteria can be broad or very specific. When you're trying to pick from among thousands of companies large and small, these tools can cut to the chase in a big way, saving you from sifting through detailed financials of thousands of companies.

We provide an assessment of the advantages, disadvantages, and the value of each site or resource. We use the old-fashioned rating scheme — good, better, and best — which has stood the test of time.

The following table summarizes the financial information resources we're about to cover in depth.

Table 5-1

Value Investing Resource Summary

Resource	Type	Description	Our Rating	Advantages	Disadvantages	Cost
Yahoo! Finance: quote.yahoo.com	Portal	Quotes, company profiles,	Good, best value	Easy, fast company snapshot, some intangibles, frequent updates	No history, not adjusted for extraordinary items	Free
Edgar Online www.edgar-online.com	Document portal	Online repository of SEC filings	Good	Complete repository, including 10-Ks	Complex site, more than average investor needs	May require subscription
Online brokers such as www.schwab.com and www.etrade.com	Online research and analysis	Data, statements, screeners	Better	Mainly free. The quality and versatility of services is improving	Sometimes a canned approach. Some sites are slow, hard to print	May require account
Quicken: www.quicken.com	Investing sub-portal	Complete set of investment analysis tools	Better	In-depth analysis from several angles, good comparisons	Can be slow, unwieldy to print	Advertising
Value Line: www.valueline.com	Subscription investing service	Complete company reports, financials, ratios, analysis	Best	Complete, concise, easy to use, much legwork done for you	Not online-oriented, but getting there. Requires paid subscription	$570 per year

Yahoo! Finance: A window to the investing world

The finance portal Yahoo! Finance is the best total package of general finance and investing information we've found. To get a quick snapshot of a stock's price and performance, the quote page is an investing standard. For the value investor, Yahoo! Finance offers a Profile page, that, for your money, provides the quickest, simplest snapshot of company performance. Key financials and a healthy list of ratios for the most recent reporting period are displayed.

The Yahoo! Finance site also provides information on analyst projections under Research. There are a few items that help develop the "intangible" picture, such as institutional buying and management ownership. There is ample press coverage, but you would be hard-pressed to develop a complete assessment of a company's market position or success. News items — through wire service feeds and company releases — are current and diverse and include such items as quarterly and annual reports. Yahoo! Finance, as the term *portal* implies, provides a window to a great deal more financial information through links to other sites, though in our experience with most portals, the quality of linked sites is a mixed bag. Interesting analyst discussion and commentary are available on the FinanceVision section.

The site lacks depth in some areas and contains little to no financial history or trend information (price, yes, but not financials). Although you can compare stock prices, there is no industry comparison for financials or ratios. Nevertheless, Yahoo! Finance is fast, cheap, easy to print, and timely. Investors of all stripes, including value investors, should bookmark this site. We rated this site a good value investing resource and best value overall.

Sites with packaged financial overviews such as Yahoo! Finance are excellent initial sources of company financials, performance, and investment potential. But be careful about the numbers. The site doesn't offer much history or context. What if a company was recently restructured or went through some other extraordinary financial event? The site goes straight into the reported numbers, and without going deeper, you would be none the wiser.

Hey, Edgar, can I please have an annual report?

The most important source of company financial information is the company's annual and quarterly reports. As required by the U.S. Securities and Exchange Commission (SEC), publicly traded companies publish these financial summaries regularly. Most companies publish fancy, glossy annual reports. They contain basic financial information, but beyond that, they've become more of a marketing brochure describing the company's products, people, markets, geographic scope, and so forth. Value investors are better served by looking at what's known as a Form 10-K annual report, which is the SEC's required version of the document. The 10-K is a longer, harder read, but it provides much more in-depth financial data, product and market data, and management discussion of the financials than does the standard annual report. The patience required is rewarded by a more in-depth understanding of the company.

To get 10-K's reliably and quickly, the SEC created a setup to make public the myriad filings it requires: "EDGAR," or "Electronic Data Gathering And Reporting." "EDGAR Online" can be found at www.edgar.com.

EDGAR has all kinds of filings available through multiple services. We frankly find EDGAR a bit confusing. Some information is available for free, some information requires a fee, and sometimes all you need to do is register. A value investor can get a 10-K for free by doing a quick search on a ticker symbol; that's probably all you need to know for now. Value investors with a deeper approach and professionals may monitor individual filings — 8-Ks of unscheduled material events, 13Fs of changes of ownership or inside buying and selling, and the like. By paying a fee, you can get these sent as real-time alerts. If you're managing billions, maybe that's okay, but it's probably not for everyone. Still, we suggest EDGAR as the most dependable source of 10-Ks and other company filings. A few caveats: Most annual reports and 10-K filings contain only limited history, maybe three years' worth. And of course, annual reports and 10-K's contain no analysis or research, and they won't tell you whether a stock is a bargain. Thus, EDGAR contains only data — but lots of it. We rate it a good, and it's mostly free.

At your online broker

Sometimes too much or too many is a good thing. The advent of the Internet and a burgeoning community of online investors led to — you guessed it — a burgeoning number of online brokerage firms. Some of these firms, such as E*TRADE, are online *only*. Others evolved from more traditional full-service brokers, such as DLJ Direct (from Donaldson, Lufkin, Jenrette) or discount brokers, such as Charles Schwab. Regardless, there are now too many for the market to sustain, and all are competing to the death for your investing dollar.

The happy result, for many investors, has been a drive to differentiate their run-of-the-mill trading platforms with a wide array of investing services, including investing information. We're continually surprised at the increasing depth and quality of services available at such sites as E*TRADE (`www.etrade.com`) and Schwab (`www.schwab.com`). Detailed financial information is supplemented by stock analyzers and screeners, often provided through Standard & Poor's and other professional investing services and made readily available to the investing public. The only catch is the "price." For the good stuff, you may have to open an account. That may not cost anything but time and a small minimum balance, but it's still a cost. For some brokerages, you may have to qualify as a preferred customer to access some services, but we haven't often found this to be a barrier. Investing gets more democratic every day. For the most part, it's free and easy.

Most online brokerage sites offer an area, often called Quotes and Research or Research and Analysis, directing you to company financials. These come either prepackaged for view in their own format or as a direct link to a published annual report or 10-K. Increasingly, you'll find stock analyzers and screeners. Charles Schwab offers screening tools, including packaged "Stock Explorer" and "Standard & Poor's (S&P) Stock Screens." These offer several packaged selection criteria and provide printable results in a matter of seconds. For example, the selection criteria available for Stock Explorer are the following:

- ✔ Growth
- ✔ Value
- ✔ Tech companies showing profits
- ✔ Earnings surprise
- ✔ Growth with income
- ✔ Growth at a reasonable price (which they refer to as "GARP" stocks)

S&P Stock Screener selection criteria include the following:

- ✔ Rising profit margins
- ✔ Companies with healthy ROE (Return On Equity)
- ✔ Superior total return values
- ✔ Recent price declines
- ✔ Exceptional earnings growth
- ✔ Notable earnings revisions
- ✔ Sizable dividend increases

These are criteria that most value investors can wrap their brains around. There is also a customizable screener for you do-it-yourselfers.

Note that stock screeners *do* have some road hazards. First, the information may not be very timely. This isn't necessarily a big problem for the long-term value investor, but generally fresh is best. Usually the way to tell whether the information is current is to look at the "price" date, if that's available. Another shortcoming of many screening sites is that you have little real control over selection criteria. Your list of superior total-return value stocks is based on someone else's interpretation of best total return value. That may be okay for most of you, but occasionally you may want to look at different criteria — or multiple criteria — which many screeners don't allow.

When using stock screeners, try to understand how current the information is and the selection criteria used. Remember, garbage in, garbage out.

Screeners that allow you to build your own selection criteria, including multiple criteria, are harder to find. We found one such screener, called NetScreen, at the Multex Investor site (www.multex.com), which also is available through Yahoo! Finance research links (yahoo.marketguide.com). You can build your own screen on up to 80 factors of choice among 13,000 companies. It's very powerful, and there is no cost, but you do encounter some advertising and pressure to register for its newsletter. A value investor looking for in-depth screening capability should take a look. Also worth mentioning is the morningstar.com "stock selector" (screen.morningstar.com). It offers flexible screening and stock grading. Although it's not as flexible as Multex, it's easy to use and relatively ad-free.

Online brokerage sites and tools qualify as better, with increased depth and analysis and selection capability. They're nicely packaged and generally easy to use and print from. On the downside, an account is often required, and many of the tools are canned and not configurable. Still, they're a good value overall.

Quicken your approach

You never know what you'll find or where you'll find it. One of the best stock and company analysis sites that we've found md available for free — is the analysis section on Intuit's Quicken Investing page. Hats off to the Quicken folks for providing complete financial information at our mouse fingertips.

You can get a multifaceted view of any major company, including its history, trends, and a comparative analysis. The do-it-yourself Stock Evaluator section allows you to look at a company through different "lenses." There is a Summary view, Growth Trends, Financial Health, Management Performance, Market Multiples, and — the one we like the best — Intrinsic Value. The Intrinsic Value screen lets you play with discount, interest, and desired growth rates to your taste, so you can build in your own bias or margin of safety into the screen. Results show the company you select compared within its industry. Easy-to-read grades of 1 to 5 that compare each company within the industry are also part of the show.

You can even do a prepackaged screen on what has been determined as the Warren Buffett approach (by Buffett student, author, and portfolio manager Robert Hagstrom).

The Quicken Investing site offers a lot of value as a company-focused investing site. It is easy to read, has good comparative and historical data, and follows the value investing approach more than most. On the downside, it is a bit slow and hard to print. The "price" is a lot of advertising, and advertising slows download and especially printing. Overall, we rank this a better value investing resource that's worth becoming familiar with.

What's my Value Line?

It's a sad fact of life for us value folks that not everything in the world is free. We just have to deal with it, don't we? Like so many life lessons, we find that if we're willing to open our wallets, possibilities expand. We also find that as the flower of possibilities begins to bloom, some petals are more attractive than others: Some give us what we want at a lower price.

The serious value investor has some interesting paid-for options to choose from . Now, we could run the gamut of monster professional database services tuned for the billion-dollar pro and costing $10,000 or more a year, but we suspect that you aren't in that market segment. So we hold the discussion to a couple of under-$1,000 per year services you may want to consider, including one in particular that has been a venerable icon of the investing community and especially value investors for 50 years: Value Line.

Value Line has been creating distinctive, one-page company summaries designed for all investors, especially value-oriented investors (was that an easy guess from the name?), for many years. The traditional *Value Line Investment Survey* package consists of sets of one-page bound reports on newsprint mailed biweekly to subscribers. Each biweekly set features five to ten industries and all companies judged to be within the industry. Sixty-plus analysts cover 1,700-plus companies in depth, usually once per quarter.

Value Line provides basic company data but smartly narrows it down to that which you need to assess business value The Statistical Array presents a composite of ratios and percentages consistent across the industry and sometimes specially tuned for an industry, for example, the insurance industry. The Value Line analyst commentary is brief and full of insight. Although Value

Line goes so far as to suggest stock timeliness and safety (and it has done well with these judgments), we think that the greatest value is delivered before it makes these recommendations. (Remember that value investors are do-it-yourselfers, but a little help never hurts.) In short, the Value Line report is a data smorgasbord ready to whet a value investor's appetite.

Recently Value Line has gone online, with data and analysis packaged for fast, real-time Web access. It also offers an Investment Survey for Windows CD-ROM version. Value Line comes as a $55 two-month starter package (recommended) and then as a $570 annual subscription to the printed survey and some online access. Additional services, recommendations, and real-time alerts cost more and may or may not be important depending on your commitment and need for investing knowledge. Many libraries and full-service and discount broker-age firms with physical offices still carry the printed *Value Line survey* on their shelves. ("That's our biggest competition," quips Value Line research director Stephen Sanborn.) Depending on where your local library or broker is, you may want to try this path before committing your dollars to a subscription.

Other "paid" investing services are out there, most tuned for the professional or semipro, full-time investor. These services offer complete packages, down-loadable data, alerts, advisories, real-time quotes, and news all bundled in. But all the services that we checked are more expensive than Value Line and are targeted more for professional investors — not packaged for the street investor. Hoovers Online (www.hoovers.com) is an example. (Don't confuse this with www.hoover.com — that will get you information about vacuum cleaners!)

We like Value Line's extensive, in-depth data and analysis, with complete (10 years plus) history, trend analysis of key financials, ratios, and percentages. The commentary is brief, to the point, and well balanced between hard facts and intangibles. Enough price information and history are available to help you make informed decisions not only about a company's value but also about value relative to price. Industry comparisons are effective, as are the many provided "batch" screen results and online screening tools, particularly against the backdrop of complete supporting information. We doubt that a value investor could get any more out of reading just one page. On the down-side, it costs money, and although the printed versions are nice, it's hard to download and print information to your specification. (VL is reportedly work-ing on correcting that problem). We look at Value Line as a best-in-class tool for the more committed value investor.

Chapter 6

Statements of Fact Part 1: Understanding Financial Statements

● ●

In This Chapter

▶ Understanding the functions of accounting and financial reporting

▶ Learning about the major financial statements

▶ Making your way through an annual report

▶ Using financial statements in value investing.

● ●

> *You should have a knowledge of how business operates and the language of business (accounting), some enthusiasm for the subject, and qualities of temperament which may be more important than IQ points. These will enable you to think independently and to avoid various forms of mass hysteria that infect the markets from time to time.*
>
> —Warren Buffett, Columbia University investing seminar, 1985

Knowledge is power. No place is that more true than in the world of investing. Value investors need to know about the companies they invest in, just as traders need to know minute-by-minute happenings in the marketplace. In either investing arena, absence of knowledge reduces investment decisions to mere guesswork.

Fortunately for the value investor, the SEC requires companies to publish complete financial information about themselves. An enormous amount of financial information about companies is available and easy to find. But unfortunately for most of us, it's *too much* information and it's way too confusing. How many of you have read an annual report from cover to cover and gained a solid understanding of the business from doing so? Not very many, right? We would guess that most of these people who open an annual report at all mostly look at the beautiful pictures. Some people read management's ebullient commentary about the strength of the company's markets, products, and financials. A few readers actually look at the colorful graphs and charts. The more curious look enviously at executive salary and option grant disclosures.

But what about the financials themselves: the goes-into's and goes-outta's indicating the true health and success of the business? The challenge — and it is a challenge indeed — is to acquire the right information about a company and then to convert it into actionable investing knowledge. Knowledge that reveals the true character and dynamics of a business, the intrinsic value, the business performance characteristics that conclusively indicate whether a company is a good place to invest.

To the untrained eye, most of the information public companies disclose is too complex and detailed to make much sense of. It appears (and often is) meaningful only to a handful of sharp-eyed accountants who live and breathe the stuff every day. The unknowing reader is unaware of what's important and may even be misled. Legally correct information can be stated in such a way as to disguise or conceal potential areas of concern to the investor.

The goal of this chapter and the next few chapters is to provide a guide for separating the wheat from the chaff. No, you will not emerge from this discussion prepared for the next CPA examination or a career in a corporate finance department. You won't be able to prepare financial statements. That's okay, right? The main idea is to know what you need to know so that you can invest wisely.

We start with a basic overview of financial statements and move forward into the balance sheet, income, and cash flow statements. From there we advance into basic financial analysis, using ratios to gain a better understanding of what the financial data tell us. The focus will be on what you need to know and how to use the info in the reports to make investing decisions. And all the while we keep a watchful eye on the tricks of the trade and creative accounting practices that can and do deceive those who haven't read this book.

Accounting Isn't Just for Accountants

Just a minute, why is accounting so important, anyway? Why does an individual investor care how a company counts its beans? The purpose of accounting is just to pay bills, collect money owed, pay taxes, and keep track of what's in the bank, right? And maybe in the course of doing so, accounting can keep an army of CPAs, clerks, and cube dwellers happily and gainfully employed.

Wrong. Accounting, and the financial reporting that emerges from accounting, serves a critical function that you, as an investor, must be aware of: It reflects the economic reality of the company and the company's business.

Accounting and accountants are supposed to project a fair, unbiased view of company performance. Accountants build financial reports according to accepted practices in the field, which dictate such principles as substance over form, conservatism, and materiality. But despite (and maybe because of) the fact that no fewer than three governing bodies decree accounting and reporting practice, a degree of latitude and flexibility exists in how reporting is actually done.

This flexibility exists mostly in the valuation of assets and determination of revenue and cost. We cover those issues in Chapters 7 through 9. Here's the upshot: As companies are increasingly under the gun to perform, and especially to perform in the short term, the art of creative accounting has emerged to help companies achieve desired levels — on paper — of performance.

Accounting is supposed to be used to measure and report business results, not to achieve them!

As a value investor, you need to be smart about what and how much to question in a financial report. The value investor who spends his time questioning the origin of every number in a financial report will never come up for air and probably will never make a successful value investment as a result. Without seeing all the background data, you can't possibly understand the origin of all those stated numbers anyway. The smart value investor knows what to look for in a statement and knows the key levers a company's management can throw to convey a certain image. It's okay to be a skeptic, but it's probably not productive to dispute every figure in the report. As with so much else in life, focus on what's important.

The State of Financial Statements

If every company were able to report information as it pleased, financial reports would be apple-to-orange nightmares, rendering all information useless to everyone. The purpose of financial reporting is to present accounting information in a comprehensible, consistent format. But one person's "comprehensible" may be another's "complex," and "consistent" doesn't mean "exactly the same." Why did financial reporting evolve this way? In part, because financial statements are used by many kinds of readers in many kinds of ways.

A whole family of readers

As much as individual investors may fantasize that all company financial information and reporting are created just for them, you should step back and realize that financial reports serve multiple masters. They aren't just for those of you who commit equity capital to a company. Those who commit debt capital (as in loans from banks, for example) have an equal, if not greater, vested interest in a company's financial health. Here's a short list of interested parties and what they want to know:

- ✔ **Stockholders** want to know about a company's short- and long-term financial health and performance to decide whether to keep or expand their investment.

- ✔ **Potential stockholders** want to know about a company's financial health and performance before they make an initial investment.

- ✔ **Value investors** need a deeper look at a company's intrinsic value in order to appraise the company's asset value, asset quality, growth and growth consistency, and intangibles.

- ✔ **Creditors and lenders** want to keep track of a company's financial health so that they know whether to keep or expand credit.

- ✔ **Suppliers** want to better understand a company's business so that they can determine product fit, know whether to extend credit, and ascertain payment.

- ✔ **Customers,** especially business-to-business customers, want information about a company's products and its dependability as a supplier.

- ✔ **Potential employees** want to understand a company's products and culture and determine whether the company is stable.

- ✔ **Government statisticians** look at financial reports to understand industries and financial performance within an industry.

What's the point? You were hoping we'd get to that. We're not trying to sell or justify the art and science of financial reporting. We simply want you, as an individual investor, to realize that you aren't the only customer. It's hard to speculate how company-published financial information would change if investors *were* the only customer, but it's unlikely that reporting will change to perfectly meet the investor's needs — let alone a value investor's needs. So go with what you have and understand it as best you can.

A slave of many masters

Imagine if the tax code were specified not only by the IRS, but also by three different agencies, public and private, who all had a hand in the matter. Well, that scenario isn't that far-fetched — it's not dissimilar to the situation faced by the financial reporter.

No fewer than three agencies are involved in creating the rules and constructs for reporting financial performance:

- ✔ The Financial Accounting Standards Board, or FASB

- ✔ The U.S. Securities and Exchange Commission (SEC)

- ✔ The American Institute of Certified Public Accountants (AICPA)

Each entity researches and publishes opinions and acts as a watchdog. The SEC can require compliance to its own dictates and to those of the others, especially the FASB. The FASB issues numbered guidelines for financial reporting that companies can choose to adopt or be required to adopt by the SEC. The SEC acts as overseer and enforcer of regulations and also cooperates with the FASB and other agencies to initiate new regulations and standards.

Again, we're not trying to prepare you to identify these agencies correctly on the next CPA exam. We simply want to reinforce the notion that many forces exist that influence the financial statements received by investors. The prudent investor keeps track of the rule changes — at least the major ones.

Value investors should watch out of the corner of their eyes for financial reporting standards changes and discussions leading towards change. Standards and standards changes deserve some attention, but not all-day and all-night vigilance. The financial newswires (Reuters, Bloomberg, and so on) usually report the big changes. For a deeper look — or to see what's coming before it arrives — a good resource is the SEC Web site, www.sec.gov.

Anatomy of an Annual Report

Enough on the background — it's time to dig in.

The many faces of an annual report

Before looking inside the annual report and the financial statements it contains, here's a look at the forms in which annual reports are published.

Hot off the press

The most popular and visible form of the annual report is the familiar, full-color marketing brochure that companies spend millions of dollars on and send out once a year. They're expensive to produce and expensive to mail. A whole industry has evolved to produce them, though we suspect that few are actually read after the initial casual glance (although we have no data to support our belief). These documents serve as useful marketing material — not only to investors, but also to lenders, suppliers, customers, employees, and the like. We've long anticipated a move away from these cash hogs into more productive marketing investments, but that change has yet to materialize.

Most printed annual reports are a bit lacking in depth and put a positive spin on everything. In the words of Clemson University professors George Thomas Friedlob and Ralph Welton, from their book *Keys to Reading an Annual Report* (Barron's, 2001), "Vague wording, colorful adjectives, and meaningless euphemisms are frequently used to conceal the fact that, in truth, the managers aren't telling you anything at all." They also warn, "The best looking reports aren't usually the most informative ones."

But we shouldn't be so negative about printed annual reports. They do contain the requisite financial information and a few graphs to help explain it. And they usually give a sketch — often a pictorial one — of a company's products and market success. For the value investor, they're a good place to start. You can obtain most printed annual reports by sending a simple postcard to the company, to the attention of Investor Relations, or by using one of the many annual report distribution agencies that are often found in financial publications. Regardless of the source, when you request a printed annual report, you won't get immediate delivery, but it should be fast enough to suit value investing objectives.

Saving paper

Another way to obtain annual reports — and often the more elaborate 10-Ks — is to go directly to a company's Web site. Most companies have a prominently displayed link to their Investor Relations or Company Information area. In our experience, using Web sites to get this information works, but we must warn you about two things:

- ✔ Many companies are slow to update their online annual reports, often because someone has to scan them in.

- ✔ Online reports can be large and cumbersome to download, even with the best of connections and the latest version of Adobe Acrobat.

Despite these limitations, company Web sites are a good way to get financial reports, and a lot of other company information, too.

How about a 10-K this weekend?

Without further ado, we present the Zeus of the financial reporting gods: the Form 10-K annual report and its quarterly brethren, the 10-Q.

One of the many goals of the SEC is to ensure that financial information about public companies is correct, consistent, regularly reported, and readily available. So the SEC created a host of reporting forms for all kinds of financial information: financial results, financial changes, and ownership changes.

The 10-K is similar to a company's printed and distributed annual report. However, it goes much further into detail, and it chucks all the glossy pictures and management hoopla. It looks like a government document because it *is* one. The reports are available from the SEC or from the EDGAR Online site at www.edgar-online.com (details on EDGAR are in Chapter 5). Documents are available on a timely basis and are quickly downloadable in a text format.

ENTERTAINMENT VALUE

Does (report) size matter?

Merrill Lynch recently did a study to correlate the size of company 10-K reports with company stock performance. Guess what it found? There is a strong correlation between the size of the 10-K report, in number of pages, and *poor* investment performance. From March 31, 2000 to March 31, 2001, companies with small 10-K filings (150 pages of text or less) lost 52 percent of stock value, while those with large (between 150 and 200 pages) or jumbo filings (200 pages or more) lost 73 percent and 78 percent of stock value, respectively. Interestingly, AOL/Time Warner's filing was 1,861 pages with the merger, but wasn't included in the study. On the plus side, Adobe Systems, which, ironically, produces software that you use to download and print 10-Ks, weighed in with an 87-page filing and lost only 37 percent. The jury is still out on whether value investors should use 10-K size as an investing criterion. The value investor should also wonder whether Merrill Lynch is getting a little desperate in its search for valid investment analysis tools!

A 10-K goes into a company's business and financials in detail in the following ways:

- ✔ It offers a detailed, objective description of a company's business, including business segments, product lines, geography, operating units, plants, property, technologies, patents, customer base and key customers, employees and employee mix, and so forth.

- ✔ It includes a description of legal proceedings. This content can take a lot of paper, but it's usually not important, unless the company is involved in asbestos issues or significant patent disputes.

- ✔ It offers a detailed, objective description of company markets — market size, market position, market growth, market share, competition, threats, and strengths. This information can help the value investor get a picture of a company's intangibles.

- ✔ It gives detailed financials. The line items are often similar to printed annual reports, but there is more history, often five to ten years' worth, deeper analysis, and more complete notes explaining certain lines in greater detail. Should you wish to understand complex financial transactions, such as acquisitions, this is the place to go.

- ✔ It provides merger and acquisition transaction details.

- ✔ It contains management's analysis of results, financial condition, and go-forward prospects. Again, the information is more detailed and less biased than that found in printed reports.

The Form 10-K annual report should be the value investor's standard source of information for company-supplied financial information.

Dissecting the annual report

Making generalizations about the construction of an annual report isn't easy, but we can safely say that most, if not all, reports contain the following elements. From one company to the next, these elements won't look the same, be the same size, be in the same order, or contain the same information. But these pieces are all present in some form.

Highlights

The highlights section is usually a one-page graphic summary of significant financial results: sales, earnings, and a few productivity measures key to a company's industry. Four or five years of history are often included. Highlights are useful for a first glance, but there's usually a lot more to the story.

Letter to shareholders

The letter to shareholders presents a chipper one- or two-page summary, usually from the CEO or chairman, describing the past year and the year ahead. Although some managers are frank in describing and confronting a company's difficulties, others are not. You can usually depend on a discussion of milestones and achievements ("We opened our 2000th store," "We maintain an in-stock level unequaled in the retail world," or "We achieved #1 position according to XYZ Industry News") without a lot of discussion of how much the achievements cost or whether they were worthwhile. The letter usually includes something about customer commitment, commitment to leading-edge technologies, and employing the best people. The value investor can assess accomplishments and the overall tone of these statements, but the letter usually doesn't provide a reason to buy a stock.

Management's discussion and analysis

Now it's time to take a trip through the financials. Better yet, with a multimillion-dollar-a-year business professional — the CEO or chairman — as a tour guide. The management discussion is usually right before the financial statements or just after the first-page summary. The discussion is a deeper, less-biased view of specific financial statement components, including sales, costs, expenses, assets, liabilities, liquidity, market expansion, and market risks. If you want a packaged tour through the financials, this is a good way to go about it. But not all tourists, especially self-sufficient value investors, like to go on tours. With tours, you see what everyone else sees, and what the tour guide *wants* you to see. Keep that in mind.

The statements

You've gone through the appetizers, and now it's time for the entrée.

The financial statement section usually consumes the last half to two-thirds of an annual report. Several versions of *consolidated* financial data are presented.

What does "consolidated" mean? You see this term in the title of most financial statements. Are they leaving something out? The answer is no. Consolidated means that (1) many legal subsidiaries including foreign subsidiaries and (2) many, many accounts are combined into a simplified reporting structure for presentation. Consolidation makes the resulting statements shorter and much easier to understand.

Normally, this section includes a balance sheet, income statement, and statement of cash flows. Sometimes the report includes a statement of shareholder's equity, a statement of working capital, or some other summary of changes in the financials. All reports contain the first three items. The others are discretionary but may be mandated by the state in which a company is incorporated. We go into more detail in Chapters 7 and 8, but here's a summary of what you can find in the financial statement section:

- The *balance sheet* captures a company's financial position at a point in time. It shows all assets, liabilities, and owner's equity, usually in clearly defined subsections. In fact, the balance sheet is often called a statement of financial position or statement of financial condition.

- The *income statement* captures a company's performance over an interval of time. Of interest here is the sales or revenues, cost of those sales, other expenses, and, of course, the difference between sales and costs — earnings. This statement is sometimes called the statement of operations or operating activity.

- The *statement of cash flows* also captures company activity and performance over a time interval, but this time it's done in cash terms. As you see in Chapter 8, cash and accounting flows can be different. Cash flows are just as the name implies — cash or checks coming in, cash or checks being paid out. Cash flows are a lifeblood flow into and out of the business. Cash flows tell you a lot about company liquidity — which refers to the presence or absence of enough cash to operate and the quality of earnings — and whether the earnings are real or a result of accounting gimmicks.

No assessment of company performance, quality, or success can be achieved without these statements and, in particular, without looking at all three of these statements together.

Before going further, consider some examples of financial statements. Figures 6-1 through 6-3 are presented from the Borders Group (book retailing) 2000 Annual Report. We use this value-oriented company as an example for its easy-to-read simplicity, although it provides only three years of history, which is not as much as many retailers provide. We refer to the Borders statements repeatedly for discussions in Chapters 7 through 10 and beyond.

consolidated statements
of operations

(dollars in millions except per share data)	Fiscal Year Ended		
	Jan. 28, 2001	Jan. 23, 2000	Jan. 24, 1999
Sales	$3,271.2	$2,968.4	$2,595.0
Cost of merchandise sold (includes occupancy)	2,354.5	2,127.6	1,859.4
Gross margin	916.7	840.8	735.6
Selling, general and administrative expenses	736.2	659.2	557.6
Pre-opening expense	6.4	7.8	7.8
Asset impairments and other writedowns	36.2	—	—
Goodwill amortization	2.8	2.8	2.9
Operating income	135.1	171.0	167.3
Interest expense	13.1	16.6	16.2
Income from continuing operations before income tax	122.0	154.4	151.1
Income tax provision	48.2	60.4	59.0
Income from continuing operations	$ 73.8	$ 94.0	$ 92.1
Discontinued operations (Note 3)			
Loss from operations of All Wound Up, net of income tax credits of $7.0 and $2.4	10.8	3.7	—
Loss on disposition of All Wound Up, net of deferred income tax credit of $8.9	19.4	—	—
Net income	$ 43.6	$ 90.3	$ 92.1
Earnings (loss) per common share data (Note 2)			
Diluted earnings (loss) per common share:			
Continuing operations	$ 0.92	$ 1.17	$ 1.12
Discontinued operations	(0.38)	(0.04)	—
Net diluted earnings per common share	$ 0.54	$ 1.13	$ 1.12
Basic earnings (loss) per common share:			
Continuing operations	$ 0.94	$ 1.21	$ 1.20
Discontinued operations	(0.38)	(0.05)	—
Net basic earnings per common share	$ 0.56	$ 1.16	$ 1.20

See accompanying Notes to Consolidated Financial Statements.

Figure 6-1:
Borders' consolidated statements of operations.

pg $\frac{24}{}$ 2000 financials

consolidated balance sheets

	Fiscal Year Ended	
(dollars in millions except share amounts)	Jan. 28, 2001	Jan. 23, 2000
ASSETS		
Current Assets:		
Cash and cash equivalents	$ 59.1	$ 41.6
Merchandise inventories	1,201.2	1,077.7
Accounts receivable and other current assets	73.7	68.9
Deferred income taxes	1.1	10.0
Total Current Assets	1,335.1	1,198.2
Property and equipment, net	562.3	558.2
Other assets	34.2	36.5
Deferred income taxes	22.3	0.1
Goodwill, net of accumulated amortization of $53.1 and $49.5, respectively	93.2	121.8
	$2,047.1	$1,914.8
LIABILITIES AND STOCKHOLDERS' EQUITY		
Current Liabilities:		
Short-term borrowings and current portion of long-term debt	$ 144.4	$ 136.1
Trade accounts payable	623.6	580.4
Accrued payroll and other liabilities	256.6	232.2
Taxes, including income taxes	93.3	79.2
Total Current Liabilities	1,117.9	1,027.9
Long-term debt and capital lease obligations	15.0	16.2
Other long-term liabilities	67.7	68.1
Commitments and contingencies (Note 7)	—	—
Total Liabilities	1,200.6	1,112.2
Stockholders' Equity:		
Common stock, 200,000,000 shares authorized; 78,649,501 and 77,687,829 shares issued and outstanding at January 28, 2001 and January 23, 2000, respectively	685.2	679.6
Deferred compensation and officer receivables	(1.0)	(3.9)
Accumulated other comprehensive income (loss)	(8.0)	0.2
Retained earnings	170.3	126.7
Total Stockholders' Equity	846.5	802.6
	$2,047.1	$1,914.8

See accompanying Notes to Consolidated Financial Statements.

Figure 6-2:
Borders'
consoli-
dated
balance
sheets.

2000 financials $\frac{24}{25}$ pg

consolidated statements of cash flows

		Fiscal Year Ended	
(dollars in millions)	Jan. 28, 2001	Jan. 23, 2000	Jan. 24, 1999
Cash provided by (used for):			
Operations			
Income from continuing operations	$ 73.8	$ 94.0	$ 92.1
Adjustments to reconcile net income to operating cash flows:			
Depreciation and amortization	95.3	83.5	66.7
(Increase) decrease in deferred income taxes	(4.6)	7.4	10.2
Increase (decrease) in other long-term assets and liabilities	6.0	8.2	1.9
Asset impairments and other writedowns	23.0	—	—
Cash provided by (used for) current assets and current liabilities:			
Increase in inventories	(136.5)	(50.4)	(140.5)
Increase (decrease) in accounts payable	45.0	(29.2)	126.5
Increase in taxes payable	35.2	60.8	2.9
Other — net	15.6	7.0	6.4
Net cash provided by continuing operations	152.8	181.3	166.2
Net cash used for discontinued operations	(14.2)	(8.3)	—
Net cash provided by operations	138.6	173.0	166.2
Investing			
Capital expenditures	(138.7)	(143.5)	(179.8)
Net investing activities of discontinued operations	(2.4)	(15.7)	—
Net cash used for investing	(141.1)	(159.2)	(179.8)
Financing			
Repayment of long-term debt and capital lease obligations	(4.2)	(1.2)	(4.6)
Increase in capital lease obligations	—	0.5	3.0
Repayment of debt assumed in acquisition	—	(2.0)	—
Proceeds from construction funding	—	—	1.3
Net funding from credit facility	21.4	1.5	9.4
Issuance of common stock	11.5	11.6	33.9
Repurchase of common stock	(9.2)	(25.4)	(51.7)
Net cash provided by (used for) financing	19.5	(15.0)	(8.7)
Effect of exchange rates on cash and equivalents	0.5	—	—
Net increase (decrease) in cash and equivalents	17.5	(1.2)	(22.3)
Cash and equivalents at beginning of year	41.6	42.8	65.1
Cash and equivalents at end of year	$ 59.1	$ 41.6	$ 42.8
Supplemental Cash Flow Disclosures:			
Interest paid	$ 15.8	$ 18.0	$ 16.2
Income taxes paid	$ 38.6	$ 6.4	$ 42.1
Debt and liabilities assumed in business acquisition	$ —	$ 6.5	$ —

See accompanying Notes to Consolidated Financial Statements.

Figure 6-3:
Borders'
consoli-
dated
statements
of cash
flow.

Common size statements

Some annual reports provide, in addition to normal financial statements, a set of *common size* statements. Common size statements are no more than standard financial reports, except that all information is presented as percentages. Thus, cash or accounts receivable are presented as a percent of total assets, and the cost of goods sold or marketing expenses are presented as a percent of revenue. As implied, common size statements are very useful for comparing companies, a frequent activity of the value investor.

Notes

Contrary to intuition, the notes part of an annual report takes more room and contains more detail than the financial statements. For the detailed financial analyst or value investor, the notes section is the mother lode of truth.

Notes describe financial information presented in the statements in greater detail. Often they have mini-statements of their own depicting some portion of company financials in greater detail. Notes not only show more detail, but also show the accounting practice a company uses in preparing a statement. A company's description of depreciation methods, option accounting, pension funding, and the like can make a world of difference in interpreting the statements. Notes also disclose one-time situations such as acquisitions, discontinued businesses, and asset write-downs in greater detail. Notes also disclose and describe changes in accounting methods. Notes can describe events or figures on any of the major financial statements.

Auditor's review

The auditor's review is normally a one-page boilerplate somewhere towards the back of the annual report. This element looks pretty much the same in every annual report (because the AICPA specifies the format) and also reads pretty much the same.

The purpose of the auditor's review is to provide concrete evidence of review and acceptance of a company's accounting and financial practices. Financial procedures are audited (sampled) for correct handling of material and money flow. Financial reporting practices are reviewed to make sure information is being reasonably captured. Whole curricula, careers, and companies have been set up around audit practice; describing it in detail is well beyond the scope of this book.

What is important is identifying *exceptions*. The standard auditor's review is three paragraphs. If the words "qualified" or "adverse" creep into the third paragraph, or if there's a fourth paragraph, watch out.

What the Value Investor Is Looking For

If you want to be a successful value investor, you have to be able to pull the relevant information out of financial statements. In Chapters 7 through 9, we explore the statements in more detail. In Chapters 10 through 17, we explore how financial information is used to value a company. In the meantime, there are five overriding themes that are supported by, or determined from, financial statements:

- **Intrinsic valuation.** The value investor uses financial statements as a base to assess a firm's intrinsic value. Intrinsic value is a composite sketch of current net asset value, net worth, and future earnings and growth potential. More detail is in Chapter 12.

- **Quality.** The investor needs to assess the quality of the business and the story around it. Financial statements can provide important clues through their very construction and use of accounting principles. More in Chapter 9.

- **Consistency.** Value investors value consistency. Financial statements can provide an important record of consistency. The more history, the better. Many annual reports show five years of history, and some of the better ones show as much as ten years.

- **Trends.** Beyond consistency, trends are extremely important. True value investors look at long-term trends, and differences in long-term trends imply vastly different business — and investing — results. Financial statements help you understand trends and undercurrents in profitability, asset utilization, and the like that serve as leading indicators of trends.

- **Intangibles.** Value investors can't and don't thrive on numbers alone. Market position, product quality, customer base, competitive position, public image, management strength, and similar attributes all function to protect or enhance future business results. As leading indicators, these factors can't be ignored. Financial statements and the reports companies construct around them, along with press releases and other communications, provide a body of information vital to the business-valuation process.

Chapter 7

Statements of Fact Part 2: The Balance Sheet

> *On numerous occasions prior to this point we have expressed our conviction that the balance sheet deserves more attention than Wall Street has been willing to accord it for many years past.*
>
> —Benjamin Graham and David Dodd, Security Analysis, 1934

*F*undamental to all fundamentalists — managers, business analysts, investors, and anyone else who looks at a company by the numbers — is the balance sheet. The balance sheet is the first topic covered by most books devoted to the subject of financial analysis. This book isn't designed to turn you into an accountant or financial analyst, only to make you familiar with basic concepts and how to use them. Consistent with our philosophy, we give a descriptive overview of the balance sheet and its contents and provide some guidance as to how you can use the balance sheet to achieve investing objectives.

A Question of Balance

You probably imagined that there is a "balance" in the balance sheet. Something must equal something else, or it doesn't balance. There must be an equation, the sum of one side of which equals the other. (Uh-oh, here we go again: *math.*)

Yes, a core financial equation (a simple one, no Greek letters, symbols, or exponents) forms the heart of the balance sheet, indeed the business enterprise itself. Follow us as we go through the equation and discuss the nature and form of the balance sheet itself.

Understanding the components of a balance sheet

The entire practice of business and business accounting is based on the relationship between business resources and their sources. A business resource is an *asset,* generally defined as any resource that can be put to use by the business to achieve business results: revenue, profit, brand recognition, and so on. These assets are acquired either by borrowing or by a contribution from the business owners.

So a generalized equation shows this relationship:

Assets = liabilities + owners' equity

Here's an explanation of each of those elements:

- ✔ *Assets* are the resources available to the business to produce and market its product: cash, investments, funds owed by customers, inventories, buildings, land, and intangibles.

- ✔ *Liabilities* represent the portion borrowed or financed by others, including short-term borrowings, amounts owed to suppliers, and longer-term financing.

- ✔ *Owners' equity* is the portion contributed by the business owners. There are many names for this: *Shareholders'* or *stockholders' equity, net worth, capital,* and *book value* are among them. Included in owners' equity are not only funds contributed directly from shareholders but also past profits retained in the business known as *retained earnings.*

It's important to reinforce the idea that a balance sheet must balance. That is, for every asset dollar, there must be contributed dollars produced by borrowing (increased liabilities) or additional funding by the owners (owners' equity) to match.

In this chapter, we examine each component of this equation in greater detail, with an eye for what's important to you as a value investor.

Taking time into account

A balance sheet is merely a listing of assets against the liabilities and equity that fund those assets, taken at a specific point in time. For investment and legal reporting purposes, generally these snapshots are taken at the end of each fiscal quarter and at fiscal year-end.

A balance sheet is necessarily a consolidation of a vast number of accounts maintained by the business. This is a good thing. Investors don't want to see the myriad separate accounts that companies likely set up for each type of physical asset or inventory for each operating subsidiary in each country! Generally balance sheets take no more than a page.

Making sense of the balance sheet

The balance sheet can be a powerful indicator of the health of a business. It is sort of a static indicator. That is, it doesn't tell much about the future of the business and particularly about future income. It tells you more about where the company has been and how well it did getting there.

Many value investors and business analysts look closely for the following in a balance sheet:

- ✔ The absolute and relative size of the numbers
- ✔ The makeup of assets, liabilities, and owners' equity
- ✔ Trends
- ✔ Quality (assessing whether stated values reflect actual values)

Each of these examinations is done with an eye towards what the figure should be for a company in that line of business. A company such Starbucks, with frequent small cash sales, shouldn't have a large accounts receivable balance. A retailer should have sizeable inventories, but they shouldn't be out of line for the industry and for its category. A semiconductor manufacturer has a large amount of capital equipment but should depreciate it aggressively to account for technology change.

To determine whether balance sheet numbers are in line, most analysts apply certain ratios to the numbers. Ratios serve to draw comparisons between companies and between companies and their industry. By doing so, they detect whether performance is better or worse than industry peers. We look at the balance sheet itself in this chapter. Because many ratios involve items found outside the balance sheet, mostly on the income statement, it makes sense to defer the discussion of ratio analysis to Chapter 10.

A Swift Kick in the Asset

An *asset* is anything a company uses to conduct its business towards producing a profit. From an accounting standpoint, an asset must

- ✔ Have value towards acquiring a return for the business.

- ✔ Be in the company's control. (A leased airplane is still an asset even if it's not legally "owned" by the company.)

- ✔ Be recordable and have value. (Employees don't show up as a balance sheet asset, though they're frequently referred to as assets in CEO speeches.)

Using Borders as an example, we walk you through an examination of the asset portion of a balance sheet (see Figure 7-1).

Borders Group reports, at the end of its fiscal year 2000 (ending January 28, 2001), a total of $2.047 billion in assets. As one might expect for a large retailer, the largest asset commitments are in merchandise inventory ($1.201 billion) and in property and equipment ($562 million), which, for a retailer, is mainly stores, store improvements, and store fixtures.

A closer look reveals something called "current assets," totaling four individual items at $1.335 billion, and then four more items making up the remainder of the asset total. This figure is typical. Most companies classify assets as current or noncurrent. Within each of these classifications lie individual asset accounts — cash and equivalents, inventories, property and equipment, and so forth. *Current assets* are short term in nature, actively managed, and directly tied to a current level of business. *Noncurrent assets* include longer-term "fixed" assets and a catchall of other types of assets not normally vital to day-to-day operations.

Current assets

Current assets are items generally held for a year or a business cycle. (If you're building a space shuttle, the business cycle, or completion of a deliverable product, is longer than a year.) Think of current assets and especially cash as the lifeblood of the business, and noncurrent assets as the body through which they circulate. The lifeblood flows to and from customers, to and from suppliers, and around to the different locations (stores in this case) to produce the greatest possible business and customer benefit. Current assets are managed pretty much on a daily basis.

pg $\frac{24}{25}$ 2000 financials

consolidated balance sheets

	Fiscal Year Ended	
(dollars in millions except share amounts)	Jan. 28, 2001	Jan. 23, 2000
ASSETS		
Current Assets:		
Cash and cash equivalents	$ 59.1	$ 41.6
Merchandise inventories	1,201.2	1,077.7
Accounts receivable and other current assets	73.7	68.9
Deferred income taxes	1.1	10.0
Total Current Assets	1,335.1	1,198.2
Property and equipment, net	562.3	558.2
Other assets	34.2	36.5
Deferred income taxes	22.3	0.1
Goodwill, net of accumulated amortization of $53.1 and $49.5, respectively	93.2	121.8
	$2,047.1	$1,914.8
LIABILITIES AND STOCKHOLDERS' EQUITY		
Current Liabilities:		
Short-term borrowings and current portion of long-term debt	$ 144.4	$ 136.1
Trade accounts payable	623.6	580.4
Accrued payroll and other liabilities	256.6	232.2
Taxes, including income taxes	93.3	79.2
Total Current Liabilities	1,117.9	1,027.9
Long-term debt and capital lease obligations	15.0	16.2
Other long-term liabilities	67.7	68.1
Commitments and contingencies (Note 7)	—	—
Total Liabilities	1,200.6	1,112.2
Stockholders' Equity:		
Common stock, 200,000,000 shares authorized; 78,649,501 and 77,687,829 shares issued and outstanding at January 28, 2001 and January 23, 2000, respectively	685.2	679.6
Deferred compensation and officer receivables	(1.0)	(3.9)
Accumulated other comprehensive income (loss)	(8.0)	0.2
Retained earnings	170.3	126.7
Total Stockholders' Equity	846.5	802.6
	$2,047.1	$1,914.8

See accompanying Notes to Consolidated Financial Statements.

Figure 7-1:
Borders
Group
consoli-
dated
balance
sheets.

Current assets normally include the following:

- ✔ Cash and cash equivalents
- ✔ Accounts receivable
- ✔ Inventory
- ✔ Deferred taxes and other items

We explore each element in more detail in the following sections.

Cash and cash equivalents

For most businesses, cash is the best type of asset to have. With cash, there is no question about its value: Cash is cash! Cash equivalents are essentially cash. They're short-term marketable securities with little to no price risk that can be converted to cash at a moment's notice.

Value investors like cash. Cash is security and forms the strongest part of the "safety net" that value investors seek. Value investors question a cash balance only if it appears excessive against the needs of the business. If Borders had a billion dollars in cash, which as you will see is almost one year of sales, you might ask "why?" Could it not put that cash to work in an investment or acquisition that might return more than the 4 or 5 percent it would get in a bank? And why isn't it being returned to shareholders? Most companies don't retain that much cash, but occasionally it becomes a value investing red flag.

It's important to recognize the total picture when companies report high cash balances. Many companies have large cash balances for a while immediately following an initial public offering (IPO). For example, at the end of the year 2000, Webvan Group had $500 million, and Gadzoox Networks had $50 million, both well over one year's sales. Why? Because they just went public. They just received a huge contribution of owners' equity in the form of cash. That's what an IPO is all about. That cash is there to be depleted (hence the term "burn rate"), hopefully to produce a favorable return But as you well know, that comes with a lot of risk in these situations. Cash is hardly a safety net in this kind of company; you need to look at cash differently.

Accounts receivable

Accounts receivable represent funds that are owed to the business, presumably for products delivered or services performed. As individuals, everyone likes to be owed money — until we're owed *too much* money. The same attitude applies to corporations.

Accounts receivable are driven by the type of industry that a company operates in. Obviously a small-sale retailer such as Starbucks operates mostly on cash — you don't give them an IOU for that double-cream latte, do you? Even when you charge something, the credit card company pays *almost* immediately, leaving perhaps a slight residual in accounts receivable. Most companies that sell directly to consumers have little accounts receivable.

Contrast this to companies that sell to other companies (b-to-b), or to distributors or retailers in the supply food chain. Most of this business is done *on account,* meaning that goods or services are delivered and invoices are then cut and sent. The billing process creates an account receivable, which goes away only when the customer pays the bill. So suppliers to other businesses or through distribution and sales channels often have significant accounts receivable.

How much of a company's asset base should be made up of accounts receivable? U.S. government data suggest that cash businesses such as Starbucks or grocery stores have 10 percent or less of their asset base in accounts receivable. Traditional retailers and other "b-to-c" (business-to-consumer) companies have 20 percent to 30 percent or more in receivables if they provide credit through their own credit card. Equipment manufacturers and other b-to-b concerns sometimes carry receivables of 50 percent or more of total assets.

For most "b-to-b" industries, accounts receivable are a part of doing business and, in a sense, a *cost* of doing business (cash is forgone to give the customer time to pay). The question is, how much commitment to accounts receivable is necessary to support the business? You should be keenly aware of situations in which companies aren't collecting on their bills or are using accounts receivable to create credit incentives for otherwise questionable customers to buy their product.

To assign value to accounts receivable, pay attention to the following:

- ✔ The size of accounts receivable relative to sales and other assets: Is a company extending itself too much to sustain or grow the business? Industry comparisons and common sense dictate the answer.

- ✔ Trend: Is the company continuously owed more and more, with potentially greater and greater exposure to nonpayment? Look at historical accounts receivable and compare them to sales.

- ✔ Quality of accounts receivable: Typically, most companies collect on more than 95 percent of their accounts receivable balances, and thus they're almost as good as cash. But if accounts receivable balances grow and particularly if large reserves show up on the income statement ("allowance for doubtful accounts" or similar), this is a red signal flare that no value investor can miss. Unfortunately, most investors don't see information on individual creditors nor can they assess their creditworthiness.

Some financial statements show "notes receivable" as a separate balance sheet item under current assets. Notes receivable are essentially a special form of accounts receivable — a promissory note for a significant amount extended to a specific firm for a specific reason. For the most part, these should be treated like normal accounts receivable, but it might be worth a quick glance at the noteholder and the terms of the note. For example, a note granted by Boeing to Pan Am or TWA might be cause for concern.

Inventory

Inventory can be a critical, make-or-break asset and factor in company valuation. Companies live and die by their ability to effectively manage inventory.

Inventory is all valued material procured by a business and resold, with or without value add, to a customer. *Retail inventory* consists of goods bought, warehoused, and sold through stores. *Manufacturing inventory* consists of raw material, work in process, and finished goods inventory awaiting shipment.

For most companies, the key to successfully managing inventory is to match it as closely as possible to sales. That is, the faster that procured inventory can be processed and sold, the better. More sales are generated per dollar tied up in inventory. Dollars tied up in inventory cost money because they could be invested elsewhere in the business.

Measuring inventory

Measuring the size of inventory assets often involves measuring turnover. *Turnover* is simply annual sales divided by the dollar amount of the asset on the books. If sales are $500 million a year and inventory on the books is $100 million, inventory turnover is 5.0. In other words, inventory turns over five times a year on average. Another way to look at it: The average item of inventory is on the books for about 2.4 months (12 @ds 5). Some would represent that figure as "months' sales in inventory." The greater the turnover, the more efficient the utilization of that asset. Turnover ratios naturally vary by industry. For example, Starbucks naturally turns over inventory much faster than Boeing. Accounts receivable are another asset that can, and often are, measured by turnover. You may choose to measure it as "days' sales in receivables." A company with a normal 30-day billing cycle that has 45 days' sales in receivables has a problem.

Moreover, inventory carries with it a significant risk of obsolescence. Changes in demand patterns, technology, or the nature of the product itself can cause valued inventory to rapidly lose value. The most extreme example of obsolescence risk is newspapers, where an inventory of today's latest edition becomes almost 100 percent worthless at the stroke of midnight. But almost any other type of inventory carries obsolescence risk, as few inventories are worth 100 percent of their purchase price or anywhere near it.

Valuing inventory

Valuing an inventory asset can be challenging. Companies don't provide much information about their inventories. About as far as you'll normally get is a breakdown of how much inventory is in "finished goods" and "purchased parts and fabricated assemblies," and even that is buried deep in the 10-K (the 10-K is discussed in Chapter 6). The value investor knows little about what those inventories really are or about their real value. A warehouse of outdated 486 computer processors probably carries a book inventory value, but they aren't worth much to the company or anyone else.

Inventory valuation is further affected by accounting methods employed by a firm. The method affects both balance sheet carrying value and cost recognition on the income statement. Mainly the choices are "first in, first out" (FIFO) and "last in, first out" (LIFO), meaning that a company assigns either the earliest stocked goods or the latest stocked goods to a sale. In a normal environment in which costs increase over time, LIFO will result in a more conservative view of earnings and inventory balances — the more expensive items are assumed to be consumed first. (This approach may not work in technology companies, where more recently purchased components are actually cheaper — LIFO may be less conservative!) The FIFO versus LIFO decision is documented in annual report notes, usually Note 1, significant accounting policies. Under normal circumstances, you probably don't need to be *too* concerned about this, unless industry price instability or inflation becomes a big factor. Also watch for accounting policy changes, which can be used to hide or inflate performance.

Further refining the reported value of inventory is the decision to carry at the lower of cost or market. *Cost* is as implied — what the material cost in the first place. LIFO or FIFO affects the cost carried. But the most conservative inventory valuation practice is to carry *at market,* which is what the company thinks the market value of its inventory is on the resale market. Normally this comes closer to a true valuation for the inventory, but it depends on the company's assessment and the recency of that assessment. Most companies carry at the lower of cost or market, but again, look for valuation practice in the notes section.

Business and inventory cycles can wreak havoc on inventory and inventory valuations. Witness Cisco Systems' $2.5 *billion* dollar write-off of raw materials in the quarter ending April 2001. In late 2000, as demand swelled for its products and deliveries were frequently missed, the company decided to grab the bull by the horns and stock up on components so as not to miss future sales and lose customers to competitors. The business cycle turned, and on top of that, many of the orders on the books were probably superfluous anyway, with customers rushing to get their orders in to make sure that they got their product in a tight supply environment. The business turn plus cancellation of some of the order backlog reduced the need for raw materials, and combined with technology shifts, the stockpile rapidly lost value. Inventory managers call this cycle the "dreaded diamond" — exaggerated demand on the up portion of the business cycle causes overordering and overstocking, and then once the demand slows on the down cycle, the downturn is further exacerbated by the cancellation of overzealous orders. Technological obsolescence makes technology companies particularly vulnerable to inventory cycles. You must recognize business cycles and watch for inventories growing out of proportion to sales. Many value investors avoid tech altogether because of inconsistency and the inability to predict the future.

You need to appraise inventory balances for economic value and efficiency of use. Look at the size of the asset in an absolute sense and relative to the size and sales of the business. Look for trends, favorable and unfavorable, in inventory balances and ratios. Look at competitors and industry standards. Where possible, look at inventory quality and past track record for inventory obsolescence and resulting write-offs. And then be conservative. It often makes sense to assign a value of 50 percent to 75 percent, sometimes less, to inventory values appearing on a balance sheet.

As in most other aspects of value investing, it is important to know something about the industry when assigning value to balance sheet assets. You may be alarmed by the $1.2 billion in merchandise inventories carried on the Borders Group balance sheet (refer to Figure 7-1), a figure that's more than half of the total assets with fewer than three turns per year ($3.2 billion in sales). But a closer look at the book industry reveals a special case: Booksellers are entitled to return nearly all inventory to publishers for 100 percent credit! Booksellers need to stock even the slow movers to get people into the stores, so publishers realize this and have created this policy to get their inventory onto the shelves. So although the Borders book inventory is large and requires significant cash tie-up, it carries with it far less risk of obsolescence and future write-offs than many of its retailing brethren. Know thy business and know thy industry.

Deferred taxes and other current assets

Most balance sheets contain small amounts for other items carried on the books. "Deferred taxes" is an item that appears frequently and results from differences between financial reporting and tax reporting requirements. For the most part, you shouldn't worry about these items; seldom do they comprise more than 5 percent of stated assets. (If they do, take a closer look.)

Bolted to the floor: fixed assets

The balance sheet entry called "property, plant, and equipment" (PP&E) is pretty clear from the name. It refers to the fixed assets — land, buildings, machinery, fixtures, office technology, and similar items owned by the firm for productive use. Depending on the industry, this item may have a different name. Retail stores, for example, don't have plants.

Valuation of PP&E can vary widely. The key to understanding PP&E value is to understand depreciation. *Depreciation* is an amount subtracted each year by accountants from an asset purchase price for normal wear and tear and technological obsolescence. Depreciation methods are discussed further under the next heading, but for now it's important to note that depreciation can affect underlying asset values substantially. Further changing the picture can be a company's decision to value at lower of cost or market value. As for other accounts, the accounting method is disclosed in the statements under the notes entry.

The value of property, plant, and equipment, of course, can vary a lot by what it is, where it is, and how it's used. These in turn vary by industry and things specific to the company itself, such as its location. A Bessemer converter probably has a smaller market value compared to its purchase price than a modern semiconductor wafer fabrication machine. An old building in downtown Bismarck, North Dakota, probably has less value than a new building in Santa Clara, California.

Although most PP&E items are subject to depreciation charges, land is not. Is the value of land overstated on the books? Hardly. Land is normally carried at purchase or acquisition value. This affords a unique value investing opportunity. Land purchased in the 1940s or 1950s is often worth much more today than back then, but it is seldom reflected in the books. Consider railroads, with vast ownership of downtown lands and land grants in the West, mostly from over 100 years ago. If one realized the value of these holdings (less the cost of an occasional environmental cleanup), the value of these investments might increase enormously. There may be some real hidden gems lurking below the balance sheets of railroad, timber, mining, and certain old-line industrial corporations.

Understanding the nature of a corporation's PP&E and its depreciation methods will help in assessing the value of this account. Generally, value investors assign very conservative values to PP&E (unless a lot of land is involved): 50 percent or less.

Appreciating depreciation

Depreciation is a methodic reduction of PP&E asset value with assignment of a corresponding dollar amount to a *period expense* — an expense recorded for a reporting period. As the name implies, depreciation represents an accounting treatment of normal wear and obsolescence on productive assets. When companies buy a capital asset, usually a purchase greater than $1,000, they don't record the entire cost as an expense in the year purchased. Instead, they gradually recognize the cost as expense in subsequent years through depreciation. At the end of the depreciation cycle (in theory at least), it is time to make another capital outlay, replace the asset, and start the cycle all over again.

There is a variety of accepted methods for assigning depreciation dollars. A detailed discussion of depreciation and depreciation methods is CPA stuff that's well beyond the scope of this book. You may find it useful to recognize two major groupings of methods for assigning depreciation dollars: straight-line and accelerated depreciation.

Straight-line depreciation is just as the name implies: Each year an equal amount of asset value is expensed until the asset value reaches zero.

Accelerated depreciation methods allow the accountant to expense proportionately more in the early years of asset life. Accelerated methods include "sum of the years' digits" and "double declining balance." The details of these methods can be found in most accounting books and aren't important here, only the effects.

Effect of depreciation on income and asset quality

Acceleration and the corresponding increase in expense — reduction in reported profit — serve the purpose of reducing taxes in early years. With the time value of money (see Chapter 4), that's a good thing. Accelerated depreciation also results in more conservative PP&E asset valuations on the books. It also may better reflect reality — because of obsolescence, that semiconductor fab machine, like your new car in the driveway, probably loses relatively more market value in the first few years.

What you should consider

The choice of depreciation methods is important. Accelerated depreciation results in the most conservative PP&E asset valuations. It also results in the most conservative view of earnings and allows more room for future net earnings growth, because you can assume that a greater portion of depreciation is behind you.

But some companies may deliberately prop up current earnings by employing straight-line methods. Watch for companies changing over to straight-line from accelerated methods. Depreciation methods are disclosed in the notes section of the statements.

Depreciation is an accounting — not a cash — expense. No check is cut for depreciation. Instead, the check is cut when the asset is purchased. Depreciation is the leading difference between stated earnings and cash flows and can mean the difference between survival and failure for a company recording net income losses. Cash flow, unburdened by depreciation, may still be positive. But look out below. Cash consumed to keep a losing business afloat may not be available the next time a key piece of equipment needs to be replaced. Reporting methods that downplay depreciation or ignore it altogether, such as the "pro forma" reporting craze, indicate trouble. For more info on this issue, see Chapter 9.

Investments: Companies are investors, too

Besides more liquid marketable securities, many companies commit surplus cash to more substantial long-term investments. These investments can serve many purposes: to achieve returns as any other investor would, to participate in the growth of a related or unrelated industry, or to eventually obtain control of the company. Favorable tax treatment of dividends and gains makes investing in other companies still more attractive, as exemplified *in extremis* by Berkshire Hathaway (see Chapter 3).

There are a lot of good reasons for companies to invest in other companies. Accepting investments as payment for goods and services rendered is probably *not* one of them. This practice became rather fashionable in the Internet boom, as companies freely paid for products and services bought from other companies with their shares. When their shares became almost worthless, well, you know the rest of the story. Watch also for technology companies making investments in startups as a way of fostering business or directing purchases their way.

There are many ways to value investments, boiling down basically to historical cost or market valuation. Market valuation is obviously better. Although investment value is disclosed in the 10-K (discussed in Chapter 6), you need to read carefully to find a statement such as the following: "... as of 10/31/00 these securities were recorded at an estimated fair value of $328M with a cost basis of $176M ... gross unrealized gains were $216M and gross unrealized losses were $64M. ..." Such a statement gives you a fair idea that the company, Hewlett-Packard in this case, is ahead on its investments. Watch out for declining fair values and particularly for large *gross unrealized losses* — future write-offs and asset value impairment loom large.

Gauge the size of investments on the balance sheet, look for detail, and understand management's intent in making the investments.

Soft assets

Asset valuation gets *really* fun for the value investor when the discussion turns to intangibles, also sometimes referred to as "soft" assets. *Intangibles* are assets that don't have a physical presence but are critical in acquiring and maintaining sales and producing a competitive edge. Intangibles include patents, copyrights, franchises, brand names, and trademarks. Also included is the all-encompassing goodwill often acquired by acquiring (and overpaying for) other companies.

Placing a financial value on these ethereal marketing assets is difficult, but accountants must and do. If there is an historical cost, accountants may carry the intangible at that cost. This is often the case with "goodwill" from company acquisitions.

Valuing intangibles

The key to assessing intangible assets is to understand (1) their carrying value and (2) the amortization technique. Intangible assets should all be amortized, since patents expire, brand value may be diluted, and so forth. Goodwill from acquisitions most certainly — at least for now — must be amortized. Like depreciation, valuation depends heavily on the method of amortization. Basically the same choice is available between straight-line and accelerated amortization, and the chosen method is disclosed in the financial statement notes. But you may not find it in Note 1, and you may need to do some digging, often in several different notes — under acquisitions, patents, and so forth.

Intangibles are subject to a great deal of discretion in their accounting, and their sources and form can be numerous and highly variable from one company to the next. Cast a skeptical eye on large goodwill accounts in particular, especially if a company seems reluctant to write them off.

Companies with aggressive acquisition strategies can be a value investor's nightmare, particularly where large amounts of goodwill and other intangibles are involved. Consider Lucent Technologies, which reports acquiring 10 major companies and 11 more small ones in the years 1998 through 2000. In the year 2000 alone, acquired intangibles reflected on the balance sheet went from $960 million to $9.945 *billion*, a tenfold increase. Add to that a major divestiture (Avaya) and a host of patents and other intangibles from the former Bell Labs, and you have a valuation nightmare. Cisco Systems reported a similar tenfold increase in acquisition goodwill to over $4 billion. The best advice here for the value investor is to stick to simplicity.

Intangibles and investing

The classical school of value investing suggested deducting intangibles from company valuation altogether. In Ben Graham's day (see Chapter 3), intangibles were subtracted directly from book value. They were considered fluff, and a conservative valuation would remove them completely. In many cases where a company simply overpays to acquire another company, this is still true. But with the advent of modern technology and marketing, the ideas of intellectual capital and brand equity are part of a company's value and cannot simply be ignored.

In fact, for some companies, these intangibles may represent their greatest value. What is the value of the Coca-Cola Company without the brand name? Or the value of Microsoft without its lock on PC operating system design? Such brands and locks often ultimately produce the best profit streams and best value. Contemporary value investors need a clear understanding of intangible assets.

An asset assimilation

As the discussion of assets on the balance sheet is now complete, it's time to impart a few parting comments and resources.

Four score and a million bucks ago

The single statement that best characterizes the nature of assets and importance of their scrutiny came from Ben Graham himself, in the book *Security Analysis:* "The liabilities are real, but the value of assets must be questioned."

This statement is the Gettysburg Address of balance sheet valuation. Aside from cash and equivalents, asset values are largely up to the company and its accounting and management philosophy. Liabilities (what is owed to others) are not subject to management control. You owe someone a buck, you owe them a buck.

The prudent value investor tries to "peel back the onion" to get a better grip on asset and thus on company value. This requires a deeper look at financial statements and the accompanying notes, and knowledge of industries and industry competitors. Without this deeper look, you're flying blind. Of course, it's a trade-off: Too much peeling back of the onion results in teary, weary eyes. This stuff is complex, and deriving meaning can take hours, if indeed it's possible at all. In business, it often seems that the more you know, the more you don't know. Eventually, you'll get good at recognizing where benefits of knowing intrinsic value aren't worth the cost of acquiring it and you'll leave behind companies that just are too complex to understand.

And finally, look at three defining characteristics of any asset: size, trend, and quality.

Assigning value to assets

Table 7-1 is useful as a simple reference to convert reported asset values to liquidating value, a conservative base for intrinsic valuation. The basis for this table once again comes straight from Graham and Dodd's *Security Analysis.* Professionals may use evolved versions, but this table is still a handy tool.

Table 7-1	Valuing Balance Sheet Assets	
Type of Asset	*% Range of Liquidating Value to Book Value*	*Comments*
Cash, cash equivalents	100%	More is better. Watch out for the post-IPO "stash."
Accounts Receivable	75 to 95%	Look at write-offs.

(continued)

Table 7-1 *(continued)*

Type of Asset	% Range of Liquidating Value to Book Value	Comments
Inventory	50 to 75%	Less for businesses with high obsolescence exposure. Look at write-offs.
Fixed assets	1 to 50%	Depends on what kind of asset and where it is. Watch for obsolescence.
Intangibles	1 to 90%	Usually lower for acquisitions, higher for patents and trademarks. Fast depreciation is better.

Does the Company Owe Money?

The last section identifies business resources in place (on the books at least) to produce income. Now you need to identify where these resources come *from*. Recall that assets = liabilities + owners' equity. Now take a look at the right side of the enterprise equation to identify what a company owes and what it owns, and what it all means to you.

Liabilities, as Ben Graham's quote, "The liabilities are real, but the value of assets must be questioned," suggests, are fairly straightforward. Although different things can be done by different people in different situations to state asset values differently, we know of no creditors that afford the same opportunity to liabilities. If you owe, you owe. Accounting and financial reporting — and the effect on intrinsic value — are straightforward.

Current liabilities

Liabilities basically come in two flavors: current and long term. Current liabilities are just what the name implies: liabilities for which payment is due normally in less than a year. The personal finance analogy is your monthly credit card or any other bill, while your 30-year mortgage is considered a long-term liability. But wait, don't you pay that every month? Yes, that shows up as a special kind of current liability known as the current portion of long-term debt due.

Payables

Almost everyone, individuals or corporations, has payables, defined as money owed to others for products purchased or services rendered. The liability is created when the service or product arrives; a cash payment follows to discharge the liability. Nearly all companies maintain a regular balance of current accounts payable, interest payable, and the like. If payment is received in advance, as with a deposit, the unearned portion is tracked as a liability. Sometimes *contingent liabilities* may be recorded, as in warranty claims expected to be paid but not yet actualized.

Payables and value investing

In personal finance, everyone wants to reduce or eliminate current payables. Books, TV shows, and experts in the personal finance world all advocate getting out of debt. And for the most part they're right. Liabilities represent consumed potential and, with prevailing interest rates, can be quite expensive.

But in corporate finance, the approach is a little different, and the mood has been shifting. Brought on in part by reduced interest costs and in part by enormously successful business models such as Dell Computer, trying to reduce liabilities — at least short-term liabilities — to zero is no longer in vogue. Why? Because companies like Dell can run their day-to-day business on someone else's money. And because most accounts payable come with a 30-day pay period, Dell and others have realized that "someone else's money," in this case, can be had for free. And the bottom line of it is relatively small equity capital requirements from the owners to support the business, and a relatively high return on equity for those owners.

There is little for you to do with current liabilities except subtract them out from intrinsic value. But also realize that current liabilities aren't necessarily a bad thing and that they can result in higher effective returns on ownership capital with relatively low cost and risk.

Long-term liabilities

Long-term corporate liabilities are really no different than those in personal finance: They represent contracted commitments to pay back a sum of money over time with interest. For the individual, they come in the form of loans and mortgages; for the corporation, they occur more often in the form of tradable notes and bonds. The result, however, is the same in both cases.

Debt and the value investor

As for short-term liabilities, you don't need to look too closely at the amount or quality of these liabilities. Trends can be important, however. Relying increasingly on long-term debt may be a sign of trouble. The company may not be making ends meet and, may be having trouble raising capital from existing or potential owners, which is never a good sign.

In addition, a company constantly changing, restructuring, or otherwise tinkering with long-term debt may be sending tacit signals of trouble. The company may be seeking concessions from lenders behind the scenes. In any event, attention paid to this kind of activity diverts attention from the core business, which is not a good thing and a warning flag for value investors.

How much is too much?

Finally, excessive use of debt signals potential danger if things don't turn out the way a company expects them to. Leverage is a good thing when things are going a company's way. Debt financing can be used to produce more product for more markets and thus more profit and, in the end, a bigger business. Return to owners is proportionately higher: Their investment stays the same while the returns grow. But as everyone knows, this can work the other way. Value investors don't like surprises, and a company with uncertain prospects and a lot of debt may not make it on to their list. Industry standards and common sense apply to debt-to-equity ratios.

Again, factor liabilities in as a negative factor in valuation and look for unfavorable trends or excessive use of long-term debt. Generally, liabilities don't require the close study that you might give to assets.

And Now, Meet the Owners

Because you're contemplating making an investment in a company, isn't owners' equity the most important balance sheet item? You and other investors, in essence, are either directly or indirectly contributing capital that is in turn converted into an asset *and then* in turn converted into revenue and profit to produce a return to the owner. You're making a decision to allocate capital to a company that in turn does the best job allocating capital to endeavors that produce the best return.

Like liabilities, the owners' equity portion of the balance sheet is critical to a company's function, but it really requires relatively little scrutiny on your part. We take you on a short tour but avoid the tedious discussions of classes of stock, par value, and the like that belabor so many finance readers. For this discussion, owners' equity consists of two things: paid-in capital, a fancy word for stock, and retained earnings.

Paid-in capital

Paid-in capital represents the total value paid into the company by its owners — its stockholders. It gets a little complicated with the discussion of par value and "additional" paid-in capital. Total paid-in capital represents capital actually paid into the company at initial or subsequent company stock sales and has nothing to do with market price or market value. In and of itself, you need to pay little attention to this item.

Retained earnings

Retained earnings are profits from past operating periods that are retained or reinvested in the business. Technically speaking, company profits belong to the shareholders, but it becomes management's prerogative to decide whether to actually pay them out. Typically, managers think that they can invest the money more effectively than their shareholders. Value investors are betting that they're right!

So long as a company's business is viable, shareholders probably want to see retained earnings as high as possible. It's a capital allocation game — the earnings are better suited to that company's purpose than anywhere else. By investing in the company, you've already decided that, so you may as well keep your money on the table.

So generally, more is better, especially if accompanied by a reasonable dividend policy in which management *is* sharing some of the spoils with the owners. On the other hand, watch for rapidly declining or, worse, negative retained earnings balances. Negative retained earnings are almost a sure sign of trouble, usually brought on by asset values declining faster than expected, excessive debt, an overinflated stock offering price, or a combination of the three. As a value investor, you should view negative retained earnings as a bright red signal flare.

A look at book value

Owners' equity is the sum of paid-in capital and retained earnings. (There can be a few other small crumbs of ownership, but they're seldom significant.) In theory, this is also the *book value* of a company — the actual net value as determined by the company's accounting for its business. The book value is the net of assets (which it can value and report with a degree of latitude), and liabilities (which occur at face value). Thus, book value reporting is done with a degree of latitude. Value investors talk about three different book value measures:

- Book value is owners' equity, or total book assets less liabilities.
- Tangible book value is total book value less all or part of intangibles.
- Book value per share is the accounting book value divided by the number of common shares outstanding.

All three of these measures crop up in value investing discussions and papers, but be careful because sometimes they're used interchangeably.

If you want a detailed assessment of book value, you can do your homework by applying asset valuation formulas presented earlier. A little less tedious approach is one used by Buffett and others: Don't get hung up on the absolute book value because you could go crazy trying to assess it with the information provided. Rather, looking at *trends* and *changes* in book value may be easier and better. You may also find it useful to examine stated book values relative to business activity and compare with the industry and competitors.

Book in, intrinsic out

Warren Buffett put it together nicely. He observed that book value is the sum of what investors put into (or leave in) the business, while intrinsic value is what investors can take out of the business. A key part of intrinsic value is the adjusted book value or net worth discussed in this chapter. But another and perhaps most important component of intrinsic value is the present and future income stream that a company can earn for the investor above and beyond the cost of capital allocated to the firm. Chapter 8 takes a closer look at income and income reporting. Once all the pieces are in place, we discuss intrinsic value and capital allocation in greater depth.

Chapter 8

Statements of Fact Part 3: Earnings and Cash Flow Statements

•••

In This Chapter

▶ Discovering the importance of earnings and cash flow

▶ Examining key parts of earnings and cash flow statements

▶ Understanding differences between earnings and cash flow

▶ How to use earnings and cash flow information

•••

> *Earnings are the honey that attracts the bees — in this case, investors.*
>
> —Janet Lowe, author, *Warren Buffett Speaks* and *Value Investing Made Easy*

*J*ust as life cannot be measured or evaluated by a single snapshot, neither can a business. Chapter 7 presents a fixed-in-time snapshot of business life: the balance sheet. From this snapshot we get a view of business resources (assets) and how they are contributed to the business (liabilities and owner's equity). But what about the business activity between snapshots? What happened between each release of the shutter? Sure, a comparison of one snapshot to another tells you something changed, just as sequential vacation snapshots show different family members in different places. But what happened to the family members between shots, and why?

This is where earnings statements and cash flow statements come in. The balance sheet is critical in evaluating the financial *status* of a business; the income and cash flow statements together measure business *activity* and *results*. Earnings and cash flow statements show the pulse of the business and explain changes among balance sheet snapshots. With these statements, the business analyst or investor can assemble a complete picture — a moving picture if you wish — showing flows into and out of the business, successes and failures, growth and decline.

Consistent with the style used in the previous chapters, we try to stick to what you need to know while avoiding expert accounting knowledge. The focus is on what you, as an investor, need to know.

The Importance of Earnings

We don't need to remind anyone of the underpinning of a capitalist society and economy: that business and economic activity are undertaken with the idea of generating a *profit*. Because we're not writing an essay on political economy, we don't go into the detail of why that is or isn't a good idea. We'll leave that to others. Investors embrace the capitalist idea. The next step is to measure the profit and allocate capital resources in such a way as to maximize it.

Profit is simply the gross revenue of an enterprise, less the cost of producing that income, over a defined period of time.

Earnings make the world go round

So much is made of earnings and earnings reports. Do you hear much about a company's cash balance, accumulated depreciation, or owner's equity during *Wall Street Week* and other financial shows? Does everyone salivate four times a year for "asset season"?

Not really. On an ongoing basis, earnings are *the* driving force and "mega" indicator of a company's success. If earnings are growing, the financial press doesn't worry much about the other stuff. Conversely, serve up a couple of double faults on the earnings front, and everybody is all over asset impairment, write-offs, debt, weak cash positions, and the like.

In the purest sense, long-term stock price appreciation is based on the growth of a company's asset base and owner's equity in that base. If a company is earning money, and particularly if it earns it at a growing rate, that's a good thing. As Buffett says, "If the business does well, the stock always follows."

Earnings tell us how well a business manages its *operations*, while the balance sheet tells us how well it manages its *resources*.

Bottom lines and other lines

You hear a lot about the *bottom line,* which refers to the net earnings or income after all expenses, taxes, and extraordinary items are factored in.

The bottom line is the final "net" measure of all business activity as measured by the chosen accounting method.

Other important lines in the earnings statement reveal key things about the business. These earnings components show important trends in the business. You'll see them in various forms on financial statements depending on the statement and sometimes the industry. Among them are the following:

- ✔ **Gross profit:** This is simply the sales less the direct cost. Direct cost includes labor, material, and expenses directly attributable to producing the product or service. Gross profit, often called *gross margin,* is the purest indicator of business profitability, because each cost dollar is directly generated by production and sale of the product. Value investors watch gross profit trends closely as an indicator of market dominance, price control, and future profitability.

- ✔ **Operating profit:** This term refers to gross profit less period expenses; that is, overhead costs not directly attributable to product production. Selling, general, and administrative expenses (SG&A) cover all the head-quarters functions, information technology, marketing, and other indirect costs. It generally excludes financing costs, such as interest, and it also excludes taxes. Amortization is usually included, as cost recovery for property, plant, and equipment is part of operating expense. Items deemed as extraordinary are not included. Operating profit gives a more complete picture of how the business is performing on a day-to-day basis. It sometimes appears as operating income, earnings from operations, or similar phrases.

- ✔ **Income from continuing operations:** This is operating profit after taxes and interest but before reporting results of discontinued business.

- ✔ **Net income:** This represents the net result of all revenues, expenses, interest, and taxes.

There are other earnings measures such as free cash flow and "EBITDA," which we discuss later in this chapter. The point is that there are many ways to measure income. Each reveals an important layer of business performance, both for determining intrinsic value and also for comparing companies. As we explore the statements (and their use to value investors), we further discuss earnings components and their importance.

Cash flow

We're sure that you're wondering what the difference is between earnings and cash flow. Why do companies have two different statements?

Good question. The answer is that the realization of accounting earnings may occur at different times from the actual realization of cash. The main differences arise from accrual accounting and from depreciation and other noncash amortizations and adjustments. A dollar earned today might not be collected until tomorrow, and a dollar earned today as cash may be diminished as earnings by a noncash amortization of an asset.

The number one guiding principle for all accounting and finance folks is to measure the business activity as closely as possible to what really occurs (what is produced and sold) in the business.

Accrual and unusual punishment

Accrual accounting sounds scary, but what it really does is divorce the business activity from its corresponding receipt or disbursement of cash. If you build a machine and sell it to another company in April but don't receive payment until June, in which month should you recognize the production cost and sale? Accrual accounting says in April, while cash basis accounting says in June. Accrual accounting is the most accurate reflection of the business activity. In this example, labor, material, and overhead were purchased in April to build the machine, and it was sold during that month. Assuming that the cash is eventually collected, accrual accounting measures the profit of the business on the sale and costs incurred in April. So because of accrual accounting, the timing of cash flows versus the recognition of revenue, expense, and earnings may be different.

Amortized to death

Likewise, depreciation and amortization are accounting transactions designed to recover the cost of large cash outlays for property, plant, equipment, and sometimes goodwill. The large cash outlay happens once, and it may be years before the expense is recognized. *Amortizations* are noncash transactions; they're simply recognition of a *portion* of an asset value as an expense during a period. Therefore, if net income is $50,000 but there is a $20,000 amortization expense recognized, all things being equal, how much cash did the business take in? The answer: $70,000.

The point isn't to challenge you up with a bunch of quiz questions but rather to illustrate the differences between income and cash flow and to explain the existence of separate earnings and cash flow statements. To summarize:

- ✔ Earnings statements measure business activity as it occurs, regardless of cash flow, and including noncash amortization and other transactions.

- ✔ Cash flow statements specifically track the movement of cash — the ins and outs of the cash and marketable securities balance sheet asset — in and out of the company.

We describe each statement. By the end of this chapter, you should know how to use these statements together with the balance sheet to understand the business.

What to look for

Used by investors and traders of all kinds, earnings statements are among the most widely examined of company publications. Even the most short-term trader trades in anticipation of earnings announcements, compares net income with projections, and trades on the result. Casual and serious investors both look at the *top line* (revenue or sales) and the bottom line. For value investors, earnings statements are indispensable. Value investors do deeper research, taking a much more in-depth look at the underlying numbers, trends, and history.

The following sections highlight a few important attributes to look for in an earnings statement.

Growth

After all is said and done, the long-term growth of a stock price boils down to growth in the business. Growth in the business means growth in the earnings — there is no other way to sustain business growth on the same ownership base. Sure, you can acquire, merge, sell more stock, and so forth to make a business larger by common definitions, but has the business really "grown"?

The value investor works to obtain a deep understanding of business growth, growth trends, and the quality of growth. Is reported growth based on internal core competencies? Or is it acquired or speculative growth based on unproven ventures? The value investor assesses growth and growth patterns, judges the validity of growth reported, and attempts to project the future.

Don't ride the cyclical

Always be wary of cyclical stocks. True, companies such as Ford may look irresistible with price/earnings (P/E) ratios sometimes approaching 4 or 5 (implying a 20 to 25 percent earnings yield or return on share purchase price). But a closer look at the long term reveals a P/E in the teens and years of marginal earnings or even losses mixed in. Look at the long term and be aware of stocks that dip as the business cycle dips. Basic industries, such as capital equipment, natural resources, paper, farm machinery, automobiles, and auto suppliers are notorious for sending signals of intermittent strength while showing little sustained growth. It is amazing how many short-term focused investors bite on these signals!

Consistency

Long-term growth should be sustainable — and thus consistent. Look for sustained growth across business cycles. A big pop in earnings one year followed by malaise for the next two does not paint a pretty picture for you as a value investor. Long, consistent, successful earnings track records get the A scores.

Beyond earnings, consistency is a desired feature for other parts of the earnings statement. Consistency in sales and sales growth, profit margins and margin growth, operating expense and expense trends is highly prized. The less consistency, the more difficult to predict the future five or ten years and beyond, and the less attractive a company looks to value investors.

Healthy components: Comparative and trends

Value investors look at individual lines in the earnings statement, not just the bottom line. Improving gross margins — especially sustained improvement — signal strong business improvement. Costs are under control, and the company is improving its market position. Likewise, improving operating margins can show better cost control, greater efficiency, and rewards from earlier expansion cycles. And value investors constantly compare companies in like industries. Gross margins of competing computer manufacturers, for instance, tell a lot about who has the best market position, production and delivery process, and business model.

Comparing the incomparable is an all-too-common investing pitfall. With earnings statements, this malady occurs in two forms:

- Earnings statements are not always broken down the same way. Although the bottom line is the bottom line, the intermediate steps may be different. One company's operating earnings may include depreciation and amortization, while another's may not. Typically, there is at least a strong similarity, particularly among firms in the same industry, but not always.

- Two companies that appear (and even are classified) in the same industry may have differences large enough to raise caution. Commercial and industrial suppliers, such as Honeywell, have consumer divisions, while consumer businesses, such as Procter & Gamble, have industrial divisions. Many businesses supply a mix of products in a mix of categories to a mix of customers. "Pure plays" in a business or industry are not always easy to find. The upshot: you must understand businesses before comparing them.

Quality

As Wall Street and its analysts exert ever-increasing pressure on companies to perform and perform to a stringent set of expectations, the idea of accounting "stretch" enters ever more into the picture. Even in complying with the rules, companies are given sufficient latitude to apply accounting principles in ways that make performance look better. Later in this chapter and in Chapter 9, we explore how this latitude can affect the quality of earnings reports.

Exploring the Earnings Statement

In this section, we explore a specific income statement and take it apart to explore its components. We continue with the example provided by Borders Group, a major book and music retailer. Note the naming flexibility: The earnings statement is presented as a consolidated statement of operations, which is shown in Figure 8-1.

Starting at the top line

The *top line* of any business is the sales or revenue figure. Normally, sales and revenues are straightforward. They represent accounting dollars generated for business products sold or services performed. (Remember, with accrual accounting it doesn't matter whether the company has been *paid* yet.) With more complex "b-to-b" businesses or for those selling into a distribution channel (a wholesaler or retailer), revenue recognition can be more complex.

Accounting revenue is normally recorded at the time of sale or service completion. But there are situations in which the process isn't complete and that may call into question the validity of the revenue. If a distributor doesn't have to pay until a product is resold, or if the manufacturer is still required to perform significant services, such as configuration, installation, and so forth, a sale to a distributor or customer may be exaggerated if recorded as a sale. Similarly, sales to subsidiaries or affiliated companies shouldn't be considered a sale.

But for the most part, sales are sales. In many businesses, such as transportation or utilities, they may be called *revenues*, but it's the same difference. Occasionally you will see an allowance for returns broken out; if not, you can usually safely assume that they're included in the sales figure as a negative amount. We're surprised — disappointed, really — that more retailers, mail order houses, and e-tailers don't give breakouts on sales returns, not even in 10-K reports.

When comparing sales figures or projecting trends, compare apples to apples. If there is a significant acquisition, divestiture, or extraordinary change in the business, make sure to take it into account.

Cost of goods sold

Cost of goods sold, or CGS, is an important driver of business success. For all but a few companies with high intellectual property or service content, CGS is the largest piece of the revenue pie. *Cost of goods sold* is the cost of acquiring goods and raw material plus labor and direct overhead expended to add value for sale.

2000 financials $\frac{22}{23}$ pg

consolidated statements
of operations

(dollars in millions except per share data)	Fiscal Year Ended		
	Jan. 28, 2001	Jan. 23, 2000	Jan. 24, 1999
Sales	$3,271.2	$2,968.4	$2,595.0
Cost of merchandise sold (includes occupancy)	2,354.5	2,127.6	1,859.4
Gross margin	916.7	840.8	735.6
Selling, general and administrative expenses	736.2	659.2	557.6
Pre-opening expense	6.4	7.8	7.8
Asset impairments and other writedowns	36.2	—	—
Goodwill amortization	2.8	2.8	2.9
Operating income	135.1	171.0	167.3
Interest expense	13.1	16.6	16.2
Income from continuing operations before income tax	122.0	154.4	151.1
Income tax provision	48.2	60.4	59.0
Income from continuing operations	$ 73.8	$ 94.0	$ 92.1
Discontinued operations (Note 3)			
Loss from operations of All Wound Up, net of income tax credits of $7.0 and $2.4	10.8	3.7	—
Loss on disposition of All Wound Up, net of deferred income tax credit of $8.9	19.4	—	—
Net income	$ 43.6	$ 90.3	$ 92.1
Earnings (loss) per common share data (Note 2)			
Diluted earnings (loss) per common share:			
Continuing operations	$ 0.92	$ 1.17	$ 1.12
Discontinued operations	(0.38)	(0.04)	—
Net diluted earnings per common share	$ 0.54	$ 1.13	$ 1.12
Basic earnings (loss) per common share:			
Continuing operations	$ 0.94	$ 1.21	$ 1.20
Discontinued operations	(0.38)	(0.05)	—
Net basic earnings per common share	$ 0.56	$ 1.16	$ 1.20

See accompanying Notes to Consolidated Financial Statements.

Figure 8-1:
Borders
Group
consoli-
dated
statement of
operations

Different accounting treatments can affect CGS. In Chapter 7, we discuss LIFO (last in, first out) and FIFO (first in, first out) as different ways of valuing balance sheet inventory. This valuation can also affect CGS — if more expensive LIFO raw material units are assumed to be consumed first, that will drive *up* the CGS and *down* the gross margin, operating income, and net income. Hence, LIFO is the more conservative reporting method except in some technology industries in which older components may actually cost more. (Note 1 in the financial statements usually clarifies accounting methods.) Value investors should be careful to understand which accounting method is used before comparing companies and watch for changes in accounting methods that may shift reporting bias. In a price-stable low-inflation environment, the LIFO-FIFO thing becomes less important.

CGS varies widely by industry and industry cost structure. For example, the physical CGS of Microsoft is tiny with respect to revenue, whereas a grocery store or discount retailer may see CGS in the 70 or 80 percent range. Apples-to-apples comparisons are critical to effective analysis.

Borders: A look at the top

Here's a look at the Borders Group top line, CGS, and gross margin in Figure 8-1.

This picture covers a relatively short period of time, three years. Normally, we'd like more time see solid trends develop.

Nevertheless, sales grew from $2.595 billion in fiscal 1998 to $3.271 billion in fiscal 2000. Nominally, this reflects slowing growth, 14 percent in 1998–99 and 10 percent in 1999–2000. As a compounded annual growth rate, this is 12.2 percent (see Chapter 4). Not bad, but slowing, at least in this three-year snapshot.

Cost of merchandise sold (another name for CGS) grew at a rate apparently tracking sales, resulting in gross margin that also seems in line with sales. A closer look will tell.

If you take gross margin in dollars and divide by each year's sales, you come up with 28.3 percent in 1998, 28.3 percent again in 1999, and 28.0 percent in 2000. This shows an ever-so-slight decline. Usually changes of less than 0.5 percent are insignificant, but in a thin-margin retail environment, is 0.3 percent significant? Next year should tell the tale. You could even take a look at the next quarter, but be careful, as seasonal patterns can mislead. If Borders clears slow moving Christmas merchandise in the first quarter, margins will be driven lower. Again, know the business, know the quarterly and annual patterns, and know the facts that support the numbers.

Note that Borders includes occupancy in its cost of goods sold. Probably its theory is that occupancy is directly proportional to sales, or sales are driven directly by the number of stores and floor space available. That's okay, and it doesn't violate accounting principles, but it also makes it harder to compare Borders to other retailers who don't report this way.

Gross margin

Gross margin, or *gross profit,* is simply the sales less the cost of goods sold. It is the basic economic output of the business before overhead, marketing, and financing costs enter the picture. Gross profit takes on added meaning when taken as a percentage. This percentage — and trends in the percentage — speaks volumes for the health and direction of the business.

Operating expenses

You can't judge a book by its cover, and you can't sell a book without operating expenses.

True, direct costs of store personnel, and in the case of Borders, even direct store occupancy costs, are included in the cost of goods sold and, as a result, in gross margin. But is that all? What about headquarters? Marketing? All those computers? The company Web site? The annual report? Recruiting and training? These are "indirect," or *operating* expenses.

No matter the business, any company incurs indirect costs, or costs of doing business not *directly* related to producing and selling individual units of product or service. Some call it overhead, but it goes a little beyond the traditional definition of overhead, and some overhead items we've seen are usually allocated to direct costs, or CGS.

Selling, general, and administrative (SG&A)

Selling, general, and administrative (SG&A) is a favorite target of value investors and more traditional investors alike. SG&A includes marketing and selling costs, including advertising, sales and sales forces, marketing and promotion campaigns, and a host of other administrative and corporate expenses such as travel, Web sites, office equipment, and the like. Many investors use SG&A as a barometer of management effectiveness — a solid management team keeps SG&A expenses in check. SG&A can mushroom into a vast slush fund and an internal corporate pork barrel that can easily get out of control. Like gross margin, looking at SG&A as a percentage is best. For an example of how to examine SG&A, see the "Practical example: SG&A at Borders" sidebar.

Research and development

Manufacturing and technology companies in particular need to invest in future products. Because these investments occur long before product production, and because many of them never pan out into saleable products, companies are allowed to expense research and development (R&D) as a period expense.

Practical example: SG&A at Borders

For Borders, selling, general, and administrative (SG&A) were 21.5 percent of sales in 1998, rising to 22.2 percent of sales in both 1999 and 2000. These numbers wave a pale yellow flag, not only for the increase but also for the absence of *decrease*. Arguably as sales increase, SG&A should decline. Why? Because of economies of scale. While business increases, at least some corporate expenses, such as corporate headquarters and staff, should remain unchanged or increase at a slower rate. Order administration cost for a 2000-copy order of the latest Grisham novel would be the same as for a 1500-copy order. As markets are established and a business grows, per-unit marketing and administrative expenses should decline. Most companies dearly seek these operating efficiencies, even to the point of seeking mergers to achieve them.

Company comparisons are appropriate here, too. But watch again for economies of scale. Although Wal-Mart reports SG&A at 16.5 percent of sales, easily beating Borders, recognize that this is measured against $191 billion, or almost 60 times the annual sales volume. Compare carefully.

A few companies, particularly software companies, have been known to *capitalize* software development costs, that is, build them into an intellectual property asset instead of expensing them, thereby inflating earnings. Accounting principles allow some capitalizing but state that the majority of R&D costs must be expensed as incurred. Companies are pretty much allowed to tell you what they want to tell you about R&D costs. Telling more may compromise their secrets, so usually they don't tell much.

Appropriate levels of R&D expense vary widely by industry. For example, software companies incur very large R&D as a percent of sales, but insurers or retailers have small R&D percentages. Because you're unlikely to know the detail of R&D expenditures, you're probably best served to watch the trend and changes in R&D as a percent of sales. Increasing R&D percentages reflect an increasing cost of doing business and possibly ineffective R&D, while decreasing R&D as a percent may reflect sacrificing the future for the present. Neither is a good thing. Watch for these changes and any explanations thereof.

Also note that companies without a significant R&D effort may not report it as a separate line. In some financial statements, it's called "product development."

Appreciating depreciation (again)

Why do we say "again"? Are we gluttons for punishment? No. We simply want you to know that in Chapter 7 we cover depreciation under "assets" on the balance sheet. But now we take up depreciation, a net effect on property, plant, and equipment, as an earnings statement item.

Depreciation and amortization represent the accountant's assignment of the cost of a long-lived asset to specific business periods. *Depreciation* is used when referring to physical fixed assets, and *amortization* is used when referring to intangible assets (such as goodwill, patents, and so forth). Some of you oil and natural resource investors bugs may run into the term *depletion:* a cost recovery for exhaustion of natural resource assets.

In our experience, depreciation and amortization expenses show up in a wide variety of ways on the earnings statement. Sometimes you'll see a specific breakout of depreciation expenses, especially for capital-intensive businesses. More often, depreciation expenses are buried in another operating expense line, often SG&A.

Do you *really* want to know what a company wrote off for depreciation in a reporting period? Then refer to the statement of cash flows. We're getting a little ahead of ourselves, but depreciation, a noncash expense, is a major source of difference between accounting income and cash flow. So, accountants almost always show depreciation as a separate add-back item on the cash flow statement.

What should you look for? The actual amount of depreciation is normally not that important. What is more important is the method and time period over which amortization occurs. Accelerated depreciation methods result in more conservative earnings statements. Companies sometimes use straight-line methods for financial reporting and accelerated methods for tax purposes — giving rise to two sets of books and a major contributor to the deferred taxes lines in the balance sheet. Watch for sudden changes in depreciation methods, and be careful when comparing companies to assure they are using comparable depreciation methods.

Impairments, investments, and other write-downs

When the value of an asset changes significantly in the eyes of management, a company can elect to take a write-down recognizing the change. The *write-down* shows up as a decrease in asset value on the balance sheet for the asset category involved and as a (usually) one-time expense somewhere on the earnings statement. The rules for when and how to take these write-downs are, shall we say, flexible. The rules for writing down investment losses, a common theme in the technology arena, are particularly complex and beyond the scope of this book. The good news is that write-downs are normally reported as a separate line and are well documented in the notes.

For you as a value investor, knowing the detail or amount may not be as important as knowing the pattern. Are these write-downs really one-time adjustments, or does the company continually overinvest in unproductive technology? Are companies quick to recognize mistakes (Borders set up Borders.com only two years before writing down part of the investment), or do they linger, pushing an ever-larger "bow wave" towards amortization and earnings oblivion? Write-down behavior provides insight into management behavior and effectiveness as well as overall business consistency and should not be ignored.

Practical example: Asset write-downs at Borders

Consider the following disclosure tied to the write-down of $36.2 million at Borders, found in Note 4 of the company's financial statement:

"In the fourth quarter of fiscal 2000, the company took a pre-tax charge of $36.2 [million] related to the impairment of certain long-lived assets and other write-downs. The carrying value of long-term assets is evaluated whenever changes in circumstances indicate the carrying amount of such assets may not be recoverable. In performing such reviews for recoverability, the Company compares the expected cash flows to the carrying value of long-lived assets. If the expected future cash flows are less then the carrying amount of such assets, the Company recognizes an impairment loss for the difference between the carrying amount and their estimated fair value. Fair value is estimated using expected discounted future cash flows. The charge taken in 2000 primarily consisted of $17.7 [M] for computer hardware and software of Borders.com and $12.5 [M] for leasehold improvements and furniture and fixture of underperforming Walden stores. The remainder of the charge was related to employee severance, cost of certain lease obligations for redundant headquarter buildings, and the write-off of certain equity investments."

So Borders recognizes the decline in value to the corporation of Borders.com technology investments and a few other asset value reductions and redundancies. In one fell swoop, the company adjusted these asset values and took care of some investment losses at the same time.

It is also critically important to understand write-offs and one-time charges when building intrinsic value models (more in Chapter 12). Many intrinsic value models base forward projections on the most recently reported net income numbers. Automated investment analysis tools, such as those provided by quicken.com and many online brokers, simply take the latest year's earnings figure from a database. If that figure was significantly reduced (or enhanced) by extraordinary items, a large (and compounded!) error in the intrinsic value assessment can occur.

Giving to goodwill

As presented in Chapter 7, intangible assets are long-lived assets that have no physical existence. Included are patents, copyrights, trademarks, franchises, and other legal protections. Also included — and attracting more interest from value investors — are goodwill assets obtained by acquiring other companies. These goodwill assets arise when more is paid for an acquired company than it is worth in hard assets. Acquired goodwill assets often have real value — brand equity, customer base, and so forth — but just as often, they don't, instead being used as a plug-in figure to account properly for the purchase.

Like other asset impairments, goodwill receives flexible accounting treatment. Companies can choose amortization schedules and periods and normally disclose them in Note 1. When derived by using quantitative methods, goodwill amortization methods can be quite complex and beyond the scope of this book. Like depreciation and impairments, goodwill amortizations are accounting phenomena and don't result in a cash transaction. Goodwill amortization affects earnings, not cash flow.

Look for aggressive and consistent treatment of goodwill. Ben Graham was particularly leery of goodwill and usually removed it entirely from company valuation, regardless of company policy. Buffett and other contemporary value investors recognize the value of patents, copyrights, brand equity, customer base, and other intellectual property and allow it to stand in valuation, so long as it's not in excess and is accounted for realistically.

Operating income

Now, finally, we can summarize how a company has performed it its basic business by examining operating income. Operating income is simply sales less cost of goods sold, less operating expenses. Because it includes noncash amortizations, it is a "fully loaded" view of operating performance in the business.

If you closely observe the effects of amortizations, special write-downs, and accounting changes, you can better understand operating income and operating income trends. For Borders Group, 2000 operating income dropped to $135.1 million from a previous year's $171 million, a significant drop in dollars and as a percent of sales. The primary reason, however, was the $36.2 million asset impairment write-down largely due to Borders.com. Value investors must decide whether such write-downs are truly abnormal or whether they're are perennial events.

Interest-ed and taxed

Interest and taxes are the corporate world's equivalent of the proverbial sure things. So not surprisingly, space is reserved for them on the earnings statement.

Companies invariably have some form of interest income or interest expense, and usually both. Interest income comes primarily from cash and short-term investments held on the balance sheet, while interest expense comes, not surprisingly, from short- and long-term debt balances. Interest reporting is usually done as a net interest, that is, by combining interest income and expense into a net figure. Taxes are quite complicated, just as they are for individuals, and the details go beyond the scope of this book. There is normally an income tax provision recorded as a single line item on the earnings statement, although this consists of myriad federal, state, and local taxes put together.

You don't need to pay too much attention to these areas except where interest expenses are disproportionately high and growing. In most situations value investors treat taxes as a given.

Income from continuing operations

What results from netting out interest and taxes from operating income is *income from continuing operations.* From this figure you can get a good picture of company performance, not only from an operating but also a financial perspective. A close look at interest costs tells you, for instance, whether operating success (operating income) comes at a financial price (high interest expense). If operating income is low or declining while financing cost (interest) is large or increasing, look out below!

Income from continuing operations tells shareholders, in totality, what their investment is returning, after everyone, including Uncle Sam and his brethren, is paid. Income from continuing operations is a good indicator of total business performance, but be aware of truly extraordinary events driving expenses or income.

A bit of EBITDA

Some companies and financial analysts like to use EBITDA, or Earnings Before Interest, Taxes, Depreciation, and Amortization, as their business health barometer. EBITDA fans consider it the truest indicator of *operating* success. EBITDA measures operating cash generated before nonoperating interest and taxes and noncash depreciation and amortization. In a sense, EBITDA is operating income before accountants, bankers, and government. EBITDA is sometimes looked at as a liquidity measure: Positive-EBITDA companies can service their debt while negative-EBITDA companies must borrow more.

Although the desire for "pure" business measures makes EBITDA compelling, many value investors look at EBITDA as a dangerous shell game. Sooner or later, a company must replace assets, as a business can't proceed on the assumption that its assets will last forever. Ironically this is especially true for the technology businesses that favor this measure but sit on top of some of the most rapidly depreciating assets! And as for interest and taxes, they're facts of business life. Who are we kidding anyway? Watch out for glowing announcements of positive EBITDA when accompanied by losses on the earnings statement.

Ordinary extraordinaries

Extraordinary items on an earnings statement are, according to accounting rules, to be tied to events that are unusual and nonrecurring. *Unusual* events aren't related to typical activities of the business, at least going forward. *Nonrecurring* events aren't expected to occur again.

Extraordinary items commonly result from business closures ("discontinued operations") or major restatements due to changes in accounting rules. They may result from debt restructurings or other complex financial transactions. They may result from layoffs and other employee transactions. Extraordinary items generally *are not* supposed to include asset write-downs (such as receivables, inventory, or intangibles), foreign currency gains or losses, or divestitures. Some companies interpret the accounting rules and guidelines more strictly than others.

In our example, Borders Group took an extraordinary charge for the discontinuance of All Wound Up, a specialty toy retailer. Borders probably considered it an extraordinary item because it wasn't related to its core bookselling business.

Our advice to you is to watch for extraordinary expenses that aren't so extraordinary. For example, companies that routinely have some kind of write-off every year or reporting period aren't doing as well as the investing community is being led to believe. If earnings are consistently a dollar a share each quarter with a consistent $4 write-off each year, the true value generated by the business is closer to zero than four.

There you have it: Net income

Sales less CGS, less operating expenses, less interest and taxes, less or plus extraordinaries give you a company's net income, sometimes referred to as income attributable to common shareholders or some similar phrase. Net income represents the final net earnings result of the business on an accounting — not necessarily a cash — basis.

Net earnings are usually divided by the number of shares outstanding to arrive at *earnings per share* — the common barometer heard in nearly all financial reports. Most analysts and investors focus on *diluted* earnings per share, which figure in outstanding employee stock options and other equity grants beyond actual shares outstanding.

In and Out of Pocket: Statement of Cash Flows

Earlier we mention the difference in timing between certain accounting transactions and related cash collections and disbursements. Build it and ship it this month and record the revenue, even though cash payments may not arrive until months later. Buy and pay for a million-dollar machine today, but expense it over its production life through depreciation. Amortize a patent and never write a check at all.

These transactions and a host of others create differences between accounting earnings and cash measures of business activity. A business needs cash to operate. A business generating positive cash flow is much healthier than one bleeding cash and borrowing to stay afloat. Because of noncash items, earnings statements don't give a complete cash picture. So value investors look for a statement of cash flows as a standard part of the financial statement package.

Sometimes the statement of cash flows is called "sources and uses of funds" or something similar. Accountants use the terms "funds" and "cash" interchangeably.

The statement of cash flow tracks cash obtained in, or used in, three separate kinds of business activity: operations, investing, and financing.

Cash flow from operations

Similar to operating income, cash flow from operations tells you what cash is generated from, or *provided by,* normal business operation, and what cash is consumed, or *used for* the business. ("Provided by" and "used for" are the terms used on the cash flow statement). Net income from continuing operations is thus the starting point: 73.8 million in the Borders Group example (see Figure 8-2).

To that figure add (or subtract) the "adjustments to reconcile net income to operating cash flow." Here is where you add back depreciation and amortization dollars; that is, dollars that came out of accounting income but had no corresponding cash payment. So far, so good.

Next comes "cash provided by (used for) current assets and current liabilities." If you look at Borders Group as an example, you can see that $136.5 million was *used* (note the parenthesis indicating a "negative" number or an *outflow*) to increase inventory — more books — on the shelf. It makes sense that an inventory increase consumed some cash.

consolidated statements of cash flows

(dollars in millions)	Jan. 28, 2001	Jan. 23, 2000	Jan. 24, 1999
Cash provided by (used for):			
Operations			
Income from continuing operations	$ 73.8	$ 94.0	$ 92.1
Adjustments to reconcile net income to operating cash flows:			
Depreciation and amortization	95.3	83.5	66.7
(Increase) decrease in deferred income taxes	(4.6)	7.4	10.2
Increase (decrease) in other long-term assets and liabilities	6.0	8.2	1.9
Asset impairments and other writedowns	23.0	—	—
Cash provided by (used for) current assets and current liabilities:			
Increase in inventories	(136.5)	(50.4)	(140.5)
Increase (decrease) in accounts payable	45.0	(29.2)	126.5
Increase in taxes payable	35.2	60.8	2.9
Other — net	15.6	7.0	6.4
Net cash provided by continuing operations	152.8	181.3	166.2
Net cash used for discontinued operations	(14.2)	(8.3)	—
Net cash provided by operations	138.6	173.0	166.2
Investing			
Capital expenditures	(138.7)	(143.5)	(179.8)
Net investing activities of discontinued operations	(2.4)	(15.7)	—
Net cash used for investing	(141.1)	(159.2)	(179.8)
Financing			
Repayment of long-term debt and capital lease obligations	(4.2)	(1.2)	(4.6)
Increase in capital lease obligations	—	0.5	3.0
Repayment of debt assumed in acquisition	—	(2.0)	—
Proceeds from construction funding	—	—	1.3
Net funding from credit facility	21.4	1.5	9.4
Issuance of common stock	11.5	11.6	33.9
Repurchase of common stock	(9.2)	(25.4)	(51.7)
Net cash provided by (used for) financing	19.5	(15.0)	(8.7)
Effect of exchange rates on cash and equivalents	0.5	—	—
Net increase (decrease) in cash and equivalents	17.5	(1.2)	(22.3)
Cash and equivalents at beginning of year	41.6	42.8	65.1
Cash and equivalents at end of year	$ 59.1	$ 41.6	$ 42.8
Supplemental Cash Flow Disclosures:			
Interest paid	$ 15.8	$ 18.0	$ 16.2
Income taxes paid	$ 38.6	$ 6.4	$ 42.1
Debt and liabilities assumed in business acquisition	$ —	$ 6.5	$ —

Fiscal Year Ended

See accompanying Notes to Consolidated Financial Statements.

Figure 8-2:
Borders Group consolidated statements of cash flow.

Then you come to "cash provided and used by changes in current assets and current liabilities." If this is familiar territory and you understand how increases in current assets and liabilities affect cash, read on. Otherwise, a stop at the sidebar "How changes in current assets and liabilities affect cash" is in order.

Finally you arrive at "net cash flow provided by operations." This is a very important figure, for although Borders generated $73.8 million in earnings, significantly it generated $138.6 million in positive cash flow. So aside from the growth in accounts payable, Borders didn't need external financing to fund its operations, which is a good sign. Negative operating cash flow is a dismal sign.

Cash flow from investing activities

Cash flow from operations tells what cash was generated in the normal course of business and by changes in current asset and liability (working capital) accounts on the balance sheet. But what about cash used to invest in the business? Invest in other businesses? What about cash acquired by selling investments in other businesses? The second section of the statement of cash flow provides this information.

How changes in current assets and liabilities affect cash

Note in the "Cash flow from operations" section in Figure 8-2 that the Borders $45 million cash *generated* by an "increase in accounts payable." You're confused. How can an increase in accounts payable (a *bigger* liability) generate cash? In your personal world, an increased Visa card balance is hardly followed by a check in the mail. Is this another dreary example of how corporations are treated better than individuals in our society?

No, not really. The confusion is caused by other accounting transactions happening behind the scenes, but it really does work out. An accounts payable increase indicates that something was bought from someone. That something — whether books, entertainment services, or washroom supplies — resulted in an increased account payable and a corresponding expense

against earnings. Without that expense, net income would have been higher, $45 million higher in this case. There is $45 million in cash floating around in the business that didn't show up in net income because of the accounting expense. Was cash paid for those items? No, an account receivable was incurred. Thus there is new cash in the business and on the balance sheet above and beyond what came from net income. In this case, it was provided or financed by creating an account receivable.

Increases in liabilities *provide* cash. Decreases in liabilities *use* cash. (This concept is easier to grasp: a single cash transaction to pay a bill.) Increases in current assets (other than cash) *use* cash. Decreases in assets (as in a net decrease in inventory) *provide* cash.

For most growing companies, while cash flow from operations should be positive, cash flow from investing activities is often negative. Why? Is this okay? Yes, because growing companies need more physical investments — property, plant, and equipment (PP&E) — to sustain growth. Generally, negative cash flows in PP&E suggest that the company is satisfied with its growth plan and feels that funds must be invested elsewhere for a positive return or returned to shareholders.

"Free" cash flow

Free cash flow sounds like what we all want in our lives, eh? Positive cash flow, and it's free. Free cash flow is a good indication of what a company really has left over after meeting obligations, and thus could theoretically return to shareholders. For that reason, free cash flow is sometimes called "owners earnings."

Free cash flow is defined as net after-tax earnings, plus depreciation and amortization and other noncash items, less annual capital expenditures, less (or plus) changes in working capital (current assets and liabilities).

Earn income, pay for costs of doing business, and what's left over is yours to keep as an owner. Pretty simple. Free cash flow is a much more realistic long-term view of business success and potential owner proceeds than EBITDA and is used by many value investors as the basis for calculating intrinsic value.

Cash flow from financing activities

Investing activities tell what a firm does with cash to increase or decrease fixed assets and assets not directly related to operations. *Financing activities* tell where a firm has obtained capital in the form of cash to fund the business. Proceeds from the sale of company shares or bonds (long-term debt) are a *source* of cash. If a company pays off a bond issue or buys back its own stock, that is a *use* of cash for financing.

A consistent cash flow from financing activities indicates excessive dependence on credit or equity markets. Typically, this figure oscillates between negative and positive. A big negative spike reflects a big bond issue or stock sale. In such a case, check to see if the resulting cash is used for investments in the business (probably okay) or to make up for a shortfall in operating cash flow (probably not okay). If the generated cash flows straight to the cash balance, you should wonder why a company is selling shares or debt just to increase cash, although often the reasons are difficult to know. Perhaps an acquisition?

Chapter 9

Games Companies Play: Irrational Exuberance in the Financial Statements

● ●

In This Chapter

▶ Understanding financial reporting: why it's important, and who makes the rules

▶ Identifying accounting and reporting "stretch"

▶ Knowing what's being done to improve reporting quality

▶ Becoming familiar with common financial statement tests

● ●

> *Some of today's practices, while perfectly legal, sail close to the wind.*
>
> —David Henry, *Business Week*

*T*ake a look at this quarterly earnings release from Kana Communications, Inc., provider of customer service software and solutions:

> "Pro forma net loss for the quarter was $38.6M, or ($0.42) per share . . . reported pro forma financial results exclude amortization of intangible assets, stock-based compensation, a restructuring charge, and a goodwill impairment charge. For full details on reported results, see the accompanying financial tables."

If you take a peek at the consolidated statement of operations (the earnings statement) for Kana Communications, the net loss reported there was $753 million, or ($8.23) per share. Hardly a subtle difference!

Now, here's a quarterly earnings release from Sun Microsystems, Inc., a bellwether computer hardware and software supplier:

> "Pro forma net income was $1.367 billion, up 19 percent compared with last year's pro forma net income of $1.146 billion. Pro forma earnings per share was $0.40, an increase of 18 percent compared to last year's pro forma earnings per share of $0.34.

> "Sun reported actual (or GAAP) net income (included realized gains/losses on Sun's venture equity portfolio, the effects of acquisition related charges, any unusual one-time items, and cumulative tax effects) for the third quarter of 2001 of $136 million or $0.04 per share, compared with $509 million or $0.15 per share for the same period a year ago."

Did Sun earn 40 cents or 4 cents? Just over $1 billion or just over $100 million? Hard to tell, and we may never be able to tell where financial reporting is headed as we open the new millennium, let alone compare one company to another or figure out its future.

Sigh. As a value investor, you need a solid, consistent set of numbers to evaluate companies. You know what the financial statements are supposed to convey, but now here are all these numbers and their withs and withouts. You thought you had the tools and the knowledge, but now you wonder just whom you can trust.

Experienced value investors have faced this issue for years. Accounting rules allow enough flexibility to give companies latitude to manage their business and decide what to recognize, when and how. Increasingly, that flexibility is being used to decide what to report and how to report it. Understanding company accounting and reporting policies — and conservative versus aggressive bias — has always been considered a good value investing practice.

Interestingly, the market events of 2000–2001 have brought the issue to greater light. Millions of investors who never before picked up nor read a financial statement save for an occasional earnings release are now wondering why their stocks, their portfolios, have cratered. They're looking for reasons. Although some grasp at straws, others have noticed the games companies play to — at least sometimes — make things seem better than they are. And when a lot of investors, large and small, notice and complain about something, the SEC usually isn't far behind. Such is the situation today with financial reporting. We thought you'd like to know the rest of the story and what's being done about it.

The bottom line in this bottom-line reporting issue is *quality*. Just as with a physical product or service, low quality or poorly represented financial reporting, whether deliberate or not, is less dependable. We don't bring this issue up to point fingers or accuse companies and their management of malicious intent, but rather to caution value-oriented investors that things may not always be what they seem.

Some Perspective on Reporting

Back in the good old days, fewer than 10 percent of the U.S. population owned common stocks. Stocks were owned, bought, and sold mainly by professionals in large institutions. They were bought and held for the long term. Business cycles were long, companies were stable and predictable, and quarter-to-quarter results variations didn't much matter. If big fund managers wanted to know more about a company's numbers or performance, they simply called the company.

Today, more than 50 percent of the public owns shares. A whole investment service industry caters to these retail customers. In an attempt to provide advice in mass-market mode, the investment service industry hires security analysts to rate securities and make quarterly and yearly projections of company performance. Effectively, they crunch the numbers so we don't have to. As the years have gone by, brokerage firms, the public, and even professional investors have come to rely on analyst projections.

Additionally, business cycles have shortened dramatically. A company with a good idea is expected to profit from it more quickly than ever. The whole world is moving faster because of technology, and because the world moves faster, companies, especially technology companies, must keep up the pace.

What happens? Companies are under tremendous pressure to meet, or even beat, analyst projections. Anything less — called a *miss* in the industry — can send a stock on a deep dive to purgatory, from which many have never emerged. Managers, who once worked for shareholders through the company's board of directors, seem ever more to work for the analysts to meet their projections. The fact that capital is allocated to companies with sustained track records of meeting their numbers isn't lost on management. Meeting the numbers means raising the share price and getting the capital that a company needs.

Add to this fact that fewer and fewer chief financial officers (CFOs) come from the ranks of professional accountants. Having a CPA no longer seems to be a professional requirement. Increasingly, CFOs rotate into the position from other parts of the business. Often their managerial skills and energy applied towards cost cutting and financial efficiency and internal control are more important to the company than rigorous financial reporting. In fact, the very compensation and reward systems they implement can stimulate aggressive financial reporting.

The end result is predictable: Management tells the story in the way that puts the company in the best light. Pressure from analysts, capital sources, shareholders, and even employees makes other outcomes unlikely.

This phenomenon has been especially evident in technology companies, where capital needs are high, business cycles are the shortest, and a full-blown company picture can be most ominous. Startup costs and initial capital outlays are huge, and often technology companies grow or fill product line gaps by acquiring other companies in lieu of incurring massive research and development (R&D) expenses and capital outlays. But although certainly not out of hand, the phenomenon does spill over to some degree into other industries and companies more likely to be in value investors' sights.

Fall into the GAAP

GAAP, which stands for Generally Accepted Accounting Principles, is a body of accounting rules evolved over many years by regulators, accountants, auditors, and companies in the private sector. GAAP rules provide the guideline for financial reporting. The SEC works with the FASB (Financial Accounting Standards Board), AICPA (American Institute of Certified Public Accountants), and other watchdog organizations to implement GAAP; they alone have statutory authority to enforce it. The SEC's role tends to be directed more towards investigation and compliance than rule origination.

You may justifiably be surprised at the rather loose sound of GAAP. Accounting seems to be a formulaic, mathematical profession like engineering, not based on generally accepted principles provided by agencies representing the very entities being regulated. Accounting instead operates more like the legal profession, where common law originates from lawyer arguments and is confirmed by a judge and a jury. GAAP is the accounting "common law," originating from practitioners and practitioner organizations and confirmed by the SEC. GAAP rules tend to be specific on some points and subject to wide interpretation on others. Interpreting and applying GAAP to company situations furnish full-time jobs for legions of financial analysts and CPAs.

Further, GAAP is sometimes criticized for allowing companies *not* to present a sufficiently complete picture of their performance. Performance indicators such as number of employees, number of managers, square-foot occupancy, sales returns, inventory composition, and so forth are routinely left out.

Still, GAAP is widely regarded as the fairest and most consistent way for companies to report. It provides a common language for reporting, even though the same concept might be communicated in different words. In the eyes of some professionals, GAAP standards don't always provide the best measurement for their business activity, but in general, the standard survives. The detail of GAAP is beyond the scope of this book.

FYI: FASB

Here's a little more about the Financial Accounting Standards Board (FASB) in its own words from its Web site (accessible at the obscure URL `http://accounting.rutgers.edu`).

"Since 1973, the Financial Accounting Standards Board has been the designated organization in the private sector for establishing standards of financial accounting and reporting. Those standards govern the preparation of financial reports. They are officially recognized as authoritative by the Securities and Exchange Commission... and the American Institute of Certified Public Accountants.

"The SEC has statutory authority to establish financial accounting and reporting standards for publicly held companies under the Securities Exchange Act of 1934. Throughout its history, however, the Commission's policy has been to rely on the private sector for this function to the extent that the private sector demonstrates ability to fulfill the responsibility in the public interest."

Accounting S-t-r-e-t-c-h

The relentless pursuit of the American corporate dream — business growth — has led to increasingly aggressive accounting practices. Some of the reasons and the tactics should already be clear by now if you read Chapters 6 through 8 and the beginning of this chapter. We thought it would be useful to explore some occasional "stretch" practices used to make business results look better.

Before you get the idea that value investors should throw in the towel on gleaning dependable information from financial statements, a couple of clarifying comments are in order. First, although GAAP legally provides stretch latitude, that doesn't mean everyone does it. The largest abuses have occurred in technology and other high-growth industries. These companies feel the most pressure to meet aggressive expectations, support high stock prices, and justify large capital infusions. But this doesn't mean it *doesn't* occur in other businesses. You can't dismiss stretch but you're more likely to favor companies that have simple, easy to understand, and conservative accounting and reporting practices.

Second, the greatest abuses (and sources of abuse) are getting more scrutiny from the SEC and its advisory boards. Several research efforts and rule changes are pending to discover and remedy financial reporting abuse. From 2001 forward, it should get better, not worse.

Sensitive stretch points occur in both revenue and expense portions of the earnings statement. We examine the following:

- ✔ Revenue recognition
- ✔ Direct costs
    - Inventory valuation: LIFO versus FIFO
    - Employee costs, including options expenses
    - Capitalizing expenses
- ✔ Amortization
    - Depreciation
    - Goodwill amortization
    - Pension funds and obligations
- ✔ Write-offs and extraordinary items

Remember that the balance sheet is a snapshot in time that captures the cumulative effects of business activity over a period. This business activity is measured on earnings and cash flow statements. As such, the balance sheet reflects the *results* of accounting policy and any stretch that may have occurred — that isn't where stretch is initially applied.

Our goal and focus is to provide a working overview of what to look for and how it can affect statements and company valuation. Technical details of the accounting standards involved and their interpretation are well beyond the scope of this book. For you bean counters in the audience, we provide references for more detailed investigation and regulatory actions at the end of the chapter in the "Watchdogs Are Barking" section.

Revenue: Sales or a bill of goods?

Recognition of revenue can be a major factor compromising financial statement quality. In a cash-only business, cash is cash, and thus revenue is revenue. But in the real world of accrual accounting, revenue recognition (at least in theory) follows the business activity, not the receipt of cash. Still, this seems simple: Deliver a product or service and record the sale. Yet it doesn't always happen this way.

There are two major sources of revenue recognition problems. The first involves timing, where revenues for long-term deals and contracts may be recognized prematurely. The second involves customer financing or price adjustments, where a customer receives an incentive or is otherwise enabled to buy a product but revenue is overstated by not recognizing the downside of such incentives.

Jumping the gun

Accounting principles state that revenue can be recognized for substantial performance of delivering a good or a service. Yet cases abound where companies, perhaps selling a three-year forward service agreement with a product, or perhaps an insurance policy, bundle downstream revenue into the original sale.

Microstrategy, Inc., a supplier of customer analytic software, got caught recognizing revenue on incomplete contracts during 1998 and 1999. In part due to the investigation that followed, its stock plunged from $333 in early 2000 to $4 in early 2001. More recently, the SEC has called into question the revenue recognition policies of Xerox, whose Latin American units allegedly sold future copier revenue streams to Citibank, thus inflating revenue and profit streams by millions. Revenue questions also emerge when companies sell to distributors but then must provide substantial services, such as installation or configuration, to complete the sale to the end customer.

Unlike at the local track meet, gun jumpers can be hard to detect. Accounting policies can provide clues, especially when appropriately conservative tactics are in place. Borders Group, for example, doesn't recognize revenue for gift cards purchased in their stores until they're used, a refreshingly conservative accounting policy. Without specific clues, value investors may provide a greater margin of safety in assessing revenue streams when looking at suspect companies selling complex products through complex distribution channels.

Mortgaging their soul

An increasing number of companies have resorted to financing their customers as a way to win deals, win customers, and bolster revenues. Although this has been common in department store retailing for years through store credit cards, it takes on new meaning when, for example, billions are lent to single customers to buy telecommunications equipment. Lucent Technologies is the unhappy poster child for this sort of activity, but it is by no means the only waif in the orphanage. The problem is, of course, that customers can go bankrupt or otherwise renege on the deal, rendering previously recognized revenue meaningless.

This problem is also hard to detect until after the fact. Lucent made a vague statement in its "Management's Discussion" about "[making] commitments or entering into agreements to extend credit to certain customers for an aggregate of approximately $6.7 billion." But this figure shows up nowhere on the balance sheet except perhaps as part of the $9.9 billion in accounts receivable. No evidence is shown as to whom the money was lent or in what amounts, or how much is collectible. When it comes to light that significant amounts were lent to the likes of Winstar Communications, Northpoint, and Teligent, three service providers in or near bankruptcy, investors might justifiably have wanted more disclosure.

When accounts receivable, and particularly bad debt reserves against receivables, start tracking higher as a percent of revenue, it's time to get suspicious. Still, Lucent described its accounts receivable increase as due to increases in longer-cycle foreign sales. Could you have known? Not for certain.

And beyond these loan arrangements, there may be problems with rebates and other after-the-fact incentives. And at the height of the dot.com frenzy, it became common for companies to accept inflated stock as payment for goods and services, and occasionally buy stakes in other companies to help influence future product sales and revenue streams. Computer hardware and software makers got caught "overinvesting" in their customers and took significant investment write-offs in 2001.

In general, you should be attentive to revenue recognition policies (usually Note 1 or Note 2 of the statements) and peculiar increases in sales, receivables, or allowances against receivables.

Inventory valuation: Get a (shelf) life

This topic is a bit simpler than revenue recognition. If you read Chapters 7 and 8, you may remember LIFO (last in, first out) and FIFO (first in, first out). In Chapter 7, we discuss those terms in the context of inventory valuation; in Chapter 8, it comes up under the topics of cost of goods sold and gross profit. LIFO typically represents the more conservative valuation, particularly in an inflationary environment. This is because recognized costs are relatively higher. However, LIFO also results in relatively *lower* inventory valuations.

Value investors should understand inventory valuation policy, normally disclosed in Note 1, particularly in an environment where costs are changing. Changes in accounting policy are particularly noteworthy. For example, was the company trying to squeeze something out to offset an otherwise dismal quarter? Policy changes should also be evident in Note 1.

Optional expenses

Compensating employees with stock options has become much more in vogue recently. Why? Sure, options serve to recruit and retain better employees.

But beyond that, they provide a rather generally accepted accounting gimmick that makes expenses *look* lower than they really are, artificially boosting earnings. Once again this technique owes its origin to the technology industry, but its application crosses over into many other industries.

Options represent a way to compensate employees without paying cash. Companies routinely omit payroll tax liabilities incurred when employees exercise these options, and they may omit the discount value of the options themselves. The practice is so widespread that FASB implemented rule FAS 123, which allows a disclosure-only option to cover fair value of options granted as compensation.

With the FAS 123 disclosure-only option, companies can submit official GAAP-compliant earnings statements that don't include these expenses. The detail of the "would-have-been" effect is disclosed only in a deeply buried note. Typically you find these disclosures at about Note 12 or 13, identified as "stock-based compensation." Some companies provide tables to make it easy to see the effects. For others the disclosure is an obscure set of numbers in a text statement, requiring you to thumb back to the earnings statement to measure the difference.

Effects can be significant, as illustrated in Table 9-1.

Table 9-1   2000 Earnings with and without Employee Option Costs

Company	Earnings as Stated		Earnings including Employee Option Costs		
	Total $	$ Per share	Total $	$ Per share	% Difference
Lucent Technologies	$1.22B	$0.37	$452M	$0.13	65%
Cisco Systems	$2.67B	$0.36	$1.55B	$0.21	42%
Starbucks Inc.	$94.6M	$0.49	$66.2M	$0.35	29%
Borders Group	$43.6M	$0.54	$31.6M	$0.39	28%
Sun Microsystems	$1.67B	$0.92	$1.35B	$0.74	20%
Hewlett-Packard	$3.67B	$1.73	$3.2B	$1.54	11%
Wal-Mart	$6.29B	$1.40	$6.23B	$1.39	< 1%

Value investors should be aware of heavy use and abuse of options as "free" employee compensation. Much of this expense isn't cash related, and the regulators seem content with the solution in place, but if changes come along requiring full inclusion into the reported financial picture, watch out. So far the biggest offenders have been high-tech and other high-growth-profile companies. But when evaluating any company, it may be worth a casual search for FAS 123 disclosure to get a better idea of the true cost — and profitability — of the business.

Capital crimes

A few companies have been caught deferring certain R&D and marketing costs into the future. How do they do it? By *capitalizing* them (that is, by recording them as an asset when incurred, rather than an expense, and then depreciating or amortizing the asset over future years).

Accounting rules are fairly firm, but not rock solid, around the notion that most R&D expenses should be incurred as they arise due to the uncertain nature of their outcome. There's no way to tell upfront whether an R&D effort will turn into a marketable product. However, where R&D is significant as a proportion of total product expense, as in the software business, certain portions are allowed to be capitalized. Imagine the wild ride if Microsoft had to report all costs of a software product development in the year it was developed and then record subsequent revenue as nearly pure profit.

AOL = accountants on leave?

Abuses in capitalizing expenses have been known to occur, and one of the more famous ones was the 1996 blowup at America Online, which spent over $350 million to distribute those ubiquitous installation disks for its latest software release. Whether it was good marketing strategy or not is unclear. But its accounting strategy was to expense only $120 million and capitalize the rest as a "marketing asset" to amortize over the next two years. The auditors accepted it, but the SEC didn't, resulting in a stiff fine and painful restatements.

Getting an explanation

To explain how key R&D or marketing expenses are handled, it's good to see statements like the following from Lucent's annual report:

> "Research and Development costs are charged to expense as incurred. However the costs incurred for the development of computer software that will be sold, leased, or otherwise marketed are capitalized when technological feasibility has been established. These capitalized costs are subject to an ongoing assessment of recoverability based on anticipated future revenues and changes in hardware and software technologies."

The "ongoing assessment of recoverability" part is still subjective and can be interpreted "on demand" to meet financial goals. As a value investor, you need to again think about a margin of safety — a buffer factor in your valuation of the company — when dealing with R&D-intensive industries or industries with exceptionally high startup marketing costs.

Depreciation and amortization: Are you getting a straight line?

Choice of depreciation and amortization methods — and time periods — can influence earnings and balance sheet statements. More aggressive depreciation results in lower earnings and conservative asset valuations, but the pressure to "meet the numbers" on earnings may lead to less aggressive depreciation. Firms have the choice of method (straight line versus accelerated) and time frame (number of years) to manage their financial reporting.

Depreciation and amortization methods are among the most clearly disclosed of financial statement "levers." Note 1 disclosures are complete with both method and time period, although frequently a mix of different methods and time periods is used for different assets. Look for how hard assets are depreciated and how goodwill is amortized.

The value investor should look for conservatism, consistency (as opposed to frequent changes), and common sense (wireless licenses amortized over 40 years probably doesn't make sense because the technology probably won't be around for that long). If a company suddenly switches to longer depreciation schedules without adequate explanation, look out.

Pension intentions

Pension fund accounting can be another source of stretch earnings in a pinch. The details of pension accounting are complex and are wisely left to the CPA community. But companies can modify pension assumptions in ways that can affect net earnings.

Suppose that a plan is targeted to reach a certain funding level in 10 years. Management has diligently set money aside with an assumption of a 7 percent return in order to achieve that long-term goal. Now suppose that management decides that an 8 percent return is more likely. Is the existing balance bigger than it needs to be to meet the obligation? You bet. The plan is said to be overfunded. Some or all of that overfunding can be recognized as income, inflating reported earnings.

Pension information is usually deep in the Notes section, usually Note 10 or higher. Check the fair value of pension assets, the projected benefit obligation, and the difference between the two. Look at the assumptions and look for changes in accounting policy, especially those not mandated by FAS (accounting standards) bulletins. Large old-line companies are more susceptible to pension stretch: the IBMs, AT&Ts, and Lucents of the world. Newer companies use the 401K approach, in which few or no pension assets or obligations are carried directly by the company.

Swallowing it whole

New rules proposed by the Financial Accounting Standard board (FASB) would end the requirement for companies to amortize goodwill incurred by acquisitions. The FASB seems to be trying to simplify accounting and to eliminate a "pooling of interests" accounting bypass that has been in place as an alternative. The result, of course, will be an increase in company earnings, particularly for companies such as GE or Cisco that have aggressive acquisitions strategies. Some investors salivate over the prospect, although you can see in Chapter 8 that it is meaningless from a cash point of view. There is no true wealth created. Worse yet, these ethereal assets could be maintained forever.

Perhaps this rule will prove value investing patriarch Ben Graham right in the end: that intangibles should be eliminated completely from intrinsic value appraisals.

Write-offs: Big baths

Pundits say, "It's better to ask forgiveness than permission." This statement may play into another fairly old accounting gimmick: write-offs. Bundling large costs into extraordinary write-offs clears the books of bad assets and bad decisions. Why? To increase earnings in the immediate future.

GAAP is fairly specific in specifying that write-offs must be unusual and non-recurring. *Unusual* means not a part of day-to-day business, and *nonrecurring* means, well, nonrecurring. Still, these terms are subject to interpretation. Are layoffs, plant closings, and restructurings unusual and nonrecurring? For some companies, yes, but such write-offs got to be almost annual events for automakers and other smokestack industries. For some companies, the December fourth-quarter write-off announcement became almost as dependable as Santa Claus himself.

Be aware of the reasons for and any regularities in such write-offs. Have they gotten to be a habit? Are they truly a cost of doing business in disguise? If Cisco writes off $2.5 billion in unused raw material components, that's an event, but who's to say that it won't happen again as technology changes and business cycles continue? Arguably, at least some of that is a normal cost of doing business.

Pro Forma Performance

If "normal" accounting stretch (that is, stretch performed within GAAP rules) wasn't enough to ruin your value investing day, consider the latest trend in aggressive financial reporting: the pro forma earnings statement. The examples of Kana Communications and Sun Microsystems at the beginning of this chapter were classic pro forma reports. Pro forma reports have become almost a public relations alternative to the classic GAAP earnings statement.

Responding in part to investor and analyst pressure and in part to a fairly loose (to date) compliance environment, companies started using pro forma reporting as a press-friendly reporting alternative. The trend started in 1999 with Yahoo! and has expanded through the technology industry and occasionally beyond.

Actually, pro forma has been in the accounting vocabulary for a long time. Pro forma statements were originally used as "unofficial" statements designed to project — not report — company performance. Companies planning to go public or merge with another company issued a pro forma set of statements to give an investor a clue to what forward-looking statements might look like. But no more are pro forma statements limited to special situations. Beyond the latitude afforded by GAAP, today's press-friendly financial reporting does an "end run" right around it.

"Everything but bad stuff"

With pro forma reporting, companies can spin their business pretty much as they please. They include certain things but leave out others they consider irrelevant to assessing performance. SEC Chief Accountant Lynn Turner calls it "EBS," or "Everything but Bad Stuff," reporting. From your perspective as a value investor, pro forma reporting not only undermines statement quality but also makes it difficult to compare one company to another.

Pro forma is really an extension of the EBITDA reporting concept made popular in the 1980s (see Chapter 8). Although EBITDA made numbers look better than they were by excluding financing costs and asset recovery, at least the application of EBITDA was consistent from one company to the next.

Companies routinely omit option costs, investment gains and losses, asset impairment or write-downs, goodwill amortization, and other "noncash" items. In that these expenses are noncash, value investors can wink and turn their heads a little — for a while. But we've occasionally seen some very cash-real expenses, such as interest expense, get written out of the pro forma.

Amazon.com made almost $200 million of adjustments between its first quarter 2001 GAAP and pro forma reports, mostly for asset impairment (closing a warehouse) and investment losses. This is significant on $575 million in first quarter 2001 revenues, especially on top of $121 million in normal operating losses. We have to applaud Amazon.com, however, for giving a clear, tabular accounting of its adjustments. In its press release, it shows side by side the pro forma statement and the GAAP statement, with the differences by line item. Most companies don't make it that easy.

The good news is . . .

Companies can release to the public pretty much any pro forma report they please. But thankfully, there is a catch: They must also provide GAAP-compliant numbers in releases and submit full GAAP-compliant reports to the SEC. So you have the pro forma reports, good enough for many investors and reflective of how companies want to see themselves. But you must dig deeper to understand the difference between the pro forma and GAAP — and why the company wants to maintain that difference.

From a value investing perspective, pro forma reports are obviously dangerous in their concealment of long-term asset recovery and similar expenses. In addition, they make it difficult to compare one company to another, as each company reports different things, and companies may report differently from one period to the next. Sorting out these differences can be very time consuming.

We never said that doing value investing from financial statements was easy.

The Watchdogs Are Barking

The SEC reports that investor complaints were up some 40 percent in 2001 regarding a host of investing and financial reporting issues. The FASB has taken note and begun research towards several recommendations and clarifications to GAAP accounting and reporting rules. So far, no rules are proposed to curb or change pro forma reporting, but that could change quickly.

Following all the proposed rule changes and their effects on financial reporting is a daunting task, even for the professional accountant. We recommend that diligent value investors occasionally surf key watchdog sites to get an idea of attitude and what may change. Major changes will probably be carried as news stories on business wires, but those reports are completely dependable.

SEC

Beginning in 1998, the SEC started to look more closely at the numbers games and created a task force to make some recommendations. Acting chair Laura Unger and chief accountant Lynn Turner hit the speaking circuit to make accountants, lawyers, and companies aware that *they are* aware of increasing use of "not so generally accepted accounting principles." Hot buttons in a recent Unger speech include undisclosed company accounting policy changes, pro forma reporting, and revenue recognition. And the commitment is clear. As Turner put it: "As a general theme, you can expect the SEC staff will be broadly directed towards obtaining disclosure of importance to value investing."

There is a 70-page list of "current finance and disclosure" issues on the SEC site, www.sec.gov, in the Accounting area. Speeches, like those of Unger and Turner cited here, are available on the site, and are long but readable. The site is worth an occasional visit from you, especially if you're a detail-oriented value investor.

FASB

The FASB has also dug into the financial statement quality issue, releasing a 135-page report, "Business and Financial Reporting: Challenges from the New Economy." This report calls for, in particular, more disclosure of nonfinancial information, more forward-looking information, and more information about intangible assets. You can obtain FASB actions, recommendations, and reports at http://accounting.rutgers.edu, but we warn again that the level of detail can be very deep.

Watching the watchdog

More or less as a public service, CPA Jack Ciesielski created The Analyst's Accounting Observer Web site, at www.accountingobserver.com, as a "research service that, simply put, provides 'remedial accounting' for institutional investors that should know better." Translated, that means that Ciesielski, an outspoken critic of current accounting practice and an occasional *New York Times* contributor, uses the site to discuss current financial reporting topics, summarize current events in the area, and, yes, educate those accountants and analysts in need of education. The site is tied to his consulting practice.

The site is targeted "to those investors who know that investing is not a 'paint-by-numbers' exercise." Some of the material is complex, but it's an insightful and sometimes fun look if you want to stay in closer touch with financial reporting and learn a bit more.

What Should a Value Investor Look For?

We cover a lot of ground in this chapter. You nonaccountants out there are undoubtedly saying "enough!" Those of you who had an accounting course or two somewhere along the way are probably now recalling why you steered clear of a public accounting career.

We understand.

It isn't reasonable — or prudent, for that matter — to examine every financial statement in enough detail to ferret out the real story. Why, it's literally impossible if you're trying to choose from among 2,000 or 3,000 companies to invest in.

The "cake test"

Some of you may be familiar with the technique of sticking a toothpick into a cake to determine whether it's done. (For those of you who haven't done this, if you stick a toothpick in a cake and it comes out clean, it's done. Try it a few times in different parts of the cake to verify your conclusion. If you don't believe it (and don't bake), then call your mother. She'd be glad to hear from you.

For value investors, particularly those of you who don't consider value investing to be their day job, we recommend a "cake test" approach to reviewing financial statements. Poke here, poke there, read some of the notes, get a flavor for financial reporting quality. Now, if you're Warren Buffett, ready to commit $2 billion to a company, you may want to take a closer look! For the rest of you, read on.

A checklist

Here are a few places to "stick your toothpick" when considering companies in which to invest:

Earnings consistent with cash flow

These two things won't be equal but should march side by side. If earnings grow faster than cash flow, that's a bad sign.

Growing current assets other than cash

Watch for increasing inventories or accounts receivable, particularly in proportion to sales.

Straight-line depreciation and amortization, long time periods

Asset recovery may be delayed through deferring depreciation and amortization in order to boost earnings. Understand what practice the company uses, and whether it's consistent with others in the industry — and common sense.

Understand asset impairments

Note which assets are "impaired" or on the block for possible write-downs, and understand why.

LIFO versus FIFO

LIFO is a more conservative approach to measuring cost of goods sold and inventory levels, as most the recent (and more expensive) stock is assumed to be consumed first. Note that this may not be true in every industry.

Reserves against bad debts change dramatically

Watch for bad debt and other reserves as a sign of deterioration in current asset quality.

Accounting policies change

Note 1 should be simple and straightforward. Look at depreciation, amortization, and capitalization versus R&D expenses. Complex, unexplained changes may spell trouble.

10-K report is longer than 100 pages

Something complex is going on. Opportunity knocks for accounting fiction and other things that are hard to understand.

Heavy employee option compensation costs omitted

If the FAS 123 disclosure shows more than 10 percent reduction in earnings then the quality of earnings might be questioned

Ugly extraordinary write-offs

If the write-offs are large or repetitive, try to understand why.

Big gap between pro forma and GAAP

Understand why. Raise the red flag higher if the company makes it difficult to understand the differences.

Understand where the revenues come from — if the company tells you

What are the major revenue "segments"? Does the company have a few big customers? Who are they? Are *their* business fundamentals sound? Does the company have channel partners? What are their selling arrangements with those partners? Do they provide financing? What are the other incentives? Are services broken out separately?

Chapter 10

On Your Ratio Dial: Using Ratios to Understand Financial Statements

> *Gentlemen, start your calculators.*
>
> —David and Tom Gardner, *The Motley Fool*

*N*umbers, numbers, numbers. Your eyes glaze over while you examine all those financial statements. You feel like you need corrective laser surgery, although you've never worn a pair of glasses in your life. How do you make sense of all this stuff?

You gaze at a company's financial statements, for example. Is accounts receivable in line or not? Is the company's inventory scaled properly to the size of the business? What about fixed assets, debt, and profitability? Is the company using capital efficiently? And does its stock price make sense? How do you know?

Ratios provide you with a pair of glasses of sorts to bring into clearer focus the many bits of information that come from financial statements. Ratios explain the relationship between two or more numbers, thus providing you with scale and context. For example, the Borders Group's $1.201 billion in inventory means nothing until you measure it against $3.271 billion in sales. The inventory-to-sales ratio of 0.37 puts company raw data into perspective, tells a story, and provides a standard for comparison with other companies and the industry.

Inventory-to-sales is one of dozens of "standard" ratios. Each ratio by itself provides a clue into some performance aspect. Taken together as a collection, ratios provide a powerful set of brushes that paint a clearer picture of a company. As you'll see, however, the brushes can't paint the picture by themselves. The artist, or investor, must supply some talent and judgment!

This chapter explores the different kinds of ratios and their use in value investing.

Ratio-nal Analysis

Before you get carried away and think, "Aha! I've found the secret tools to automate success," we need to go on record with a brief discussion of ratio analysis and its practical strengths, limitations, and applications. It's easy to think that ratios provide mathematical insight to true company performance and value. Maybe so, but it's also easy to overestimate their potential as the be-all-end-all analysis tool.

Knowing what "station" you're looking for

Ratios can be kind of fun. Whip out the calculator, warm up the fingers, open the annual report, and divide away! Can this effort be productive? Yes, but you should have an idea of where you're going before you get started. Here are some things to think about as you develop your ratio "play list":

- ✔ **Stick to the standards.** It's good to stick to standard ratios (which we describe later in this chapter in the section "Ratio Stations on Your Dial"). First, they're likely to tell you something important. Second, standard ratios can be compared across companies and with industry standards.

- ✔ **Tune in to the good stuff.** As a value investor, you should decide what you want to know. We group ratios into four families: asset productivity, financial strength, profitability, and valuation. When evaluating a company from scratch, you may want to look behind all four of these "doors." When focusing on one aspect — for instance, profitability — you obviously want to focus on ratios that describe that particular aspect.

- ✔ **Choose your music: jazz, news, classical, modern rock.** We just mention four families of ratios. Different financial texts assign different categories and different names, but for our purposes the following four categories make the most sense:

- **Asset productivity:** In Chapter 7, we define assets as resources used in a business to produce a profit, or return. This group of ratios describes how effectively those assets are deployed. Some analysts call these ratios *efficiency* ratios. How much inventory, accounts receivable, or fixed asset investment does it take to support a given volume of business? Are these assets being managed effectively with proper controls?

- **Financial strength:** Company resources are provided either by company owners (shareholders) or by creditors (debt holders or holders of other obligations). This set of ratios measures to what extent company resources are provided by sources other than the owners. It also assesses the company's ability to pay its creditors. And some financial ratios tell you about financial or capital structure — and how financially *leveraged* a company may be.

- **Profitability:** Profits make the investing world go 'round. How profitable is the company? Sure, there may be a lot of business activity. But how much profit is produced? Per dollar sold? Per dollar invested? Some analysts refer to these ratios as *management effectiveness* ratios, as they indicate management's overall success in generating returns for the enterprise.

- **Valuation:** The first three ratio families examine internal business fundamentals, or "intrinsics." When the valuation curtain opens, stock price makes a glorious and long-awaited entry. Valuation ratios, as the name implies, relate a company's stock price to its performance. The ubiquitous price-to-earnings (P/E) ratio shows up here, as do its lesser siblings price-to-sales and price-to-book.

Knowing where to dial in

Anybody with an annual report and a calculator can analyze ratios. Almost all ratios take a pair of numbers from a company's balance sheet, earnings statement, or both

Ratio analysis can be cumbersome and time-consuming, particularly when you're looking at a group of companies or an industry. Services that "do" the numbers, and particularly the comparisons, for you are hard to find — for free, anyway. A great deal of comparative industry ratio data is available to professional financial and credit analysts, but they pay hefty subscription fees to get it. The challenge is finding it for free (or nearly so). We value investors like that sort of challenge, don't we?

Here are the best sources of ratio data and comparison we've found:

- ✔ **Free:** Multex's Market Guide sits behind Yahoo! Finance and is — for now, anyway — free. Tricky to find but easy to use, it's a useful resource for cost-conscious value investors. See "Turn On, Tune In, Compare Ratios" at the end of the chapter to learn how to access and use Market Guide.

- ✔ **Almost free:** Other packagings of financial data from Multex and other financial data providers sit behind specially constructed screens available from online brokers. Typically, the cost is opening an account. Charles Schwab, for example, displays a predesigned set of fundamental ratios for different industries and their constituents from Multex.

- ✔ **For a modest fee:** Value Line Investment Survey (www.valueline.com) offers a window to many key ratios. Value Line doesn't present as many ratios or compare as much as Market Guide, but it gives you many years of history, which in many ways is more important. A basic subscription to Value Line costs $570 per year but offers a lot more than just ratio analysis. (See Chapter 5.) Well-equipped value investors (the non-professional ones, anyway) might use both services: Market Guide for simplicity, ratio breadth, and comparisons and Value Line for history and greater depth of company information.

If you have access to Dun & Bradstreet or Standard & Poor's industry financial comparisons, don't hesitate to use these rich, complete, and up-to-date resources as well. They may be out of reach of the average investor due to cost. If you work with a full-service or hybrid broker, you may be able to get access to some of these services.

Fine-tuning

What does a value investor look for when doing ratio analysis?

- ✔ **Intrinsic meaning:** What does the ratio tell you? If the debt-to-equity ratio is 3 to 1, the company has a lot of debt. If the inventory-to-sales ratio is greater than 1, the company turns its inventory less than once per year. A price-to-earnings (P/E) ratio of 50 implies a 2 percent return on invested capital ($1 returned per $50 invested). These numbers tell you something without looking at any comparisons or trends.

Want an early test for determining whether a ratio is good, bad, or ugly? Just think of the company's ratio as it would apply to your personal finances. A household with three times as much debt as equity is in dire straits, as is a household that turns over inventory (say, groceries) only once a year, as is a household that achieves only a 2 percent return on its investments or a household that's owed a third of its annual income. You can't apply this test to all ratios, but where common sense tells you something, use it!

✔ **Comparisons:** For many analysts, and especially credit analysts, trying to get a picture of a company's health, comparative analysis is the most important use of ratios. A ratio acquires more meaning when it's compared to direct competitors, the company's industry, or much broader standards, like the S&P 500. A profitability measure, such as gross profit margin, reported at 25 percent tells more when direct competitors are at 35 percent plus. Analysts make similar comparisons with asset utilization, financial strength, and valuation ratios.

When doing comparisons, be in tune with what you're comparing. Companies can be in many different businesses at once. It's tough to find pure plays in any industry. Realize that Dell Computer is almost 100 percent in the PC business, while Hewlett-Packard derives only 25 percent of revenues from PCs. A company mostly in the health insurance business may be difficult to compare to a company that sells mostly life insurance. Borders Group and Amazon, while classified in the same industry, have very different business structures. While the resulting ratio differences may in part be valid, they also may lead you to believe that an apple is bad when it really isn't. Compare apples to apples, compare red apples to green apples with caution, and avoid apples-to-oranges comparisons altogether.

✔ **Consistency:** The hallmark of good management, as well as of an attractive long-term investment, is consistency of results. If profit margins are consistent and changing (hopefully growing) at a consistent rate, the company is predictable — and most likely in control of its markets. Inconsistent ratios reflect on inconsistent management, competitive struggles, and cyclical industries, all of which diminish a company's intrinsic value.

✔ **Trends:** Better than consistency alone is consistency with a favorable trend. Growing profit margins, return on equity, asset utilization, and financial strength are all very desirable, particularly if valuation ratios (P/E and so on) haven't kept pace. A value investor who studies trends carefully has information that most investors don't.

Ratio Stations on Your Dial

Enough of the preliminaries. On to the main event. We present some of the key ratios in each category identified earlier in this chapter. We offer examples from the Borders Group 2000 financial statements, which appear in Chapters 6 through 8.

Note: When using items from the earnings statement in the numerator or denominator of a ratio, the figure used typically represents either the *previous fiscal year* or the *trailing 12 months* (TTM) of business activity. Balance sheet items come from the most recently reported period. The terms *sales* and *revenue* are used interchangeably.

Asset productivity ratios

Asset productivity ratios describe how effectively business assets are deployed. Typically, you look at sales dollars generated per unit of resource. Resources can include accounts receivable, inventory, fixed assets, and occasionally other tangible assets. Occasionally, you may apply similar analysis to non-financial capacity resources, such as square footage, employees, number of facilities, and airplane seat miles.

Receivable turnover

Receivable turnover measures the size of unpaid customer commitments to a company. Specifically, it measures how many times a year this asset turns over; that is, is cleared out and replaced by similar obligations from other customers. Rapid turnover, not lingering old debts, is what you want to see. Here's the formula:

Receivables turnover = sales $ ÷ accounts receivable $

For Borders Group, $3.271 billion ÷ $73.7 million = 44.3, a very high turnover, which you would expect for a cash-and-carry retail business. For every dollar invested in receivables, $44.30 comes back to the company in sales.

Accounts receivable is a resource at a company's disposal like anything else and must be paid for, essentially, by sacrificing cash that otherwise would be available to fund the business. A company selling direct to consumers with cash sales or bank credit card sales will have lower receivables turnover than an industrial supplier. Watch for consistency and compliance with normal billing policy for the industry.

Average collection period (or days' sales in receivables)

A slightly different way of looking at receivables is to show the average number of days that a given receivable dollar lives on the books. To find this number, you divide the receivable turnover ratio (from the preceding section) into 360 to put it on a daily scale:

Average collection period = 360 ÷ receivables turnover

So for Borders, 360 ÷ 44.3 gives 8.1 days of life for the average receivable dollar on the books. For an industrial supplier with a standard 30-day billing cycle, there should be 30 days or less worth of sales in receivables.

If, based on industry comparisons or stated billing cycles, the collection period is higher than it should be (or growing), watch out. The company may be losing control of its collections or selling to customers who have questionable credit. This ratio is also sometimes called *days' sales in receivables*.

Inventory turnover

Inventory turnover works like receivables turnover, only you plug in balance sheet inventory in place of receivables. Here's the formula:

Inventory turnover = sales ÷ inventory $

As with receivable turnover, the higher the number the better. High numbers indicate that stuff is flying onto and off of shelves at a rapid rate. Less dust collects on less stuff in fewer warehouses. Also, there's less risk of obsolescence and write-offs and fewer clearance sales — a good thing for any business.

Borders had $3.271 billion in sales on $1.201 billion in merchandise inventory for an inventory turnover ratio of 1.96 — not a particularly good number. But if you know something about the bookselling business, you know that shelf inventory is fully returnable to publishers, mitigating inventory risk, providing reader selection, and justifying higher levels of inventory. Know thy industry!

Extra credit: How many days does the average book sit on the shelf? If you guessed almost six months, you're getting it. (360 ÷ 1.96 gives 183.7 days, a shade over six months.) This "days sales in inventory" or "average inventory shelf life" is another ratio sometimes shown to help put inventory levels in perspective.

Fixed asset turnover

This ratio is straightforward:

Fixed asset turnover = sales $ ÷ fixed asset $

Obviously, all else being equal, the company that produces the most sales or revenue per dollar of fixed assets wins.

Total asset turnover

Again, straightforward:

Total asset turnover – sales $ ÷ total asset $

Here we get a bigger picture of asset productivity as measured by the generation of sales. For the first time, intangible assets are included. Again, industry norms are the benchmark. Comparing a railroad to a software company probably won't make any sense.

Non-financial productivity ratios

We find some of these capacity utilization ratios quite interesting, yet inconsistently measured and applied in businesses. If the raw data is even available in company statements, finding it can be a difficult task. Calculated ratios are even harder to find, although Value Line and other analysis services make it a point to present certain non-financial operating data. These measures vary by industry, as capacity and operational inputs vary by industry. Here are some examples:

- ✔ **Sales per employee:** This ratio tells you how productive a company is in regard to investments in human resources. We think it's worth a look in almost all industries, particularly those that are labor intensive, such as retail, transportation and other service industries.

- ✔ **Sales per square foot:** This ratio is especially important for retail and similar businesses where occupancy investments are large and sales can be tied directly to them.

- ✔ **Average selling price (ASP):** Many financial reports don't present the number of units sold because they don't have to and they want to keep selling prices secret. But sometimes this data is available (for example, from Boeing and other very-large-ticket manufacturers), and it can be quite revealing as to the direction of a business.

- ✔ **Industry specials:** Airlines and airline investors pay close attention to seat miles and revenues per seat mile flown. Railroads may look at revenue per track mile or car mile. Other service businesses such as banks, mail order retail and similar might look at sales or revenue per *customer*.

"Foolish Flow"

Tom and David Gardner of the Motley Fool (www.fool.com) do a commendable job of presenting investment facts and analysis in an enlightening and fun way ("To Educate, Amuse and Enrich" is their clever motto). They also give us a few gems in the form of new ways to look at old things.

Take, for example, their Foolish Flow ratio. As a formula, it's simple (foolishly simple?):

Foolish Flow = current assets $ – cash ÷ current liabilities $

Behind this seemingly benign formula is a powerful and somewhat contrarian level of understanding of a business. A business that runs on relatively few non-cash current assets (inventory, accounts receivable, and so on) *and* can stretch out payments to suppliers is making efficient use of cash resources. Effectively, it's living off of someone else's cash. Put another way, it has control over its operations, markets (doesn't have to extend precious receivable dollars or put inventory on shelves to lure customers), and suppliers (can stretch payments). In this view, assets are liabilities and liabilities are assets! A Foolish Flow ratio of less than 1 is a good sign; greater than 1 is weaker. Companies like Dell Computer base their entire business model on this notion. Others are looking at it. In any case, Foolish Flow is anything but a foolish way to look at a company's strength.

Financial strength ratios

This set of ratios goes by many names (liquidity, solvency, financial leverage), but they all point to the same thing: What is a business's financial strength and position? What is its capital structure? A balance sheet–oriented value investor looks closely to make sure that the company will be around tomorrow (as many investors did in the 1930s). Today's value investor most likely looks at financial strength ratios for glaring danger and then bases the bulk of his or her intrinsic value analysis on business-strength or market-strength measures like productivity and profitability.

Current and "quick" ratios

These commonly used liquidity ratios help you evaluate a company's ability to pay its short-term obligations. Here's the formula:

Current ratio = current assets ÷ current liabilities

The current ratio includes all current assets, but since inventory is often difficult to turn into cash, at least for a reasonable price, many analysts remove it from the equation to arrive at a *quick* ratio. The quick ratio emphasizes coverage assets that can be converted to cash quickly:

Quick ratio = (current assets – inventory) ÷ current liabilities

You sometimes see another related ratio: cash to debt. The calculation is self-explanatory. It takes a still more conservative view of coverage assets (cash only) and a more pointed view of what needs to be covered (total debt, current and long-term portions).

The traditional thinking is that the higher the ratio, the better off the company. Greater than 2:1 for the current ratio or 1:1 for the quick ratio is good and safe; less than 2:1 or 1:1 is a sign of impending problems meeting obligations. Borders Group, for example, has a current ratio of 1.2 ($1.34 billion ÷ $1.12billion) but a "quick" ratio of only 0.12 [($1.34 billion – $1.20 billion) ÷ $1.12billion], implying some coverage problems. But this implication quickly disappears when you remember that bookstores can return books to publishers for nearly full credit (know thy industry!).

More recent thinking, exemplified by the Foolish Flow ratio discussed in the sidebar, doesn't always hold liquidity in the highest esteem. It's better to live off the assets of others than off your own — if you can get away with it.

The value investor's general rule (as with most other ratios): Compare liquidity to industry norms and watch for unhealthy trends. Liquidity ratios don't tell you so much what to buy as what *not* to buy.

Debt to equity and debt to assets

Now we move on to the so-called *solvency,* or *leverage,* ratios. Effectively, these ratios measure what portion of a firm's resources, or assets, are provided by the owners versus provided by others.

Financial leverage can be a good thing — to a point, and as long as things are going well. If you put up $1, borrow $9, and invest the $10 total to achieve a 10 percent return, your profit is $1. Your return on equity is 100 percent (your $1 profit divided by the $1 invested). But what if you lose $2? Your creditor still wants his or her $9 back and is entitled to it. You lose your entire investment and then some. On top of that, your creditor demands (and is entitled to) a fixed level of interest payments, which is a constant expense to your enterprise regardless of results. Leverage is thus a double-edged sword.

Too much long-term debt costs money, increases risk, and can place restrictions on management in the form of restrictive lender covenants governing what a company can and can't do, minimum performance levels, and so on. The two most common ratios used to assess solvency and leverage are *debt to equity* and *debt to total assets.* Here's the formula for debt to equity:

> Debt to equity = total debt ÷ owner's equity

Note that current liabilities, such as accounts payable, typically are not included. From this point of view, Borders is very solvent and not highly leveraged with a debt-to-equity ratio of 0.1 ($82.7 million ÷ $846.5 million).

Here's the formula for debt to assets:

> Debt to total assets = total debt ÷ total assets

Making a sweeping statement about what these ratios should be for a given company is difficult. When a company has more debt than equity (debt to equity > 1 or debt to total assets > 0.5), yellow flags fly. But again, industry comparisons are important. Economic value achieved should exceed the cost and risk incurred with the debt. Sounds good in theory, but precise appraisal can be complex. As with liquidity measures, solvency measures probably deliver a stronger signal for what *not* to buy than what to buy.

Cash flow ratios

Because cash is really the lifeblood of a business, financial strength assessments typically look at cash and cash flow ratios. But there's a hidden agenda behind these ratios: to assess earnings quality.

Overall cash flow ratio

This powerful ratio tells whether a business is generating enough cash from its business to sustain itself, grow, and return capital to its owners. Here's the formula:

Overall cash flow ratio = cash inflow from operations ÷ (investing cash outflows + financing cash outflows)

Operating cash flows represent, as the term implies, cash generated by normal business operations. They should be positive. If not, the company isn't generating enough cash to cover current expenses, let alone replace assets. *Investing* cash flows signify the acquisition or disposal of physical assets and are usually negative, assuming that the company is investing in its business or replacing fixed assets. *Financing* cash flows include proceeds from financing transactions, such as the sale of stock or debt (bonds). They can be either negative or positive, depending on current financing needs and strategy. See Chapter 8 for details.

If the overall cash flow ratio is greater than 1, the company is generating enough cash internally to cover business needs. If it's less than 1, the company is going to capital markets or is selling assets to keep afloat. Borders Group is basically cash flow neutral, with (+)$138.6 in operational cash *in*flow, (–)$19.5 million in financing cash *in*flow (careful, the signs are tricky), and (+)$141.1 million in investing cash *out*flow. The resulting 1.14 ratio tells you that things are okay. From the numbers, it can be implied that Borders invested $141 million in its business (probably opening stores), financed $138 million of that investment from operations, and went to the capital markets for $19.5 million; in so doing it raised its balance sheet cash slightly.

Cash flow and earnings

Now let's talk quality. In Chapters 7, 8, and 9, we bring up the idea that different accounting methods can produce different results on earnings statements. Earnings can be managed up or down, depending on depreciation, amortization, non-cash write-offs, revenue recognition, and so on. Cash flow comparisons with earnings can be used as a quality audit to see how much non-cash accounting stretch went into a report.

You want to see cash flows to accompany earnings. If earnings increase without a corresponding increase in cash flow, earnings quality comes into question. A base measure is the following:

Cash flow to earnings = cash flow from operations ÷ net earnings

Because depreciation and other non-cash amortizations vary by industry, it's hard to hang a specific goal on this measure. Consistency is good. Favorable industry comparisons also are good. Further, it's good when period-to-period earnings increases are accompanied by corresponding cash flow increases.

Profitability ratios

Asset productivity and financial strength reflect business basics, neither of which you can do without, but neither of which alone can point you to good companies and good investments. Because profit is the yardstick of capitalism, profitability ratios form a core set of bottom-line ratios that are crucial to all investment analysis.

In this section, we take a look at four profitability ratios. Each is typically based on net earnings, but occasionally you see variations using cash flow or operating earnings.

Typically, items related to extraordinary charges or discontinued operations are excluded. If you're using calculations from a financial information package, check out the basis. If it doesn't tell you, check a few numbers from the company's own financial statements.

Return on sales

This ratio is just as it sounds:

> Return on sales = net earnings ÷ sales

Return on sales (ROS) tells you how much profit a firm generated per dollar of sales. This figure is much better known as the *net profit margin.* Closely related is gross margin, which we cover in Chapter 8:

> Gross margin = (sales – cost of goods sold) ÷ sales

Obviously, gross margin is a key driver of return on sales and is the driver perhaps most strongly connected to the organization's operational effectiveness. Some analysts also look at operating margin:

> Operating margin = (sales – cost of goods sold – operating expenses) ÷ sales

where SG&A (selling, general, and administrative) expenses, amortizations, and asset recovery are factored in.

For Borders Group, you see a return on sales, or net profit margin, of 2.3 percent ($73.8 million net profit from continuing operations ÷ $3.271 billion in sales). Gross margin is 28 percent [($3.271 billion – $2.354 billion) ÷ $3.271 billion], and operating margin is 4.1 percent ($135.1 million operating profit ÷ $3.271 billion sales).

Too many apples and oranges will turn your profitability metrics into lemons. Regardless of the measure used, return-on-sales measures are key to understanding a company's success. Value investors watch consistency, trends, and comparisons closely.

Stay on the same frequency

Here we go again with that apples-to-oranges thing. In the "Return on sales" section, we calculate the Borders Group gross margin at 28 percent and the operating margin at 4.1 percent. Yet when we look at these ratios on the Value Line Investment Survey, they come in at 30.9 percent and 8.2 percent, respectively. What gives?

The difference goes back to how Borders reports its earnings and how Value Line looks at gross and operating margin. Borders includes occupancy in cost of goods sold; Value Line removes it to keep things comparable to other companies. Borders (like most companies) includes depreciation and amortization in calculating operating earnings, and it lumps asset impairment write-downs into that line. Value Line doesn't include these non-cash items, seeking a more "pure" reflection of operating earnings as sales less cost of goods sold less SG&A. (Note the similarity to EBITDA, which we discuss in Chapters 8 and 9.) These purifications would be difficult for a value investor to achieve on his or her own, and they make comparison much easier. Such is the advantage of using a service like Value Line to go beneath the surface and standardize these calculations for you.

Return on assets

How much profit is generated per resource dollar invested? Return on assets, or ROA, provides the answer:

Return on assets = net earnings ÷ total assets

This measure is especially important in asset-intensive industries, such as retail, semiconductor manufacturing, and basic manufacturing. We take a closer look at ROA in Chapters 13.

For Borders, ROA is $73.8 million ÷ $2047.1 billion, or 3.6 percent — not a very high number, but only a tiny bit below the industry. (How did we know that? We'll get to that when we talk about ratio comparisons at the end of this chapter.)

Return on equity

Return on equity, or ROE, may be the most important ratio an investor looks at. It *is* the bottom line. Here's the formula:

Return on equity = net earnings ÷ owner's equity

ROE is the true measure of how much a company returns to its owners, the shareholders. It is the bottom line after all else is factored in (asset productivity, financial structure, and top-line profitability). ROE is important as an opportunity benchmark. What else could an investor invest in to get a better return? Again, consistency, trends, and comparisons are critical.

Return on invested capital

Debt, while raising ROE in good times, also can lead to financial disaster. As a result, many investors look at return on invested capital (ROIC), measuring profit as a percentage of combined owner's equity and debtor's investments. Here's the formula:

> Return on invested capital = net earnings ÷ (owner's equity + long-term debt)

Frequently, you see ROE and ROIC side by side in ratio charts and discussions. Sustained ROE of 20 percent or more is considered very good, and ROIC should be higher, since debt increases the size of the business on the same equity base. See Chapters 13 and 16 for more on ROE/ROIC.

Valuation ratios

The ratios presented so far in this chapter are aimed at appraising a company's performance — and thus its intrinsic value. Productivity, financial structure, and profitability are sections in a value investor's orchestra pit. The total sound produced depends on the individual sounds made by individual instruments (ratios) and how they work together.

But as a music buff, how much would you pay to listen to it? That's the question that valuation ratios answer: How much would you pay (and how much are others paying) for tickets to this concert? Here, finally, we introduce *price*. Here, finally, we get to the most popular ratio of all, the one in the newspaper, at parties, on license plates: the price-to-earnings (P/E) ratio. Tagging along for the party sophisticates are price to sales, price to book, and a couple of boutique variations on P/E.

When in doubt, should you average?

Occasionally, you see a variation in the formulas for ROE and sometimes ROA. Because these ratios use snapshot balance sheet items in the denominator, some people feel that you get the most accurate financial picture by adding year-end and year-beginning equity or asset values and dividing by 2. Thus ROE would be

ROE = net earnings ÷ [(beginning equity + ending equity) ÷ 2]

Many information sources and services use the averaged formula, but important references such as Value Line don't. The important thing is to understand how a served-up number is calculated and to use consistent numbers in assessing value.

Price to earnings

Price to earnings is just as you would expect: the ratio of a price at a point in time to net earnings in a period, usually the trailing 12 months (TTM). Here's the formula:

Price to earnings (P/E) = stock price ÷ net earnings per share

A high P/E, say, 20 or higher, indicates a relatively high valuation; a low P/E, say, 15 or less, indicates a relatively low or more conservative one. If you have investing experience, you're probably familiar with P/E, so we won't go into detail or show sample calculations. Rather, we'll share a couple of useful derivatives: earnings to price and price-earnings to growth. P/E is explored in detail in Chapter 16.

Earnings to price

Earnings to price is simply the reciprocal of P/E, or 1 divided by the P/E. Why do we go here? Earnings to price is the functional equivalent of a stock's *yield*, comparable to an interest rate on a fixed income investment. Because we're talking earnings and not dividends, this yield doesn't usually come your way in the form of a check, but it's useful just the same to determine how much return your dollar paid for a share is generating. Many people call this figure *earnings yield*.

Take Borders, for example: TTM earnings per share from continuing operations was $0.94. A recent price was $18, giving a P/E of 19.2. Still with us? Now on to the earnings yield: Calculated at 1 ÷ 19.2 (a one-button push on most calculators), it comes to 5.2 percent. What's the significance? This investment could be compared to a Treasury security (today yielding about 5.1 percent) as a prospective investment. Which investment is better? An investment in Borders is riskier but affords the opportunity for gain through growth.

Price-earnings to growth

You still don't know whether Borders' P/E ratio of 19.2 makes sense. Sun Microsystems is at 45, while Ford Motor Company is at 8. Why is one so much higher than the other? The primary reason is growth. Investors pay higher P/Es for companies with greater growth prospects. Greater growth prospects mean greater earnings and greater earnings yields *sooner*. So a recently popularized way to normalize P/E is to compare it to the growth rate. From this comparison, you get price-earnings to growth, or PEG:

Price-earnings to growth (PEG) = (P/E) ÷ earnings growth rate

If Sun Microsystems has an earnings growth rate of 30 percent, while Borders's is 20 percent and Ford's is 5 percent, then PEG is 45 ÷ 30 or 1.5 for Sun, 19 ÷ 20 or 0.95 for Borders, and 8 ÷ 5 or 1.6 for Ford. Now you can say that Borders is the best investment of the three, while Ford is the worst.

Market cap

When calculating price-to-sales ratios or other valuation measures, it's sometimes easier to look at aggregates rather than per-share amounts. Sales are reported as an aggregate figure, not as a per-share figure. So to compare apples to apples (oh no, not that fruit thing again!), you look at aggregate share valuation instead of the per-share price. This aggregate figure is known to investors as *market capitalization*, or *market cap* for short. Market cap is simply the number of shares (usually the fully loaded number, including options and equivalents) times the stock price. Divide total market cap by total sales, and you have the price-to-sales ratio.

Now we get into some sticky stuff in the denominator earnings growth rate. What rate should you use? What the company has already achieved? What do analysts project it to do? Over what period? When will the growth rate run into the law-of-large-numbers wall (see Chapter 4)? Much has been said and written about the use of growth rates and PEG; you'll see PEG and growth rates in the next few chapters.

Price to sales

Per dollar of shareholder value, how much business does this company generate? Price to sales (P/S) is a straightforward way to answer this question. Here's the formula:

Price to sales = stock price (total market cap) ÷ total sales (revenues)

P/S is a common-sense ratio. The lower the better, although there's no specific rule or normalizer like growth. Somewhere around 1.0 usually is considered good. 2.0 isn't out of hand, but the business had better grow consistently and be prepared to grow into valuation. P/S can be a way to filter out unworthy candidates, such as Cisco, whose P/S once approached 20 (while its P/E approached 100, already a trouble sign). For Borders, P/S is about 0.42 ($1.404 billion ÷ $3.271 billion) — very healthy, but typical for the retail industry, where high sales dollars are offset by low margins.

Price to book

The price-to-book ratio is getting varying amounts of attention from investors in different sectors. Here's the formula:

Price to book = stock price (total market cap) ÷ book value

Recall from Chapter 7 that book value consists of the accounting value of assets less (real) liabilities — sort of an accounting net worth or owner's equity of a corporation. This figure has greater meaning in financial services industries, where most assets are actual dollars, not factories, inventories, goodwill, and other hard-to-value items. Some book value measures include intangible assets, and others exclude them.

Value investors use price to book a bit like price to sales: as sort of a smell test for obvious lack of value. A price-to-book ratio of 1.0 is very good — unless the asset base is a bunch of rusty unused railroad tracks. P/B of less than 1.0 signifies a buying opportunity — if book assets are quality assets. A price way out of line with book had better be justified by conservative asset valuation or by the nature of the industry. In the software industry, for example, if R&D (research and development) is properly expensed and intellectual capital intangibles are aggressively amortized, book value and P/B will be low. Trends and especially comparisons are important.

Turn On, Tune In: Compare Ratios

We saved the comparative part of ratio analysis for the end of the chapter on purpose so that you would be more familiar with the ratios involved. This comparative ratio analysis is the only truly free one we know of, as available through Yahoo! Finance from Multex Market Guide. Getting there is a trick in itself:

1. **Get a stock quote for the stock you want to compare to its industry.**

   Simply type the ticker symbol of the company you're looking for and then click the Get Quotes button.

2. **In the "More Info" column, click the "Profile" link.**

3. **Scroll down the Profile page until you see the "More From Market Guide" heading on the left. Click on "Ratio Comparisons."**

   The Statistics at a Glance box is worth a look, too; some of the popular ratios are there, but no comparisons.

What this tool doesn't do (easily, anyway) is compare one company to another. If you want to compare Borders to Barnes & Noble, for example, you have to enter each company separately, print the results, and then compare them.

For company side-by-side comparisons with industry data, Charles Schwab and other online investment houses, as well as the Quicken investment site (www.quicken.com), enable company comparisons, usually in a list with industry data included. These lists are handy but don't go as deep as the Yahoo! Finance table in that they don't show as many ratios. For Charles Schwab (account required), go to Quotes & Research, then to Industry, and then to Fundamentals on the pull-down menu. Although the ratio list is skimpy and uncustomizable (a shame, because the data source is the same as Yahoo!'s Multex), it shows the important ones — and ones from each category, asset productivity, financial strength, profitability, and valuation.

Part III
So You Wanna Buy a Business?

The 5th Wave   By Rich Tennant

OUT OF BUSINESS

Main Street CHINA SH

"What made you think you were the one to own and operate a china shop, I'll never know."

In this part . . .

We help you to assess or *appraise* the value of a company and relate that value to the stock price. We examine some of the proven methods of business value assessment, including intrinsic value, book value, discounted cash flow, and the strategic profit formula. Then we sprinkle in a dash of intangibles (investors shouldn't live by numbers alone) and discuss buy and sell decisions. To bring these tools and techniques together into a system, we use none other than the full example of the master, Warren Buffett. Finally, to provide practice and reinforcement we present case studies of value, and for further reinforcement we resort to the age-old technique of showing opposites: examples of *un*value.

Chapter 11

Appraising a Business

The key to valuing a public company is to determine how much and how quickly a company can return profits on your behalf.

—Timothy P. Vick, *Wall Street on Sale*

If you compare *Value Investing For Dummies* to a fancy restaurant meal, then Chapters 1 through 10 provide the table, dishes, silverware, menu, appetizers, wine, and bread. They give you the value investing context, basic tools, and a menu of financial statements and ratios that are commonly used to evaluate a company's performance.

In this chapter, we move on to the main course: using what you find out about a company to appraise the company. For your investing to be consistent with the value investing approach, you must understand what a company is worth before you make an investment decision.

Sounds easy, right? Serve entree, pick up knife and fork, and dig in. If only it were so simple. As you'll see, the main course could be a *college* course. Valuation has been the subject of vast theoretical study and debate — as well as experience and learning — in the investing community. Business valuation is at best an inexact science that no two people do exactly the same way. Our goal is to expose you to some of the techniques and underlying principles. Whether you apply them rigorously to every investment decision or just keep them in the back of your mind is up to you.

In this chapter, we outline a system for business valuation. We discuss two major valuation approaches: *intrinsic* and *strategic* valuation. In the chapters that follow, we provide a practical framework for applying these approaches and a set of tools that a nonprofessional value investor can use.

Comparing Business Valuation to Stock Valuation

So you think you know how to value a business? Just look at the price-to-earnings (P/E) ratio, then maybe price-to-sales (P/S) and price-to-book (P/B) ratios, compare to its closest competitor, and *voilà* — you've valued the business. Right?

If you guessed "no" (and that's logical, since we're pointing you in that direction), you're on the right track. P/E, P/S, and P/B are *valuation* ratios (see Chapter 10) to be sure, but they value the stock, not the business. They compare the stock price to a top- or bottom-line attribute of the business. They suggest whether the stock price is reasonable in the context of that attribute, but they don't tell you what the business itself is worth.

We're not saying that stock valuation ratios have no place in value investing. Valuation ratios play into a good value investment system, usually in two ways:

✔ You can use valuation ratios at the beginning of value analysis to screen companies for deeper analysis. As you can imagine, performing a detailed evaluation of 1,700 companies would take way too long.

✔ You can sometimes use valuation ratios after completing the company value assessment as a tool to determine whether the price and timing are right to buy.

But beware: Relying on valuation measures alone can give you a superficial view of company performance, especially if unusual items like one-time write-offs color the numbers. If you don't understand the underlying fundamentals and trends, you may hitch your wagon to the wrong horse.

Understanding What Goes into the Valuing of a Business

Plain and simple, the value of any business is the sum of all the cash you receive from the business now and in the future. The two questions left to be answered are "how much?" and "when?" You ask these same questions whether you buy a lemonade stand, write a book, or buy the Coca-Cola Company. The importance of "how much" is obvious, and the importance of "when" refers to the time value of money. A sum received today has more value than the same sum received 20 years from now.

If you knew how much and when, you'd be able to nail the business value with accuracy. But unfortunately, life isn't so simple — you have to piece together the "how much" and "when" from what you know, and what you can infer, about the business and its value *as a business*.

Other factors: Drivers

Business value is created and driven by the following factors:

- ✔ **Income:** Profits — and cash flows exceeding profits — are a good thing. A company starting at a loss and banking on future profits is starting in the hole, particularly considering the time value of money.

- ✔ **Income growth:** If income is steady but unlikely to grow, there is value. Steady future cash flows have value and are worth paying for. But without growth, time depreciates earnings value over time. There's little to make a stock price rise unless the market values the income stream incorrectly in the first place.

- ✔ **Productive capital investments:** It's important that a company be able to invest additional capital productively — at a greater return than it would get by putting the capital in the bank. And it goes without saying that a company should invest capital more productively than *you* can; otherwise, it makes sense for you to invest your capital elsewhere. If the company doesn't have productive places to invest but pays you a good return (dividends), the company has value, but reasons for share price growth may be absent.

- ✔ **Rising productivity and falling expenses:** A good business makes better and better use of assets and creates more output per unit of input. Businesses that can do so are likely to generate more income sooner than other less productive businesses.

- ✔ **Predictability:** Generally, a business with a predictable, steady income stream is more valuable than a company that has erratic or cyclical earnings. The erratic company may return as much money in the long run as the steady company, but the uncertainty surrounding the earnings stream requires a higher discount rate or margin of safety because you just don't know. The higher discount rate reduces value.

- ✔ **Steady or rising asset values:** Asset growth, particularly current assets, should ultimately lead to higher shareholder returns. If assets (for example, cash) aren't distributed directly to shareholders, the company may become a more attractive takeover target. A company with falling assets is suspicious, unless its productivity gains are significant.

✔ **Favorable intangibles:** Many, many things can affect or serve as leading indicators of business value. Management effectiveness, market presence, brand franchises, intellectual property, and unique skills and competencies all play a part in driving business value. By nature, these items are hard to quantify, but they are very much a part of the valuation playing field.

You can compare these business value drivers to your personal situation. If you have predictable income, it's growing, you're investing your income and savings productively, your expenses are falling, and your assets are going up in value, you, as a "business," are doing okay. In the business world, it's no different — just a little more complicated to evaluate.

Appraising Business Value

You know what you have to achieve: an appraisal of business value through factoring in a whole bunch of diverse inputs. A true business value assessment could be a never-ending process. You could unearth more and more detail that could affect value, and by the time that Input Z was measured, Input A would change. And there are enough subjective points to the valuation process (such as discount rates and intangibles) that peeling back *every* layer of the onion just doesn't make sense. The old adage may apply: The more you know, the more you don't know.

Intrinsic and strategic valuation

If you've read other books or articles about value investing, you realize that dozens of valuation approaches are out there. One writer uses a set of ratios, another looks at acquisition value, and a third projects earnings based on sales growth, margins, and P/E ratios. All these approaches make sense. Our goal in this book is to take the best of what's out there and make it understandable and practical for you. To help, we propose a valuation system built on two component approaches: *intrinsic* valuation and *strategic* valuation.

✔ **Intrinsic valuation** attempts to place a dollar value on future income or cash flows based on growth, timing, and discount rates. Intrinsic value formulas result in a value per share of the company. But because of predictive uncertainty and the nature of underlying assumptions, intrinsic valuation is far from precise. It can give a wide range of valuations, depending on the assumptions that you make in the valuation process. Still, whether or not you as an investor choose to run detailed intrinsic value calculations, understanding intrinsic value principles will help you judge company value.

✔ **Strategic valuation** backs up a step from intrinsic valuation to look at factors that drive and ultimately create intrinsic value, and thus shareholder value. Most of these factors are influenced or controlled by specific management strategies, hence the term *strategic value.* There are two components of strategic value: strategic financials and strategic intangibles.

Strategic financial value starts with *return-on-equity (ROE),* a core driver of shareholder value. From ROE, fundamental strategic valuation works backward to assess major ROE drivers of profitability, productivity, and capital structure. Then, moving farther back into the value food chain, you examine strategic *intangibles,* which influence the ROE drivers.

Strategic valuation doesn't give a single figure for company value, but it tells you how many of the arrows point in the right direction and whether management is pulling the right levers to create shareholder value — and eventual shareholder returns.

The two approaches are not altogether unrelated. Strategic value affects intrinsic value. A company with high and growing profit margins, return on assets, and a good franchise will not only maintain strong ROE but also produce high returns on invested dollars and a high intrinsic value.

Intrinsic value gives a specific dollar business value, albeit with a wide range, for each share of a company's stock. This value is of little use for comparison *except* with the company's stock price; that is, if the stock price is far less than the intrinsic value per share, the stock is a good buy. On the other hand, strategic value is much more comparative; you can use it to compare Company A to Company B and decide which one to buy.

Developing a value investing system

In the end, if you have the time, you're probably well served to calculate intrinsic value and then flavor it with strategic value assessments and intangibles. But the difficulties and vagaries of intrinsic value calculations make strategic valuation probably the more practical of the two approaches.

You may be disappointed that we provide no absolute system or set of formulas to pick the surefire winners. (If we had such a system, we'd be sitting on some South Seas island instead of writing this book.) We provide formulas and tips, but developing a value investing system is pretty much up to you. It depends on your time, appetite for numbers, goals, and, ultimately, what your experience shows works for you.

Having said that, we'll offer this value investing system as an example or model that could become *your* system, with or without modifications. This system is designed for non-professionals who may have just a few hours a month to sit down to review and select investments.

1. **Screen companies.**

   Using P/E, P/S, or other chosen ratios, get a list of companies to evaluate. The list can include industries considered timely by popular investment analysts, companies you read about in the financial press, or companies you deal with in everyday life that appear to have their act together. In addition, online stock screeners, introduced in Chapter 5, are useful for this step.

2. **Calculate the companies' intrinsic value.**

   Using formulas we present in Chapter 12, derive an estimate of intrinsic value for each company. As you gain experience, you'll arrive at a set of assumptions that you can always apply. Getting good at this step may take practice.

3. **Assess each company's strategic value.**

   Develop a checklist, similar to Ben Graham's checklist in Chapter 3, for key business performance measures (return on assets growing, return on equity constant, profit margins growing, sufficient liquidity, and so on). We show you such a list in Chapter 13. Then, add a checklist and evaluate intangibles, as we do in Chapter 14.

4. **Decide whether the price is right.**

   Compare current price to intrinsic value, sprinkle in strategic value assessments, and bake in a dash of judgment. Look at valuation ratios (P/E, P/S, and P/B, both current and historic) to decide whether the price is right and whether a margin of safety exists. Check to see whether price can grow to meet your investment objectives. We walk you through this process in Chapter 16.

This four-step process is only an example; you may end up doing something totally different. It may make sense to place more emphasis on one step or another, depending on the amount and reliability of the information available. Steps 2 and 3 can be reversed. You can evaluate strategic value and then use intrinsic value as a reality check to validate your selections. It all depends on what works for you: what is time efficient and produces results.

Chapter 12

Running the Numbers: Intrinsic Value

> *This method takes a lot more work than simply dividing a stock's price by its per-share sales or earnings, then deciding if the result is reasonable . . . you get a picture of how such variables such as growth and interest rates will affect the value of a stock.*
>
> —Carol Marie Cropper, *Business Week*

*W*hat is something really worth? Regardless of what you buy — or invest in — this nagging question ruins sleep for value types. You pay six figures for that house, realizing the impossibility of counting nails, two-by-fours, sheets of plywood, and roof shingles, not to mention the work required to get them there. The house has a value, and the whole has greater value than the sum of the parts. The value to you as a buyer is related not just to nails and boards, but also to what the house returns to you as a living space now, in the future, and compared to alternatives.

Investments can be looked at in much the same way. You can round up all the buildings, trucks, pallet jacks, and PCs that a company owns, assign a value to each, and add it all up. Yeah, right — hardly. Instead, here's what's really important: What does all that stuff produce in the form of investor returns? *Intrinsic valuation* is the art and science of placing a fair value on current and future investment returns. When assets are deployed productively, you don't care about the value of pallet jacks. The return is the main thing! If healthy returns stopped coming, then and only then are investors concerned about their residual asset value for liquidation.

Value investors think of the asset base as a minimum, or *floor,* for intrinsic value. True measured value comes from the returns. Intrinsic value formulas help value investors measure a business value from today's facts and data. As you will see, intrinsic valuation depends on assumptions, many of which elude precise identification. A wide range of projected values can result. As a result, some value investors choose to avoid the intrinsic value calculation. But that doesn't mean you should avoid this chapter. Value investors should understand the principles and purpose behind intrinsic value, whether or not they attempt specific calculations.

The Intrinsic Value of Intrinsic Value

Intrinsic value is a present dollar value placed on net returns generated by a business over time. This is the financially correct theoretical value of a security. It's the net present value of all future returns from investing in a productive asset — in this case, a business.

As a practical matter, wouldn't it be great if you could quantify "present dollar value" precisely? For fixed income or bond investments, it's relatively easy. Save for default, you know what you're going to get back: a fixed return or "coupon" — a fixed payment. As an investor, you must decide how much that return is worth. Current interest rates, alternative investments, and default risk play a role, but calculating the return on a bond is fairly straightforward.

But what about equities?

Valuing business equity investments is a trickier task. There is no guaranteed return. Instead, returns vary year by year with fluctuations in sales, sales prices, costs, and internal productivity. Market factors, competitive factors, operating efficiencies, financing costs, and a wide range of other factors affect profits — and thus returns — on equity investments.

Further, not all returns are paid to shareholders. Aside from dividends, returns are reinvested in the company for future returns, which are also unpredictable. These returns may not be paid back to shareholders for years, even decades, depending on the life of the company. The company may choose to keep reinvesting, hopefully with success. A more common outcome for all but the biggest companies is that the continuing value of a company is paid to shareholders in the form of cash or securities in a buyout or merger. But it may not happen for 20 years.

The reality of intrinsic value models

The reality is that you *can* assign an intrinsic value to a company by mathematically estimating future returns and their present value. But (and you were waiting for the *but*) there is a great range of possible outcomes, depending on what assumptions you use.

Intrinsic value models depend on estimating growth rates and growth periods and assigning a discount rate to bring future returns back to present value. These inputs elude precision, and the outcome is extremely sensitive to the inputs. So once again, there's no one-shot formula for securities valuation. But an understanding of the model and its behavior can contribute mightily to investment analysis.

We make the point earlier that if all investing boiled down to simple, precise mathematical formulas built on perfect knowledge, there would be no difference of opinion on company values, and thus no market. The whole equity world would function like a bond market, except that your investments would rise or fall dollar for dollar with every incremental change in company fortune. There would be no reason for investment books — the same stock valuation formulas would be on your PC or calculator and everyone else's alike. Superinvestors such as Warren Buffett wouldn't become superinvestors, because they couldn't make better judgments than the next investor. Markets would no longer fire up the competitive juices of cocktail-partygoers. It *would* be a bit boring.

There are many ways to use intrinsic value principles and models. Intrinsic value models and principles should be carried in every value investor's golf bag. They will be used at different times for different reasons:

- **Thought framework:** Intrinsic value principles serve as a thought framework, or investing "conscience." Successful investors constantly weigh future returns, risk and uncertainty, and alternative investments. It's like playing with a full set of clubs, though only a few may be used.

- **Entry point:** Intrinsic value models provide a good entry point for investment analysis. By playing with the assumptions, you get a picture of a stock's logical range and of the factors that could cause a stock to exceed the range in either direction. Tee off with intrinsic value, approach with strategic financials, putt with intangibles, and you just may par the hole.

- **Reality check:** There are different ways to get to the business valuation "green." Intrinsic value models can help you decide whether you're on the right fairway. As a reality check, look to see whether calculated intrinsic value is below or close to share price.

Intrinsic Value Ground School

Theoretically and practically, the value you get out of owning a business or a security is the amount you receive in return for your investment. That return may come as a single payment at the end of the ownership period for selling the stock or business, or as payments at regular intervals during ownership, or (often) as a combination of the two.

You may at first glance say that it makes no difference — money is money. But growth and time value of money have a major impact on the final valuation of equity investment returns. In fact, intrinsic valuation is a lot about assessing the effects of future growth on future returns and then assigning a *present value* to those returns.

A checklist of how's

The following "how" questions can guide your assessment of business returns.

How much?

How many dollars of return will the business produce, either to distribute to shareholders or to invest productively in the business? Key drivers are profitability and growth rates — and all the business factors that drive the profitability and growth.

How soon?

Big payoffs are nice, but if you have to wait 30 years for them, they aren't as valuable. Remember the time value of money. If two companies produce the same return but one does it sooner, that company has more value, because those dollars can be reinvested sooner for more return.

How long?

Although future returns have less value than current returns, they do have substantial value, and 20, 30, or 50 years of those returns can't be ignored, particularly in a profitable, growing business.

How consistent?

A company producing slow, steady growth and return is usually more valuable than one that's all over the map. A greater variability, or uncertainty, around projected returns calls for more conservative growth and/or discounting assumptions.

How valuable?

Finally, after assessing potential returns (how much, how soon, how long, how consistent), you must assign a current value to those returns. That value is driven by the value of the investment money as it might be used elsewhere. A return may look attractive — until the investor realizes that he can achieve the same return with a bond or a less risky investment. Valuing the returns involves discounting (using a discount rate) to bring future returns back to fair current value. The discount rate is your personal cost of capital — in this case, the rate of return you expect to deploy capital here versus elsewhere.

Sooner isn't *always* better. A business producing quick, short-term bucks may not be more valuable than one that produces slow, steady growth. The quick-bucker may be cyclical and go through years of diminished or even negative returns. Even though the quick-bucker produces a lot of value in the first few years, that may not be better than sustained growth and value produced later on by the slower, steadier company. It's a combination of how much, how soon, how long, and how consistent. The tortoise often beats the hare.

Airspeed, altitude, amount, and timing

Yes, that's right. Intrinsic value boils down to amount and timing. Just like flying, intrinsic value seems pretty simple — until you try to do it yourself!

Before climbing into the intrinsic value cockpit, you need to do some more preliminary navigation work to (we hope) simplify the flight plan.

Dividends? We don't need no stinkin' dividends

Dividends represent a direct cash payment of a portion of company profits to its shareholders. A dollar paid to shareholders comes directly out of retained earnings — and future book value — of the company. For many investors, a dividend check "bird in the hand" is worth more than two reinvest-in-the-future "birds in the bush," and some regard dividends as a reaffirmation of management commitment to producing returns for shareholders. But dividends paid are money taken out of the business, possibly attenuating future growth in dollars and future business returns.

As part of intrinsic value, dividends are counted as part of yearly investment returns and grown and discounted in the same way as earnings retained in the business. But deducting dividends reduces the growth base of retained earnings and book value kept in the business. Companies with a high growth rate and return on equity often yield greater intrinsic value if all earnings are retained and reinvested, which is why you often see just that — no dividends in high-growth companies.

To keep it simple, the examples we use later in this chapter include no dividends.

Returns

What returns are we talking about, anyway? There are earnings, which as you see in Part II of this book, can be as much an accounting story as reality. Do you want to place your faith in the accountants? Or as a measure of returns, do you want a more real measure of what you really get as cash flows? EBITDA? Free cash flow? The debate rages on.

Cash flow (CF) or discounted cash flow (DCF)

Cash flows, which we cover more closely in Chapter 8, are yearly cash returns into a business, without accounting adjustments for asset write-downs, amortizations, and the like. Earnings depend a great deal on how the company values and adjusts the value of assets. At the end of the day, cash accounts grow — and checks are written — on cash flow. Many sophisticated security analysis models, including intrinsic value models, operate on cash flow. These models are sometimes referred to as *discounted cash flow* (DCF) models.

EBITDA

EBITDA (Earnings Before Interest, Taxes, Depreciation, and Amortization) is an approximation of cash generated by business operating activities. Okay, but interest and taxes are real, and depreciation "chickens" come home to roost someday when depreciated fixed assets need to be replaced.

Free cash flow (FCF)

Free cash flow is essentially cash flow generated from operations *less* interest, taxes, and capital investments. Much better.

Net free cash flow (owner earnings)

The most realistic version of free cash flow is plain old free cash flow with an additional adjustment for working capital changes. If persistent growth in accounts receivable or inventory is required to sustain business levels, the cost or cash invested in those assets should be deducted from that returnable to owners.

> Net free cash flow =
>
> operating earnings
>
> less interest and taxes
>
> less capital investments
>
> less (or plus) net working capital requirements

Warren Buffett uses net free cash flow to do his assessments and wisely calls it *owner earnings* to represent the annual earnings truly available to business owners.

Any one of these cash flow streams can be used as an input to an intrinsic value or DCF model, and they are probably more robust than reported earnings. But they are harder to identify for the nonprofessional investor. Most free data sources provide little in the way of cash flow figures, and if they do, they aren't adjusted to accommodate fixed or working capital investments. It takes a deep understanding of a company to properly time fixed and working capital investment outlays into an intrinsic value computation. Therefore, most investors use earnings as the most readily available proxy for business returns. It's a good place to start. Understanding earnings quality and the differences between earnings and cash flow goes a long way towards producing valid results.

When using earnings streams to project future returns, remember to make sure to understand quality and one-time extraordinary gains or losses. Especially when occurring in the base year, extraordinary earnings items can mess up the intrinsic value calculation. Be especially careful when using a "canned" package, as it picks up whatever is on a company's source earnings database, ordinary or otherwise. To their credit, analysts and Value Line usually filter out these abnormalities when making projections.

Future investments: Continuing climb?

No airplane — or business — climbs forever. Soon the air thins, fuel runs low, instruments start to fail, safety margins diminish — and we must level off.

We stated that true intrinsic value is the total of *all* future investment returns. This year, next year, 5, 10, 20, 40, 80 years from now. C'mon, how can you possibly project a company's return 77 years from now? Heck, it's hard enough to do it for this year! How do you play years 77, 78, 79, and 80 into the intrinsic value calculation? Especially with a knowledge of gravity and the understanding that growth rates inevitably level off?

First stage: Off the ground

Intrinsic value models are set up to specifically value a first stage in detail, year-by-year. Typically the first stage is 10 years, although in some analyses it may be more or less. Typically, the first stage is assumed to have a higher growth rate and a lower discount rate than the second stage. Why? High altitude attenuates high growth rates as time goes on, while risk and uncertainty call for higher discount rates farther out into the future.

Second stage: To infinity — and beyond?

The second stage covers the more nebulous period of business life that comes after the first stage. Second-stage returns are harder to project with any degree of accuracy, so intrinsic value models use one of two assumptions — you can think of them as tricks — to estimate what is known as *continuing value:*

✓ **Indefinite life:** The indefinite life model assumes ongoing returns and uses a mathematical formula to project returns, really to infinity. We share that formula in a minute. It really isn't too bad.

✓ **Acquisition:** A convenient way to bypass mathematical approximations is to assume that someone will come along and buy your business after the first stage at a reasonable valuation. Returns include all future payouts, including lump sums, so this method works too, so long as you're reasonable in projecting resale value.

To summarize, for each stage, you have a growth rate and discount rate applicable to that stage. You apply one growth rate and one discount rate to the first stage and another growth and discount rate to the second stage. You calculate growth-compounded, discounted earnings specifically for each year in the first stage, while applying a generalizing formula, either indefinite life or acquisition-based, to the second stage.

The value attributed to the second stage is known as *continuing value.*

Jets and Props: Intrinsic Value Models

Now, out of flight school and into the cockpit! It's time to examine the models themselves, in what we hope to be a straightforward, practical treatment. Remember that textbooks have been written on this stuff! We write about some of the models available and what results you can expect.

Outcome: A safe landing

So what is the output of an intrinsic value model? A buy order delivered electronically to your Internet broker? A red, yellow, or green light on your screen? Not quite.

The finished product is simple, but the work isn't done. Intrinsic value models conveniently provide a single-figure result: the estimated per-share value of the company. One single number: For example, Borders Group is worth $23.44. If (and it's a big if) you're satisfied with this number and the assumptions going into it, you can compare this intrinsic value with current market price and make a buy decision. But, as we point out earlier and as you'll see by the end of this chapter, the results can vary widely according to your assumptions. It's best to at least consider the strategic financials and intangibles (see Chapters 13 and 14) before hitting the buy button.

Three airplanes in the hangar

In this section, we introduce three intrinsic value model sources you can use:

- A build-your-own model using a spreadsheet (like Microsoft Excel)
- Prepackaged models on the Web
- A single equation developed by Ben Graham in *Security Analysis* (see Chapter 3)

Build your own spreadsheet

The standard intrinsic value model is relatively easy to construct with an Excel or Lotus spreadsheet. We supply the formulas for educational purposes, and you can create your own intrinsic value models. Two different versions are presented, one for each continuing value approach — indefinite life and a ten-year acquisition.

A prepackaged Web model: the Quicken Stock Analyzer

Intuit Corporation, through its excellent Quicken Web site (www.quicken.com), provides a nicely packaged intrinsic value calculator. This solution saves you time by accessing publicly available data and suggesting growth and discount rates based on current analyst projections and going rates. You can run an intrinsic value calculation in less than a minute. It also allows flexibility to select growth and discount rates from among several pull-down choices, or you can supply your own rates. Likewise, you can accept the automatically sourced base earnings level or supply your own. Finally, the package does a good job of explaining assumptions and interpreting results.

Our build-your-own approach uses the same formula as the Quicken analyzer, except that Quicken has no acquisition form of continuing value.

The Graham classic

In Chapter 3, we present the original formula created by Ben Graham, dating back to his classic 1934 book *Security Analysis*. The formula, though simpler and not quite as adjustable as other models, yields surprisingly comparable results.

High-octane fuel

To run a model, you need a base, first- and second-stage growth rates, and first- and second-stage discount rates.

TIP

Fun with Quicken

Here's how to get to the quicken.com intrinsic value model:

1. **Open your Web browser and type in** www.quicken.com.

2. **Click the Investing tab.**

3. **Find "Evaluate Investments" on the left navigation bar.**

4. **Click on "Stock Evaluator."**

5. **Enter a ticker symbol in the "Getting Started" page.**

6. **Select the "Intrinsic Value" evaluator ("#5" on the screen).**

7. **Read about the model, select parameters, and GO!**

Or for a bookmarked shortcut, www.quicken.com/investments/seceval gets you to the ticker symbol entry.

Remember, this package is a good shortcut for building and testing assumptions, even if you prefer to build your own intrinsic value model.

Also required are long-term debt (to net out what's actually *yours*) and, to run the ten-year acquisition model, a ratio of price-to-book value that the supposed acquirer is willing to pay.

Where do you get these numbers? We show you in greater detail as we describe each section of the model.

Contact! Crank Up the Intrinsic Value Spreadsheet

Cleared for takeoff, let's go. We gun our engines a bit and show the build-your-own intrinsic value spreadsheet as calculated for Borders Group, using the indefinite life assumption for continuing value. See Figure 12-1. Note that dollar figures, except per share amounts, are in millions.

Not bad, really! Only a half page. And you thought those half-million-dollar-a-year securities analysts used gigantic, multipage monsters infiltrated with macros. Well, maybe they do for some things.

Deciphering the intrinsic value worksheet

The intrinsic value worksheet has nine parts. We examine each more closely, including formulas and data sources. Really, you can build this one yourself!

INTRINSIC VALUE WORKSHEET
indefinite life model

Growth and Discount assumptions

first stage growth	14%	g1	your assumptions
second stage growth	6%	g2	
first stage discount rate	12%	d1	
second stage discount rate	15%	d2	

Earnings, shares outstanding, EPS

beginning earnings	$ 73.60	E	from statements or Value Line
number of shares (M)	79.9		
beginning EPS	$ 0.92		

Calculated 10-year earnings stream

year 1	$	74.91
year 2	$	76.25
year 3	$	77.61
year 4	$	79.00
year 5	$	80.41
year 6	$	81.85
year 7	$	83.31
year 8	$	84.80
year 9	$	86.31
year 10	$	87.85

beginning earnings

* compounded for growth *multiply E by* $(1+g1)^n$

* then discounted *divide by* $(1+d1)^n$

Total discounted return, first 10 years

discounted 10-year value	$ 812.30	sum years 1-10

Continuing value beyond 10 years

continuing value (> 10 years)	$ 1,112.78	$\dfrac{[E*(1+g1)^{n+1}]/(d2-g2)}{(1+d1)^n}$

Total future returns value, discounted

$ 1,925.08	10 year + terminal value

Long term debt adjustment

$ 15.00	from statements or VL

Net future returns value

$ 1,910.08	subtract LT debt

Per share intrinsic value

$ 23.91	net future value / # shares

implied P/E	26.0
implied PEG	1.9

Figure 12-1: Intrinsic value worksheet — indefinite life.

Growth and discount assumptions

Not surprisingly, here at the very top of the worksheet is where you can do the most damage — or the most good — to your analysis. Those of you familiar with the time value of money and the power of compounding readily recognize the potential effects of these assumptions carried over 10 years, 20 years, 50 years, and so forth.

Recall from earlier that we choose a set of earnings growth and discount assumptions for the first stage — in this model, ten years. Then we choose another set of earnings growth and discount assumptions for the second stage. Because this is the indefinite life version, the second stage covers year 11 through, really, infinity!

Choosing a growth assumption

Uh-oh. You're thinking that you can't even pick a show horse for the next race, and you're being asked to choose business growth assumptions from now to eternity? Scary stuff, for sure. You can rely on outside sources such as analysts or Value Line. You can eyeball the numbers yourself and pick a number that makes sense, even with conservative bias. Or you can dig deeper and do what the analysts themselves do (hopefully, better than they do it!) and derive earnings growth estimates by projecting sales, profitability, productivity, and so on. The point is, you need a number — a number you feel comfortable with. Again, it's art *and* science.

Table 12-1 identifies approaches to assessing growth rates.

Table 12-1	Approaches to Assessing Earnings Growth		
Rating	*Approach*	*Advantages*	*Disadvantages*
Good	Using analyst projections (from the financial press, Yahoo! Finance, and so on)	Simple, readily available	Analysts tend to overestimate
Good	Select from Quicken.com Stock Evaluator choices	A simple, wide variety of selections; saves time and provides a place to start	Still mainly based on analysts; industry or sector growth rates may be irrelevant or too general; may be out of date
Better	Value Line projections	Solid research, long history	Sometimes overly optimistic
Better	Project your own earnings or cash flow growth from history	You get the best overall feel, can include own conservative bias	Sufficient history hard to find, must filter out extraordinaries

Rating	Approach	Advantages	Disadvantages
Best	Derive earnings growth from sales growth, profit margins, and operating expense projections. Examine market share, business and brand strength, capital requirement, and earnings quality.	You get the deepest understanding. This is the true buying-the-business approach	Time consuming; some information may be elusive and hard to get

Growth assumption examples

We now share examples of three resources we used to get growth assumptions for Borders Group. These resources are illustrated in Figures 12-2, 12-3, and 12-4. The first is from Yahoo! Finance (Figure 12-2), the second is a set of selections from the Quicken.com Stock Evaluator (Figure 12-3), and the third is from Value Line (Figure 12-4).

The Yahoo! Finance (click "Research" after entering a ticker symbol) figures represent a composite survey of security analysts who follow and rate the company.

Figure 12-2: Analyst growth projections from Yahoo! Finance.

Earnings Growth								
Calendar Year Figures	Past 5 Years	This Quarter (Q2)	Next Quarter (Q3)	This Year (2001)	Next Year (2002)	Next 5 Years	Price/ Earn	PEG Ratio
Borders Group Inc	11.7%	N/A	N/A	14.5%	N/A	15.0%	12.6	0.84
Industry	N/A	11.8%	11.8%	24.3%	19.8%	16.19%	27.86	1.72
Sector	N/A	-46.2%	0.0%	-15.9%	37.6%	13.47%	37.20	2.76
S&P 500	N/A	-17.2%	14.0%	-5.5%	19.2%	13.34%	23.55	1.76

Quicken Stock Evaluator growth assumptions for intrinsic value are shown in Figure 12-3. They are from the pull-down menu under "Earnings growth rate." See the "Fun With Quicken" sidebar to learn how to access

You can see the wide range of available assumptions. These are based on company history and analyst projections. Careful: it would be dangerous to use the industry or sector assumptions unless you were sure that Borders tracked the industry or sector closely. Watch for the effects of one-time write-offs — in this case, for Borders.com (see Chapter 8). And now for Value Line, shown in Figure 12-4.

quicken.com Stock Evaluator GROWTH RATE selections		
Source	**timeframe**	**Borders Group**
		BGP
Analysts	5 year average	17.0%
	5 year low	15.0%
	5 year high	22.0%
Company history	3 year	-23.4%
	1 year	-72.7%
Industry	10 year	31.4%
	5 year	-2.9%
	3 year	-24.7%
	1 year	-68.9%
Sector	10 year	14.2%
	5 year	5.6%
	3 year	-4.6%
	1 year	-31.0%
S&P 500	10 year	13.7%
	5 year	9.4%
	3 year	11.7%
	1 year	2.2%

Figure 12-3: Quicken Stock Evaluator growth assumptions.

ANNUAL RATES of change (per sh)	Past 10 Yrs.	Past 5 Yrs.	Est'd '98-'00 to '04-'06
Sales	– –	10.5%	9.5%
"Cash Flow"	– –	16.0%	11.0%
Earnings	– –	20.5%	14.0%
Dividends	– –	– –	Nil
Book Value	– –	10.0%	12.0%

Figure 12-4: Value Line growth assumptions.

From the Annual Rates breakdown on the left of the Investment Survey page, you can see that the estimated 1998–2000 to 2004–2006 *earnings* growth rate is 14 percent. This is what we used in the sample model, although Value Line's projection covers only five to eight years, not ten years. We could well have gone more conservative. In the model, it is easy to change growth assumptions and compare one to another (which we show later in this chapter).

Regardless of how you decide to formulate your growth assumptions, it is important to be consistent. Comparing two businesses by using different approaches to growth and discounting assumptions can lead to trouble.

First- and second-stage growth

The tools and techniques just presented are useful for projecting first-stage growth, but start to fall apart when assessing second-stage growth. Not even the most self-assured analysts try to pin down growth rates beyond ten years!

You have to be careful with this one. Excessive second-stage growth rates will really distort results because so much time is involved. And no matter what the company is, sooner or later it will exhaust market growth and penetration opportunities. Second-stage growth rates should be less than first-stage growth rates and less than 10 percent, probably no more than 5 percent or 6 percent. Conservative is better.

If you're uncomfortable with second-stage growth rates and their effect on valuation (and many investors are), you can use the acquisition model presented in the section "Making the acquisition assumption," later in this chapter. Although this model implies an acquisition will definitely happen that, in reality, may not happen, it does reduce sensitivity to input assumptions.

Choosing a discount assumption

We now go where many, many others have gone before — tackling what discount rate you should choose to assign value to future earnings streams.

There is no easy or exact answer.

In theory, the discount rate should be your own personal cost of capital for this kind of investment. If you have a million bucks and can invest it with no risk in a Treasury bond at 6 percent, your cost of capital is the risk-free 6 percent you would forgo by not investing in the bond. So the implied cost of your dollars made available to invest in Business XYZ starts at 6 percent. Financial types refer to this opportunity cost as the *risk-free cost of capital*.

But implicitly, Company XYZ common stock is riskier than the bond investment. Sales, earnings, and myriad other intrinsic things can change, as can markets and the market perception of XYZ's worth. So an *equity premium* is added to the risk-free cost of capital rate. In effect, the total cost of capital is your required compensation, or *hurdle*, for the opportunity you've lost by not buying the bond, plus the assumption of risk by investing in XYZ.

Here's where we depart from the stacks of research papers and finance textbooks. Much has gone into identifying appropriate risk premiums and the like. Modern portfolio theory and its reliance on *beta* — a measure of relative stock price volatility — doesn't really do much for us, nor for most value investors (price doesn't determine value, right?).

The keep-it-simple approach used by most value investors, including Warren Buffett, involves using one of two approaches:

✔ Discount at the bond rate (6 percent in our example). This gives a relatively high valuation. Then create a margin of safety by buying at a significant discount to intrinsic value.

✔ Discount at a consistent and relatively high rate (Buffett uses 15 percent as a hurdle). If intrinsic value still looks attractive, you're on the right track.

At this point, we again introduce choices provided by the Quicken.com Stock Evaluator (see Figure 12-5):

Figure 12-5:
Quicken
Stock
Evaluator
discount
assump-
tions.

quicken.com Stock Evaluator DISCOUNT RATE selections	
1 year T-bill	5%
30 year long bond	6%
S&P long term return	11%

At the Quicken.com Intrinsic Value model (for access, see the "Fun With Quicken" sidebar earlier), find the pull-down menu under Discount rate that shows the following:

1-year T-bill	5%
30-year long bond	6%
S&P long-term return	11%

As you build and run models, you'll see firsthand how the discount rate affects the resulting intrinsic value. Here are a few points to remember:

✔ The higher the discount rate, the lower the intrinsic value — and vice versa.

✔ The second-stage discount rate should always be higher than the first stage. Risk increases the farther out you go.

✔ If you choose an aggressive growth rate, it makes sense also to choose a higher discount rate. Risk of failure is higher with high growth rates.

✔ If the discount rate exceeds the growth rate, intrinsic value will be low and implode quickly the larger the gap. Aggressive growth assumptions with low discount rates yield very high intrinsic values. You can find examples under "The Wide World of Intrinsic Value Results."

If you're worried about earnings and earnings growth consistency and want to factor it in somehow, but don't want to do a deep statistical analysis on a zillion numbers, Value Line does one for you. At the bottom right corner of the Investment Survey sheet is a figure called "Earnings Predictability." It's really a statistical predictability score normalized to 100 (100 is best, 0 is worst). A score of 80 and above indicates relative safety; below 80 means that you may want to attenuate growth rates or bump up the discount rate to account for uncertainty.

So, with all of that behind us, here again is the set of growth and discount assumptions we use for this example. Remember that consistency is important as you apply this model to different companies.

First-stage growth	14%
Second-stage growth	6%
First-stage discount rate	12%
Second-stage discount rate	15%

Earnings, shares outstanding, EPS

All that, just to cover the first box in the intrinsic value spreadsheet. Where are we going with this? Should there be a separate *Intrinsic Value For Dummies* book?

The reality is that the rest of the worksheet, even with formulas, is relatively simple. You will make or break the analysis with the four numbers you supply for the first block.

Earnings, number of shares, and EPS come straight from the statements. We use Value Line for simplicity and consistency.

We've chosen to project total, rather than per share, earnings streams, mostly so that at the end we can easily subtract out total (not per share) long-term debt. You may choose to base growth and discounts either on total or per share earnings — it's up to you.

When loading beginning earnings, remember to adjust for one-time or extraordinary gains or charges.

Calculated ten-year earnings stream

Here we go with the first of two sets of formulas. This section projects growth during each year of the first stage and then discounts the resulting value back to the present. The spreadsheet formulas are straightforward:

For each year

> Multiply beginning earnings by $[(1 + g1)n]$
>
> where **g1** is the first-stage growth rate
>
> and **n** is the year number of the future year.

Then

> Divide that figure by $[(1 + d1)n]$
>
> where **d1** is the first-stage discount rate.

The resulting figures represent projected earnings for each year, discounted to the present. Remember again, dollar figures, except per-share amounts, are in millions.

Year 1	$74.91
Year 2	$76.25
Year 3	$77.61
Year 4	$79.00
Year 5	$80.41
Year 6	$81.85
Year 7	$83.31
Year 8	$84.80
Year 9	$86.31
Year 10	$87.85

Total discounted return, first ten years

We get to the sum of the first 10 years discounted earnings stream by summing the figure for each year. This represents the total discounted value of first stage:

Continuing value

Here comes the biggest mathematical ugliness. We must calculate a value for all future returns, ostensibly from here to eternity. Without even touching the mathematical basis for the approximation, here is the formula:

$$[E \times (1 + g1)^n + 1] \div (d2 - g2) \text{ all divided by } (1+d1)^n$$

where

E is beginning earnings

g1 and **d1** are first-stage growth and discount rates, respectively

g2 and **d2** are second-stage growth and discount rates, respectively

n is the number of years in the first stage, in this case, 10

Just close your eyes and put this formula in the spreadsheet. Then ask your neighbor's 14-year-old son to explain the math behind it. (When you get the explanation, mail it to us.)

So what you have here is a single value approximating discounted value of *all* future returns for the business beyond the first stage:

Continuing value beyond 10 years = $1,112.78 million

Total discounted future returns value

The next step is to add first-stage and second-stage *continuing* discounted value — $812.30 million and $1112.78 million. You get $1,925.08 million

Long-term debt adjustment

Normally you'd be done, but earnings not owned free and clear must be recognized. To arrive at the net intrinsic value, you must subtract long-term debt (from Value Line or statements), which in this case is $15 million.

Net future returns value

Net of what you owe, this is the total intrinsic value, based on future returns, of our business: $1,910.08 million ($1925.08 total discounted value less $15 in long term debt).

Per share intrinsic value

Divide net future returns value by the number of shares outstanding to get a per share intrinsic value. This is the magic number you can use to compare with market price and to compare the differential to market price to other companies: $23.91.

And you're done!

Making the acquisition assumption

If the continuing value formula makes you nervous, and if the idea behind it of trying to project to eternity makes you equally nervous, there is another approach. The approach is to assume that someone else will buy the business from you at a fair value at the end of the first stage. So in essence, you get continuing value in a lump sum payment, which of course must also be discounted for time value.

Before we show the model, here are a few things you should know:

- ✔ Growth and discount assumptions are the same as the indefinite life model.

- ✔ The price paid by the acquirer is the key challenge that makes or breaks this model. That price is calculated based on a ratio of price to book. Earnings during the first stage are used to grow the base book value. (Watch out: If the company pays dividends, those earnings don't accrue to book value but must be tracked and discounted as a separate income stream in valuation.) You then supply an assumption of what price-to-book value is appropriate ten years down the road and use that to determine the cash-out price.

- ✔ Because book value is already net-of-debt, you don't have a long-term debt factor.

- ✔ This calculation is based on per-share earnings and book value, again because you don't have long-term debt.

Figure 12-6 shows the ten-year acquisition version of the intrinsic value worksheet.

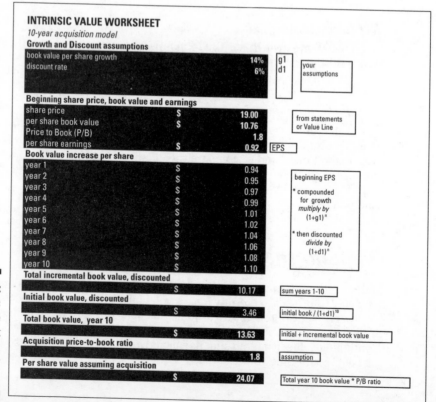

Figure 12-6: Intrinsic value worksheet for a ten-year acquisition.

INTRINSIC VALUE WORKSHEET
10-year acquisition model

Growth and Discount assumptions

book value per share growth		14%	g1
discount rate		6%	d1

your assumptions

Beginning share price, book value and earnings

share price	$	19.00
per share book value	$	10.76
Price to Book (P/B)		1.8
per share earnings	$	0.92

from statements or Value Line

EPS

Book value increase per share

year 1	$	0.94
year 2	$	0.95
year 3	$	0.97
year 4	$	0.99
year 5	$	1.01
year 6	$	1.02
year 7	$	1.04
year 8	$	1.06
year 9	$	1.08
year 10	$	1.10

beginning EPS

* compounded for growth *multiply by* $(1+g1)^n$

* then discounted *divide by* $(1+d1)^n$

Total incremental book value, discounted

$	10.17

sum years 1-10

Initial book value, discounted

$	3.46

initial book / $(1+d1)^{10}$

Total book value, year 10

$	13.63

initial + incremental book value

Acquisition price-to-book ratio

	1.8

assumption

Per share value assuming acquisition

$	24.07

Total year 10 book value * P/B ratio

If you followed the indefinite life version, you'll find this one fairly straightforward. Growth and discount assumptions are the same. Base values are share price and per-share book value, which are used to calculate an initial price-to-book ratio. You then supply a per-share-earnings figure to begin growth and discounting operations.

The book value is assumed to increase by each year's grown and discounted earnings. (Again, if dividends are in the picture, subtract them out and value them as a separate income stream.) The formula for growing earnings and discounting to the present is the same, except that you apply it to per-share earnings instead of total earnings.

To figure out what happens in the tenth year, when the supposed acquisition takes place, here's what to do:

1. Sum up the discounted increments to book value, much as you discounted incremental first-stage earnings earlier.

2. Take today's book value and assume that it remains intact ten years from now. This value is discounted back to the present. One factor favoring this version of the model is that some value is explicitly placed on productive *assets* owned by the business.

3. Total the estimated ten-year book value.

4. Now comes the fun part: figuring out the acquisition price based on the price-to-book (P/B) ratio. What price-to-book should you use, anyway? We suggest using today's P/B — unless it is excessively high. Markets have a way of diminishing P/B ratios over time, as book values are expected to grow and premiums related to growth and newness decline. We suggest capping the ten-year P/B ratio at 3.0 by using a MAX formula. In Microsoft Excel, you can use the @MAX function to assign a maximum value, or limit, to the result. In this case it's 3.0, and the formula would be @MAX (3.0, beginning P/B).

5. Multiply the total ten-year book value by acquisition P/B and, *voilà*, there's your intrinsic value.

The indefinite life model and ten-year acquisition models yield similar results!

A few hours of flight: Comparing companies

To get a better feel for the intrinsic value model and its spreadsheet version, we prepared a comparative table for ten popular companies, including the Borders example highlighted in this chapter. The model used in Figure 12-7 is the indefinite life version.

INTRINSIC VALUE COMPARISON	Source	Microsoft MSFT	Borders BGP	Hewlett-Packard HWP	IBM	Oracle ORCL	Sun Microsystems SUNW	Wal-Mart WMT	Gillette G	Coca-cola KO
Growth and Discount assumptions										
first stage growth	Value Line	14%	14%	14%	13%	23%	17%	14%	9%	10%
second stage growth	assumption	6%	6%	6%	6%	6%	6%	6%	6%	6%
first stage discount rate	assumption	12%	12%	12%	12%	12%	12%	12%	12%	12%
second stage discount rate	assumption	15%	15%	15%	15%	15%	15%	15%	15%	15%
earnings predictability	Value Line	85	70	80	35	80	80	90	85	75
Earnings assumptions										
beginning earnings	Value Line	$ 9,421	74	3,600	8,093	2,055	1,725	6,295	1,251	3,669
number of shares (M)	Value Line	5,382.0	79.9	2000	1760	5613	3260	4470	1054	2485
beginning EPS	calculation	$ 1.75	0.92	1.80	4.60	0.37	0.53	1.41	1.19	1.48
Discounted 10-year earnings stream										
year 1 (all $M)	calculation	$ 9,589.23	74.91	3,664.29	8,165.26	2,256.83	1,802.01	6,407.41	1,211.91	3,587.10
year 2	compound earnings growth	$ 9,760.47	76.25	3,729.72	8,238.16	2,478.48	1,882.46	6,521.83	1,174.03	3,507.03
year 3	discounted	$ 9,934.76	77.61	3,796.32	8,311.72	2,721.91	1,966.49	6,638.29	1,137.35	3,428.75
year 4		$ 10,112.17	79.00	3,864.11	8,385.93	2,989.24	2,054.28	6,756.83	1,101.80	3,352.22
year 5		$ 10,292.74	80.41	3,933.11	8,460.80	3,282.82	2,145.99	6,877.49	1,067.37	3,277.39
year 6		$ 10,476.54	81.85	4,003.35	8,536.35	3,605.24	2,241.80	7,000.30	1,034.02	3,204.23
year 7		$ 10,663.62	83.31	4,074.84	8,612.56	3,959.33	2,341.88	7,125.31	1,001.70	3,132.71
year 8		$ 10,854.05	84.80	4,147.60	8,689.46	4,348.19	2,446.42	7,252.54	970.40	3,062.78
year 9		$ 11,047.87	86.31	4,221.67	8,767.05	4,775.24	2,555.64	7,382.05	940.08	2,994.42
year 10		$ 11,245.15	87.85	4,297.05	8,845.32	5,244.24	2,669.73	7,513.88	910.70	2,927.58
Discounted 10-year value	total years 1-10	$ 103,976.61	812.30	39,732.06	85,012.62	35,661.52	22,106.70	69,475.93	10,549.36	32,474.22
Continuing value (> 10 years)	continuing value formula	$ 142,438.58	1,112.78	54,429.35	111,057.96	71,671.31	34,706.50	95,175.76	10,978.97	35,618.88
total value future returns	years 1-10 plus terminal value	$ 246,415.18	1,925.08	94,161.41	196,070.58	107,332.83	56,813.21	164,651.69	21,528.33	68,093.11
Long term debt	Value Line	$ -	15	3,402	18,371	303	2,183	15,655	1,650	835
Net value future returns	total returns less LT debt	$ 246,415.18	1,910.08	90,759.41	177,699.58	107,029.83	54,630.21	148,996.69	19,878.33	67,258.11
Intrinsic value per share	Net value / # shares	$ 45.79	23.91	45.38	100.97	19.07	16.76	33.33	18.86	27.07
Recent price	June 2001	$ 70.00	19.00	30.00	115.00	16.00	17.00	51.00	28.00	48.00
Intrinsic value and P/E										
implied P/E	intrinsic value/ TTM earnings	26.2	26.0	25.2	22.0	52.1	31.7	23.7	15.9	18.3
implied PEG	implied P/E / first stage growth	1.9	1.9	1.8	1.7	2.3	1.9	1.7	1.9	1.9

Figure 12-7:
Intrinsic value comparison of selected companies.

Interestingly, you'll notice that some of the more growth-oriented technology companies, notably, HP, Oracle, and Sun Microsystems, were priced close to, or below, intrinsic value in 2001, while value stocks such as Coke, Gillette, Wal-Mart, and Quaker were selling at premiums to their intrinsic value! Quite a turnaround from 1999–2000. Maybe the analysts *do* know what they're doing (finally) with tech stocks? Or maybe our growth and discount assumptions are still too aggressive?

Anyway, it's a fun — and useful — sort of table to prepare when examining intrinsic value for a group of related or unrelated companies. It can tell you which ones merit further study.

The Quicken Jet

The preceding few sections take the spreadsheet version for a spin to accomplish two purposes: to get you familiar with the model construct and to (hopefully) provide enough information so that you can build your own.

Now we hop over into the Quicken.com cockpit to illustrate this tool and to also show the wide variety of results you can get when flying any intrinsic value "aircraft."

What the Quicken intrinsic value model looks like

Dial up www.quicken.com/investments/seceval, enter a symbol, and look for the intrinsic value model to see the Quicken.com model.

If you didn't tour this area of Quicken.com earlier, when checking out their growth and discount assumptions, you can see the drop-down boxes offering growth and discount assumption choices. These can be selected using the radio buttons furnished. Happily, you can also supply your own assumptions. You can even supply your own initial earnings if you want. Otherwise, you rely on whatever is in the Quicken database.

An interesting feature is Quicken's automatic discount rate assignment. It takes a risk-free return and adds an equity risk premium that is driven by the number of years the company has been in existence. Shorter existence equals a higher discount rate. Interesting, but as Borders was spun off from Kmart eight years ago, the discount rate skied to 17 percent because of the short life — probably a bit too conservative. You're the pilot, so take control.

The model used is the same as the indefinite value spreadsheet. It's easy to exercise the model with different assumptions, and Quicken provides a handy price-to-intrinsic-value comparison and Insights and Walk through sections discussing the result. By clicking on the blue Intrinsic Value link in the text, you can also review mathematical formulas, if you're so inclined.

Remember that this is a canned model, and you'll get canned results if you don't manage it carefully. Garbage in, garbage out.

The wide world of intrinsic value results

You can exercise the intrinsic value model by using the Quicken calculator to obtain a range of growth and discount assumptions, all within a degree of reasonableness.

With a range of aggressive, moderate, and conservative growth and discount assumptions, you can quickly arrive at a fantastic variety of intrinsic values, even for a relatively stable company such as Borders. Intrinsic valuations range from $5.47 a share all the way to $173.16. If you adjust base earnings to remove extraordinary write-downs, you end up with a range of $7.29 to north of $228!

Can you base an investment decision on such a wide range? It's like trying to find a runway in a 200 mile-an-hour wind. Such is the reason — now made plain on your radar screen — why these simple spreadsheets don't provide the panacea that many investors seek. We can take off or land with intrinsic value. With a reasonable, stable set of assumptions, these models have value. But a deeper understanding of the business is in order before committing hard-earned dollars, and our "flight plan" for developing more understanding is to examine strategic financials and intangibles.

The Ben Graham Model

We also want to look at intrinsic value through the eyes of Ben Graham, based on his 1930s formula:

Intrinsic value = Earnings × [(2 × growth rate) + 8.5] × [4.4 ÷ bond yield]

Well — how about this — a simple straight-line formula, no exponents, no first- and second-stage stuff, no discount rate? Could it work? Take a look at Borders Group:

Intrinsic value = 0.92 × [(2 × 14%) + 8.5] × [4.4 ÷ 6%]

By way of explanation, we use the first-stage growth rate, which is the assumption that Graham calls for. The bond rate is 6 percent. We also use the full $0.92/share earnings before extraordinary items, and arrive at:

$24.62

which is quite within range of the $23.91 from the indefinite life and the $24.07 from the ten-year acquisition models presented earlier. Actually, Graham would have arrived at a slightly smaller number, preferring corporate bond yields as his benchmark. A more conservative 7 percent bond benchmark yields an intrinsic value of $21.10.

So the Graham model, derived from the more complex model but philosophically aligned to it, can be used as computational shorthand. It doesn't allow for stages and uses a more simplistic discounting assumption. Moreover, it produces the same wide range of results as the other models. But it is a good shortcut — one you may be able to do in your head when looking at a number of investment choices.

Book value and intrinsic value

A final note — to help lock down the notion of intrinsic value in our brains — comes in another observation from Warren Buffett. Apparently tired of answering questions about how to use book value to make investment decisions, Buffett pointed out the difference between book value and intrinsic value: "Book value is what the owners put *into* the business, intrinsic value is what they *take out* of it." In another explanation offered in an annual report from 1996, he likened book value to college tuition paid, with intrinsic value being the income resulting from the education. The education and the dollars spent on an education mean nothing unless there is a resulting financial return. The point: Many investors put too much emphasis on book value and not enough on intrinsic value.

Chapter 13

Running the Numbers: Strategic Financials

After all, if a focus [investor] hasn't got the economics right in the portfolio, it is unlikely Mr. Market will ever find the occasion to reward the selections.

—*Robert Hagstrom,* The Warren Buffett Portfolio

Chapter 12 shows that profits and growth drive intrinsic value. For any fairly priced asset to increase in value over time, the value of the returns must grow. You may or may not indulge in calculations to estimate intrinsic value. But be aware that earnings and growth *do* matter. The time value of money and the value of alternatives *do* matter. When you look at a business, you seek consistent, growing returns on a quality asset base — achieving reasonable returns without taking on unreasonable risk.

If it isn't easy to pin down growth and the value of growth, it gets a little easier to step back and identify business traits that drive growth. Sustained return on equity (ROE) implies sustained growth and blares out loudly "well managed company!" In this chapter, we examine ROE and its component drivers: profitability, productivity, and capital structure. These strategic financials represent knobs and levers that management can shape and control to achieve growth, ROE, and, hence, intrinsic value.

Yes, we indulge in another formula: the *strategic profit formula*. This formula breaks ROE down into component parts for better understanding and examination. We look at each component and what factors drive it. We finish up with a sample checklist that you can employ. And there is no complex math!

It's All about ROE

ROE is, when all is said and done, a capitalist's bottom line. Simply, it represents the return on owner's equity invested in the business. As a practical matter, although it can be jiggered somewhat through accounting policy and practice, it's a good barometer to determine whether the company is on the right track and whether management is doing a good job.

ROE in the scheme of things

Unlike intrinsic value, ROE from the beginning doesn't purport to estimate the value of a company. You can't go through a series of calculations, out of the bottom of which pops a shiny new per-share value estimate. But ROE — and its components — can tell whether things are going the right way. Although intrinsic value is an absolute measure of company value, ROE and its components tend to be relative to past performance and to the performance of other businesses.

As in the adage "where there's smoke, there's fire," we believe that where there's ROE, there's intrinsic value. Likewise, where there's sustained ROE, solid and improving strategic financials and intangibles lurk just below the surface.

Growing to stay the same?

On the surface, a steady ROE would appear to indicate a ho-hum business. Same old, same old, year in and year out. But quite the contrary. Many investors, Warren Buffett himself included, get pretty excited when they see steady ROE over a number of years, particularly when already at a high level, say, greater than 15 percent.

Why?

ROE is defined as net earnings divided by owner's equity. What happens to net earnings, each year, in well-managed companies? They become part of owner's equity as retained earnings. Where are we going with this? Well, as time goes on, the denominator of the ROE equation goes up, as earnings become equity (unless a portion of earnings are paid out as dividends). Here are a couple maxims worth highlighting:

✔ Maintaining a constant ROE percentage requires steady earnings growth.

✔ A company with increasing ROE, without undue exposure to debt or leverage, is especially attractive.

In fact, over time, ROE trends towards the earnings growth rate of the company. A company with a 5 percent earnings growth rate and a 20 percent ROE today will see ROE gradually diminish towards 5 percent. A company with a 20 percent earnings growth rate and a 10 percent ROE will see ROE move towards 20 percent, as the numerator grows at a faster rate than the denominator.

We spare you detailed examples, but you can try this yourself with a spreadsheet (or in the shower if you're a mental math type!)

Big green in Big Blue

As we searched our research and experience to find an example of ROE excellence, we naturally let our fingers do the walking through Berkshire companies (those with public reporting, anyway, such as Coke and Gillette). We also examined Borders Group, the subject of frequent earlier examples. Although all these companies exhibited strength in ROE and its driving numbers, one slight dark horse of a company jumped out at us: good old Big Blue — IBM!

If you look at IBM's track record over the past ten years, it's clear that CEO Louis Gerstner has placed particular emphasis on managing ROE, among other things. When Buffett and others look for excellent management, they look for managers who manage the owner's bottom line, rather than sales growth, record earnings reports, and the like. Gerstner seems to have taken ROE to heart.

What has IBM done? Simply, ROE has moved on a near-steady up-and-to-the-right path, from about 5 percent to almost 40 percent as reported for 2000, as shown in Figure 13-1.

Is this a fluke? Did IBM simply borrow its way to improved owner returns? The numbers say no, and in fact, IBM has sneaked quietly past the industry in profit margins and asset productivity, as we soon explore in more detail. Significantly, while raising the earnings bridge, IBM also lowered the equity river not by borrowing, but by deliberately and religiously using earnings to buy back stock.

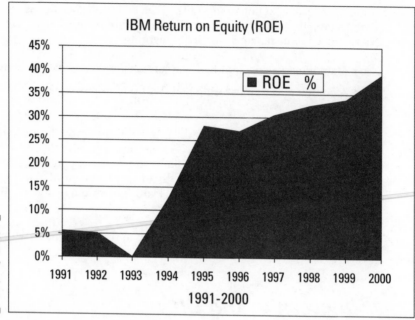

Figure 13-1:
IBM Return on Equity (ROE), 1991–2000.

Shares outstanding have declined almost a quarter, from 2.3 billion to under 1.8 billion in the ten-year period. Stock buybacks aren't always a good thing, as they sometimes tell a story of a bad business with few productive investments. But IBM through this period has grown sales, profits, profit margins, return on assets, and a host of other things, indicating good business and good strategic decisions from the helm.

ROE versus ROTC

ROTC? Military service to become a value investor? Before entertaining visions of value investors marching around parade grounds in brightly colored uniforms, be clear that we're talking about another measure of owner returns: *return on total capital*. What's that? Owner's equity plus long-term debt. Why? So that we can see through the effects of leverage. If a company is growing ROE but not ROTC, chances are, the company is doing it by borrowing to fund growth producing assets, thus leveraging the company (this *can* be a good thing in moderation). So look at ROTC and ROE together. They should march side by side and change in unison. Many information services such as Value Line provide both figures simultaneously.

The Strategic Value Chain

There is a chain of events that underlies ROE. ROE doesn't just happen all by itself. A series of business fundamentals, all linked together, leads to respectable, sustained, and growing ROE. In a minute, we represent the chain by — ugh! — another formula. (For those of you with weak mathematical stomachs, have no fear. This one isn't too bad. If you made it through ratios, you'll do all right. And like other math stuff presented in this book, it's the principle that counts!)

Strategic fundamentals

The links in the strategic value chain are the business fundamentals that directly influence ROE and are controlled or influenced by management. The links are profitability, productivity, and capital structure. When all three are strong and tight, ROE outcome is destined for success. If there is a weakest link (a business fundamental that is poor or failing), it can weaken the entire chain and hamper ROE indefinitely.

Strategic fundamentals are manageable business fundamentals that management can influence or control to maintain or increase ROE.

And now, the formula

Although this formula surfaces in business schools around the country, it owes its origins to the real world. Some years back, it originated in the finance department at DuPont. It's called the "strategic profit formula" and, in some circles, the "DuPont formula."

Return on equity = [profits/sales] × [sales/assets] × [assets/equity]

It's easy to see the links in the chain: profitability, productivity, and capital structure, in sequence. Good managers work on each one, and we talk about how to do so in a minute.

The formula is like one of the easier high school chemistry or physics formulas in which you take the numerator on the first term and the denominator on the last term and cancel out everything in between. Only here, we don't cancel out intermediate terms, because they tell us so much about the health of the business. For each intermediate term in the formula, we want to know its value, in what direction it's going (trend) and how it compares to others in the industry.

Three tiers for ROE

Each link in the ROE chain has its own component drivers. For instance, gross margins and expenses drive profitability. Asset levels, quality, and turnover drive productivity, while debt and new capital requirements drive capital structure. To create a useful evaluation framework, we define first- and second-tier fundamentals. *First-tier fundamentals* define a ROE value chain link; that is, profitability or productivity. *Second-tier fundamentals* drive or influence the first tier and are usually measurable. *Third-tier fundamentals* are usually intangibles that drive or influence the second-tier metrics (see Figure 13-2).

So for instance, net profit percent is the first-tier metric for profitability. From this measurable figure, go a step backward to define gross margin as a measurable second-tier driver of net profit. Then, go another step backward in the chain to examine items that affect gross margins. For example, consider market position, price power, franchise or brand value, cost of inputs, cost of doing business — many of which are intangibles. Third-tier drivers may also give a quality check, for instance, cash flow or book value checks on earnings quality.

The value investor works backwards through the ROE value chain to find good or bad in ROE drivers and the things that influence those drivers. (You can find out more about intangibles in Chapter 14.) Later on, we present a structure and checklist that you might use to analyze businesses.

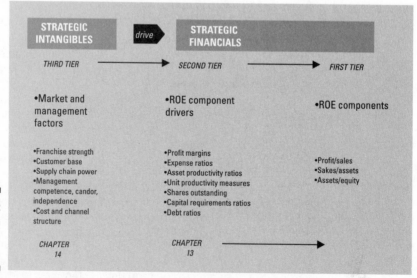

Figure 13-2:
The Strategic Value Chain.

"Drug tests"

If you apply for a job, you may have to take a drug test. Does passing the drug test mean that you get the job? Nope. Does failing the drug test mean that you won't get the job? Yep. So how does this apply to investing?

When you look at strategic financials and fundamentals, some characteristics of the business are normally expected to be okay, but if they're off course, they may raise red flags. They can be looked at as sort of a final analysis quality check. For example, low debt doesn't necessarily indicate high value, but frequent trips to the capital markets for debt or stock sales may indicate capital starvation and "un-value." And continuing with the drug test metaphor, the "substances" you "test" frequently are addictive to bad managements: overuse of acquisitions, write-offs and write-downs, debt, and stock sales, which are used to pad numbers and fix problems arising from bad performance.

We do "drug tests" for each of the first-tier components of ROE. Drug tests are usually painless pass/fail tests, not detailed assessments.

A Big Blue Example

Formulas, numbers . . . okay, you may as well as get it over with. Figure 13-3 shows a set of numbers for IBM for the last five years.

IBM ROE and STRATEGIC PROFIT FORMULA

		2000	1999	1998	1997	1996
PROFITABILITY						
Revenue	$	88,396	$ 85,748	$ 81,667	$ 78,508	$ 75,947
Gross Profit	$	32,424	$ 31,929	$ 30,872	$ 30,969	$ 30,539
Gross Margin %		*36.7%*	*37.2%*	*37.8%*	*39.4%*	*40.2%*
SG&A	$	15,639	$ 14,729	$ 16,662	$ 16,634	$ 16,634
SG&A %		*17.7%*	*17.2%*	*20.4%*	*21.2%*	*21.9%*
Operating Profit	$	11,634	$ 11,927	$ 9,164	$ 9,098	$ 8,596
Operating Profit %		*13.2%*	*13.9%*	*11.2%*	*11.6%*	*11.3%*
Net Profit	$	8,073	$ 7,692	$ 6,308	$ 6,673	$ 5,409
NET PROFIT / SALES (a)		*9.1%*	*9.0%*	*7.7%*	*8.5%*	*7.1%*
PRODUCTIVITY						
Total Assets	$	88,349	$ 87,495	$ 86,100	$ 81,499	$ 81,132
SALES/ASSETS (b)		*1.00*	*0.98*	*0.95*	*0.96*	*0.94*
CAPITAL STRUCTURE						
Total Equity	$	20,624	$ 20,511	$ 19,433	$ 19,816	$ 21,628
ASSETS/ EQUITY (c)		*4.28*	*4.27*	*4.43*	*4.11*	*3.75*
RETURN ON EQUITY (a*b*c)		*39.1%*	*37.5%*	*32.5%*	*33.7%*	*25.0%*

Figure 13-3: ROE and Strategic Profit Formula numbers.

Finding the data

The set of numbers in Figure 13-3 provides all that you need to start a strategic financial analysis of Big Blue. The numbers are *almost* all available on Value Line. Unfortunately, for some reason, VL doesn't provide figures on total assets and, somewhat less importantly, on selling, general, and administrative expenses (SG&A). If VL went the extra distance to include these figures, we would have 15 full years of history at our fingertips. Still, Value Line is an excellent source for ROE, sales, and profit margin components to start your analysis. Where did we get the other figures? From the Multex Investor Market Guide" supplement on the Yahoo! Finance Profile and Ratio Comparison pages. It's a good source and free (for now), but it offers less depth and only five years of history. Sometimes you take what you can get. Note: these resources are discussed in greater detail in Chapter 5.

Be wary of extraordinary items and write-offs that can corrupt individual numbers and trends. When asset productivity gains result from cutting out slop (not from better utilization), it doesn't count as much. It may be unsustainable and may even mask bad management practice.

Running the numbers

Now for the math. Here's the formula:

Return on equity = [profits/sales] × [sales/assets] × [assets/equity]

The components for fiscal year 2000 (dollars in millions):

Profitability: profit/sales = $8073 ÷ $88396, or **9.1**%

Productivity: sales/assets = $88396 ÷ $88349, or **1.001**%

Capital structure: assets/equity = $88349 ÷ $20627, or **4.28**%

Multiply these together, and you get 39.1 percent, the reported ROE figure for 2000.

Okay, so now what?

As you become familiar with this sort of analysis, you'll come to realize that none of the intermediate ratios — profit/sales, sales/assets, or assets/equity — in and of themselves, are truly outstanding. True, profitability as net profit margin is higher than the industry (9.1 percent versus 6.61 percent, from Multex Market Guide/Yahoo! Finance ratio comparison table), but there's nothing outstanding in the other numbers. Assets at four times equity imply a lot of leverage, but a closer look at the balance sheet reveals use of short-term liabilities ($36 billion) and not too much long-term debt ($18 billion). (You may recall the Foolish Flow ratio presented in Chapter 10).

What is compelling is the steady, *coordinated* strengthening in all drivers: profitability, productivity, and capital structure. The business appears to be hitting on all cylinders in balance. Now we take a look at each ROE driver independently and comment on some important factors within each driver.

Profitability

The primary, or first-tier, measure for profitability is net profit percent. No surprise here. For IBM, growth in net profit percent from 7.1 percent to 9.1 percent in five years is a good story, but it isn't the whole story. It's a better story than just nominal earnings dollar or EPS growth; it says that the business is becoming more productive in generating earnings. The ten-year story, readily available from Value Line, tells a stronger story still.

The second tier

When looking at profitability, the second tier measures a clearer view of the dynamics behind net profit percent. We look at gross margin, SG&A, and operating profit percent.

Gross margin

Gross margin tells a lot about a business's success in managing its sales and direct costs of producing product and services. A company on top of its marketing and production game usually produces improving margins.

But market characteristics and selling aggressiveness can work against margins. Intuitively, you might guess that increased volumes lead to increased margins, as fixed costs are absorbed and economies of scale work in their favor. However, this isn't always the case. A company often must make price concessions to achieve sales goals. And aggressive volume building also takes its toll on operating costs (not part of gross margin) in the form of marketing expenses and sometimes interest expense to expand the level of business.

To some extent you must understand the industry in which you want to invest. For example, anyone around computers knows that there is heavy competition in that industry and that aggressive market share building campaigns based on price have long been underway. This intangible phenomenon has clearly affected IBM's gross margin, which has actually declined to just under 37 percent from just over 40 percent in five years. This sends a pale yellow flag, but these gross margins are still higher than most of their competitors (32.7 percent industry average based on a broad definition of the industry, as shown later in Figure 13-6).

Selling, general, and administrative

Selling, general, and administrative (SG&A), although not directly tied to net profit percent, tells a lot about how management controls expenses and how expenses are tied to business production. SG&A normally includes marketing expenses such as advertising and customer incentives, in addition to more traditional selling salaries, commissions, and so on. SG&A percentage is the total SG&A cost divided by sales or revenues. You have to calculate this one yourself, as few information sources provide this one. It is an important part of total operating expenses — and thus operating profit percentage. Also be aware that different companies define SG&A differently. so look to annual reports for clarification.

When SG&A increases faster than sales, that's a dark yellow or orange flag. Although investors tolerate short-term expenditures in marketing campaigns, store openings, or customer relationship management platforms, these can't go on forever. Chronic SG&A percentage increases are a red flag.

In fact, if a company is realizing the benefits of economies of scale, SG&A expenses should *grow* at a rate *less* than sales. SG&A growth persistently matching sales is a yellow flag. As a general rule, most analysts look for sustained SG&A *growth* rates at 80 percent or less of the sales growth rate.

IBM successfully trimmed the SG&A percent from almost 22 percent to less than 18 percent.

Operating profit

SG&A is part of this important figure, but certainly not all. Depreciation, amortization, and certain facility and employee costs can all influence operating expenses. A company in control of gross margin *and* operating expenses will show increased operating profit. Even though IBM endured deteriorating gross margins, focus on *total* profitability and tight control of SG&A and other operating expenses resulted in growth of operating profit percentages from 11.3 percent to 13.2 percent.

Drug test

It's up to you to define your profitability "drug tests." We suggest three:

- Overdependence on acquisitions for growth. Companies sometimes get so caught up in building the top line that they resort to painful and expensive acquisitions to do it. Profitability usually suffers.

✔ Deferred, unaggressive amortizations. Slow asset depreciation and goodwill amortization indicates a management trying to pad or "save" an earnings number, particularly if policies have changed in that direction.

✔ Cash flow and changes in book value march with changes in earnings. If earnings rise but cash flow doesn't and book value doesn't, over time, one must question the quality of earnings.

The third tier: Intangibles

We've mentioned a few intangibles and dig further into the subject in Chapter 14. But it's worth reinforcing the key intangibles that drive profitability, particularly gross margins. Market position is a vital influencer. Market leadership, brand dominance, public image, and pricing power bear the seeds of improved gross margin, while resource acquisition power directly affects costs, which also defines gross margin. Businesses dependent on tight markets for supply invariably suffer in profitability, whether labor, fuel, money (as in banks), or you name it.

We raise many questions about earnings quality throughout this book. Reporting quality qualifies as an intangible attribute of profitability. So a quick spot check of cash flows and changes in book value as they relate to earnings is worthwhile. And once again it's important to understand write-offs and extraordinary items that may affect the analysis.

What to look for

Look for improving profitability measures and be able to explain those that aren't improving. You also need to understand market forces and intangibles that drive profitability factors and look at them as leading indicators of future performance. Finally, check with the neighbors to see how other businesses in the industry are faring.

Productivity

Productivity measures tell us how well companies deploy and use assets. Assets are resources there for a single purpose (to generate sales), so you may as well measure how well this is done. All things considered, a dollar of sales produced on 50 cents worth of assets is better than the same company producing a dollar of sales on a dollar of assets. Such an observation shows prima facie asset efficiency and also indicates less asset amortization expense later (higher profitability). Obviously, asset productivity figures vary by industry as different industries require different assets to do business.

The first-tier measure of productivity is sales/assets: the amount of sales generated per asset dollar employed.

First-tier metric: Sales/assets

IBM did almost exactly one dollar in sales for every dollar in assets. Not too bad, and in fact comparable to slightly below larger competitors. The good news is the trend: Sales to assets has crept up to 1.00 from 0.94 five years ago, reflecting better utilization.

Here are the two traps to avoid when looking at sales/assets:

- Misinterpreting large changes due to write-offs. If IBM or any other company took the plunge to purge a big chunk of overvalued or nonexistent assets from the books, that would show up as an "improvement" in sales/assets. Not! Be careful to distill out major changes in asset deployment that create no change in the business.

- Reading too much into the absolute numbers. Sales/assets will be huge for a Microsoft or Oracle, reporting high sales on a small asset base, while a large industrial corporation, railroad, or electric utility requiring a large asset infrastructure will appear to have poor asset utilization. Be careful about comparing across industries.

Deconstructing ROA

In Chapter 10, we discuss return on assets, or ROA. Many popular information services show ROA. If you're wondering why ROA doesn't make the grade as a first-tier measure, here's why: ROA really does too much.

ROA is net profit divided by total assets, which you'll recognize as the first *two* links in the ROE chain *combined*. (Profit/assets = profit/sales × sales/assets, for you math types.) We don't dispute the validity and value of ROA but prefer to look at the two links separately. The first measure, profit/sales, has more to do with market power and cost structures, while the second, sales/assets, has more to do with resource requirements and deployment. Deconstructing ROA provides a more bottoms up, inside-out view of the business.

The sharp reader will note that if ROA and profit margin figures are supplied by an information portal such as Yahoo! Finance or Value Line, one can deduce asset productivity. Bad ROA and good margins equal bad productivity.

Deconstructing sales/assets

An obvious key to understanding total sales/assets is to understand utilization for individual assets making up the total asset base. Accounts receivable, inventory, and fixed assets are the major "food groups" in this value chain.

The analysis is similar to the top-line sales to assets computation. We look at the turnover ratios, essentially sales/accounts receivable, sales/inventory, sales/fixed assets. (For a review, see Chapter 10.) If you "deconstruct" into these tier two measures (see Figure 13-4), you can see an exciting story for IBM — better than the top-line measure would lead you to believe (we get to *why* in a minute).

Accounts receivable turnover

How many dollars in sales does the business generate per dollar of accounts receivable investment? A business on top of its receivables generates more and more, through faster collections and extending less credit altogether. IBM goes the right way in flying colors. In 1996, it generated $3.41 in sales per dollar of accounts receivable (A/R); in 2000, this more than doubled to $8.46.

When examining statements for accounts receivable, use "trade" accounts receivable — those that arise from and support the normal course of business. IBM shows a significant and growing "other" receivable, probably resulting from a business sale or financing. Although these financings can be important to monitor, they don't come from business as usual.

Inventory turnover

This works the same as accounts receivable in principle. A business in control of finished goods, raw material, and production inventories shows greater sales per dollar invested in inventory. IBM went from $12.90 in sales per dollar of inventory to $18.50 — a 50 percent improvement.

Fixed asset turnover

And another turnover measure, this time for fixed assets or PP&E (property, plant, and equipment), IBM got to $5.36 in sales for every dollar of PP&E from $4.36. Not bad — and again in the right direction.

Figure 13-4: Deconstructing Sales/Assets for IBM.

DECONSTRUCTING SALES/ASSETS: IBM	2000	1999	1998	1987	1986
Sales (Revenue)	$ 88,396	$ 85,748	$ 81,667	$ 78,508	$ 75,947
Total Assets	$ 88,349	$ 87,495	$ 86,100	$ 81,499	$ 81,132
SALES/ASSETS	*1.00*	*0.98*	*0.95*	*0.96*	*0.94*
Trade Accounts Receivable	$ 10,447	$ 9,103	$ 18,958	$ 16,850	$ 22,236
Sales/Accounts Receivable	*8.46*	*9.42*	*4.31*	*4.66*	*3.42*
Inventory	$ 4,765	$ 4,868	$ 5,200	$ 5,139	$ 5,870
Sales/Inventory	*18.55*	*17.61*	*15.71*	*15.28*	*12.94*
Fixed assets (PP&E)	$ 16,714	$ 17,590	$ 19,631	$ 18,347	$ 17,407
Sales/PP&E	*5.29*	*4.87*	*4.16*	*4.28*	*4.36*

Why so modest a sales/asset gain when the big three components — accounts receivable, inventory, and fixed assets — showed larger improvements, up to 50 percent? In many cases (not IBM, unfortunately), this is due to increased cash, which is also an asset and part of the denominator base. If a company shows stubbornly little improvement in asset productivity as reported, sometimes it's because of cash accumulation, which is normally a good thing. With IBM, it was because of other assets. Scrupulous value investor should check to make sure what those other assets represent.

Unit productivity measures

If the figures are available, you can go into sales per facility, sales per store, same-store-sales growth, revenue per mile of track or passenger seat flown, or sales per square foot, depending on the industry. For IBM, you could look at sales per employee as a tangible metric, although finding meaningful historic data to build this as a trend is elusive, so we didn't do it. These productivity metrics are good for comparing with other firms in the same industry.

Drug test

You might go farther than we did here, even including some of the unit productivity measures (such as sales to employee) as a drug test. We chose only to look at asset write-downs. If write-downs are excessive and persistent, asset quality — and really, asset acquisition — problems are evident. On the flip side, a company not taking sufficient write-downs may also be suspect. If technology changes, capital equipment is overbought, or sales are declining, asset write-downs not taken may spell trouble. The telecommunications industry is a recent example.

The third tier: Intangibles

Many factors support, verify, or could be leading indicators of asset productivity. As you can see in Chapters 7 through 9, asset quality is greatly influenced by depreciation and amortization policies. Channel structure (direct, single-tier retail, two-tier wholesale-retail, OEM, or other) can greatly influence the amount of assets required, particularly receivables and inventory. And of course, the base nature of the business — the cost structure — can tell a lot. A steel mill has different asset needs and utilization than a nail salon.

What to look for

Looking at trends within individual metrics makes sense — improving values at all tiers is a healthy thing. Give special credit to consistent improvement through business cycles. Depending on the industry, you might balance emphasis on inventory, accounts receivable, and fixed assets differently. For example, you might give more attention to inventory and store utilization when looking at a retailer, while paying more attention to accounts receivable when evaluating an industrial supplier. And it never hurts to compare companies to other companies, so long as you're comparing apples to apples.

Capital Structure

When looking at capital structure, you're trying to determine two things:

✔ Is the business a consumer or producer of capital? Does it constantly require capital infusions to build growth or replace assets? Warren Buffett tends to shun businesses that cannot generate sufficient capital on their own. In fact, one of the guiding principles behind Berkshire Hathaway is the generation of excess capital by subsidiary businesses that can be deployed elsewhere.

✔ Is the business properly leveraged? Overleveraged businesses are at risk and additionally burden earnings with interest payments. Underleveraged businesses, while better than overleveraged, may not be maximizing potential returns to shareholders.

First-tier metric: Assets/equity

The first-tier measure for capital structure is assets/equity. Per dollar of owner's equity invested, how many dollars of productive assets are deployed in the business?

For IBM, approximately $4.28 of assets is deployed for every $1 of owner's equity on the books. Five years ago, it was $3.75, so the asset base has been growing faster than the owner dollars invested in the business. As we will see, IBM has been steadily buying back shares and returning capital to some owners while increasing owner returns for remaining shareholders.

Second-tier metrics: Is more capital needed?

Capital-hungry companies are sometimes hard to detect, but there are a few obvious signs. Companies in capital-intensive industries, such as manufacturing, transportation, or telecommunications, are likely suspects. Here are a few indicators.

Buying (back) the farm?

The number of shares outstanding can be a real simple indicator of a capital-hungry company. A company using cash to retire shares — if acting sensibly — is telling you that it generates more capital than it needs. A big part of the IBM ROE story is the retirement of almost 600 million shares (2.3 billion to 1.7 billion) in the last five years.

When evaluating share buybacks, make sure to look at actual shares outstanding. Relying on company news releases alone can be misleading. Companies also buy back shares to support employee incentive programs or to accumulate shares for an acquisition. Such repurchases may be okay but aren't the kind of repurchases that increase return on equity for remaining owners.

Cash flow ratio

Recall from Chapter 10 the cash flow ratio, where you see whether cash flow from operations is enough to meet investing requirements (capital assets being the main form of investment) and financing requirements (in this case, the repayment of debt). If not, it's back to the capital markets. This figure is pretty elusive unless you have — and study — statements of cash flow.

Lengthening asset cycles

If accounts receivable collection periods and inventory holding periods are lengthening (number of days' sales in accounts receivable and inventory — see Chapter 10), that forewarns the need for more capital.

Working capital and Foolish Flow

A company requiring steady increases in working capital to support sales requires, naturally, capital. Working capital is capital. Foolish Flow (see Chapter 10) measures the ratio of current assets less cash to current liabilities and is an indicator of whether the business — net net — is successful in living off the capital *of others* as opposed to having others live off the capital of *it*.

The capital of *it*? Who would have thought of such an Addams Family-esque way to explain a valuation concept? Our apologies for the "fester"-ing confusion.

Foolish Flow for IBM actually goes from slightly less than one at 0.97 in 1996 (net user of others' working capital) to 1.10 in 2000. But this is colored by the "other" items mentioned earlier. If you factor out the "other Receivables (do so with care), Foolish Flow drops to 0.64, a healthy user of the capital of others. To some degree, this probably enabled the stock buybacks.

Second-tier metrics: Leverage

Leverage and debt assessments are perpetually subjective and are bandied about continuously by financial and credit analysts. Some debt is usually regarded as a good thing, for it expands the size of the business and hence the return on owner capital. But too much is too much. Where do you draw the line?

Guiding principles include comparative analysis and vulnerability to downturns. Debt must always be paid back, whether business is good or not — so debt stops being okay when it's too large to cover during a downturn or business strategy change.

Here are a couple second-tier metrics:

Debt to equity

This old standard is used over and over to get a feel for indebtedness and particularly for industry comparison. The calculation is simple, but remember that we're talking long-term debt here. IBM has reached a little, incurring a debt to equity (D/E) of 0.84 versus an industry average of 0.46. Overextended? Not really. When you look at IBM's credit ratings and cost against the industry, it is so favorable, that why not borrow a little and use it to buy shareholders out and increase ROE for remaining shareholders? Still, a deteriorating D/E over time is a bad sign unless you understand the context. A worsening D/E without a reduction in shares is less healthy.

Interest coverage

We don't cover this ratio in Chapter 10. Digging it up is a little harder because interest expense often isn't easy to find as a separate line item. One measure of interest coverage is the ratio of earnings to annual interest, a rough indication of how solvent or burdened a company is by debt. IBM covers its interest 17 times versus 15 for the industry and only 9 for the S&P 500 (see Multex Market Guide Ratio Comparison), so one would assume no problem there.

A good question to ask is, what happens to coverage if, say, business (sales) drops 20 percent, as in a deep recession? We're starting to edge out onto intangible ground.

Drug test

One could develop a whole checklist of drug tests in this category. In fact, the older Depression-influenced checklists of Ben Graham and followers placed great emphasis on financial strength, liquidity, debt coverage, and so on. It was the tune of the times. Credit analysts today continue to check all manner of coverage and debt ratios, but for most companies reporting a profit, we regard that as overkill. Still, a few checks provide a margin of safety and a further test of whether the company has an insatiable demand for capital:

- ✔ Current assets (besides cash) rising faster than business. This ties to the asset productivity and turnover measures discussed earlier in this chapter, but it's worth one last check to see whether a company is buying business by extending too much credit. More receivables result from extending credit, while losing channel structure and supply chain battles (customers and distributors won't carry inventory, suppliers are making them carry more inventory) result in increased inventories. The risk is greater capital requirements and expensive impairments downstream.

- ✔ Debt growing faster than business. Over a sustained period, debt rising faster than business growth is a problem. If the owners won't kick in to grow the business, and if retained earnings aren't sufficient to meet growth, what does that tell you?

- ✔ Repeated financings. If the business continually has to approach the capital markets (other than in startup phases), that again is a sign that internally generated earnings and cash flows aren't sufficient. Once in a while it's okay, but again you're looking to weed out chronic capital consumers.

The third tier: Intangibles

Several intangibles enter in here. Some are specific and some are conceptual. We start with credit ratings and changes in credit ratings. Declining credit ratings mean that someone somewhere is less secure with the capital structure as currently deployed. Capital intensity is another, particularly changes in capital intensity. The semiconductor business happily churning out DRAM chips becomes less happy when equipment must be replaced with more expensive equipment more often. Such shortening product cycles can similarly stoke the capital requirement fires for software companies and the like. And finally, there's the whole quality thing — again. A company that faces its finances head on is in better shape than one that plays games, delays write-downs, uses "good" debt to finance "bad" assets, and the like. There are specific indicators and a lot of general ones, such as the thickness of 10-K reports we mention in Chapter 6, the tone of press coverage, the departure of CFOs, and so forth.

We dig deeper into the intangibles for all three ROE links in Chapter 14.

What to look for

Again, look for signs that the company will be a healthy user and producer — and not a chronic consumer — of capital. Trends, comparisons, drug tests, and a good understanding of "goes-inta's and goes-outa's," particularly from the statement of cash flows, are good to have.

A Valuation Checklist

We end this chapter by sharing a construct and examples of a checklist you can use to evaluate strategic financials. It's shown in Figure 13-5.

Figure 13-5:
Standard checklist: for strategic financials.

VALUE APPRAISAL CHECKLIST   Strategic Financials

Company: [_____]

Enter:
"+" if positive
"-" if negative
"0" if neutral
"blank" if not evaluated

First Tier   Second Tier

First Tier / Second Tier	Number	Trend	Comparison	Total	Comments
RETURN ON EQUITY					
PROFITABILITY — Net Profit / Sales%					
Gross Margin%					
SG&A%					
Operating Profit%					

Drug Test: Depending on acquisitions for growth? Deferred or "unaggressive" amortizations? Book Value & Cash Flow track earnings? — pass? ☐☐☐

PRODUCTIVITY — Sales/Assets					
Sales/Accounts Receivable					
Sales/Inventory					
Sales/Fixed Assets					
Unit productivity measures 1. 2.					

Drug Test: Excessive or recurring writedowns? — pass? ☐

CAPITAL STRUCTURE — Assets/Equity					
Share Buybacks?					
Cash Flow Ration					
"Foolish Flow"					
Debt/Equity					

Drug Test: Current asset growth > sales growth? Debt growing faster than business? Repeated financings? — pass? ☐☐☐

SUMMARY					

You can clearly see the first tier, second tier, a placeholder for the third-tier intangibles, and the "drug tests." Cells are provided for values, trends, comparisons, and a total assessment for each attribute. Score by using a +, −, or 0, but you can also leave something blank, especially for a first-pass analysis. We don't want to be bossy and make everything mandatory! Putting a complete checklist together does take a fair amount of time.

An example

Figure 13-6 shows what the strategic financials checklist might look like for IBM:

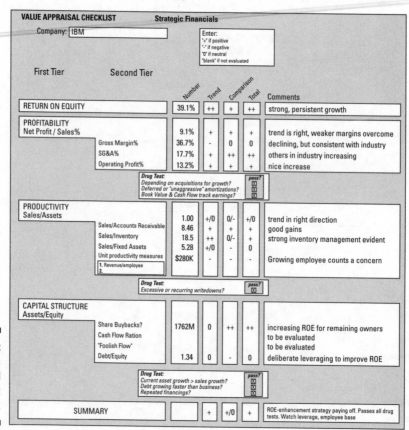

Figure 13-6: Strategic financial checklist: IBM.

From a strategic financial viewpoint, IBM looks pretty good. There are no failed "drug tests" and a lot of positives on the ROE front. But you aren't done, and it isn't time to log into your brokerage account — not quite yet. Although the fundamentals point to good value, it's important to review intangibles — the leading indicators. A check of intrinsic value (Chapter 12) is always a good idea, and also check valuation ratios, price appreciation potential, and alternative investments to compare price to value (Chapter 16) before pushing any buttons.

Chapter 14

Beyond the Numbers: Strategic Intangibles

> *If you gave me $100 billion and said take away the soft drink leadership of Coca-Cola in the world, I'd give it back to you and say it can't be done.*
>
> —Warren Buffett

Chapter 14 spells relief — relief for those of you who slogged along with us through the nitty-gritty numbers world of investment in Chapters 12 and 13. As you explore with us the more humane, cerebral world of marketing and management *intangibles,* you can surface for much-needed air.

Why intangibles? Because so much of what makes excellent businesses excellent transcends the arcane world of factories, storefronts, products, and packages. Anyone can make a hamburger, a cup of coffee, or a beverage with water, sugar, and a few flavorings. Anybody with a few tens of millions can start an airline or retail chain. But everyone knows that there's something more that turns the McDonald's, Starbucks, and Coca-Colas of the world into the great businesses they are. That "something" is the set of intangibles. Intangibles are often the greatest, most powerful, and most productive set of assets any company can own.

We're talking about the difference between "viable" and "greatness," between Michael Jordan and all those other guys. Although the original Ben Graham value school set its sights on cheap, safe assets, the evolved Buffett school goes beyond that to identify, appreciate, and appraise the intangibles that make great businesses great. The words of the late money manager and Buffett disciple George Michaelis, discussing newspapers and television stations, say it all: "Such businesses tend to have a high return on book equity. Why? Because they are earning not only on their tangible assets but on the intangible ones as well."

Intangibles come in all shapes and sizes. Every company has different intangibles. This chapter discusses marketing and management tenets that separate "great" from "good." Marketing tenets include franchise, brand, position, and customer power. Management tenets include competence, independence, and style. Other tenets include ownership and a few financial intangibles. These intangibles are clearly strategic in the creation of value in the business and return for the shareholders. And most of them can be controlled or influenced by good management.

In this chapter we will show a framework for appraising a company's intangible value. At the end, we'll provide a checklist to help you do it yourself.

Lollapalooza

What was that word again? You probably do feel like you have surfaced for air! You've come all the way from "compounded, discounted returns on investment" to "lollapalooza."

Lollapalooza effects are the "really big effects that come from large combinations of factors." Charlie Munger used the term and defined it this way for an executive seminar to describe the ascent and future of Coca-Cola. Engineers use it to describe flight, doctors use it to describe treatments, and art critics use it to explain the success of really great art. We follow Munger's path to learn to evaluate the "whole is greater than the sum of the parts" synergies that really great intangibles add to really great businesses.

Lollapalooza *(noun, slang)* is defined as an extraordinary or unusual thing, person, or event, or an exceptional example of something.

Beyond the numbers

Of course, when the whole is greater than the sum of parts, it defies calculation. That's good news for you with the weak math stomachs, right? There will be no formulas in this chapter.

Quantifying intangibles is elusive and really beside the point. Such things as market share, degree of management ownership, and control can be quantified.

But these numbers are merely details. The point is to size up marketing and management phenomena and assess the lollapalooza potential in your mind. Market and customer psychology, history, and personality finally move to center stage.

Like other parts of the value framework, status, trends, and industry comparisons are important. But at last, you're into something that the human mind can do better than a desktop PC.

Before the numbers

Intangibles often enhance value. Market power allows greater prices to be charged for the same product produced at greater cost efficiency, producing more profit and return on equity. If you start with labor, material, and overhead and add lollapalooza, you get above average profits and returns.

That's the point, but it isn't the only point. Those that caught on to the last three chapters realize that intangibles can be a good leading indicator of things to come — and numbers to come. Good and improving brand image, reputation, and popularity beget better sales, stronger pricing, and other good things downstream. Ignoring actual numbers for a minute, can you see the potential for a Starbucks or a Krispy Kreme built on reputation, popularity, and word of mouth?

On the flip side, a blown public reputation spells disaster. Who thinks owners of Bridgestone/Firestone, Ford, or Alaska Airlines will benefit from any lollapalooza effects in 2001? For those companies, business and share value will be the sum of the parts, nothing more, and quite likely something less until investors feel the storm has passed.

Before deciding what revenue and earnings growth numbers to apply to value a company, a conscious appraisal of intangibles is in order.

Beyond your windshield

How do you do a lollapalooza assessment? Pure information sources are few and far between. Mainly, the idea is to keep your antennae up and tuned in at all times. Tune into the business world by reading company communications, checking out companies' Web sites, and following the commentaries of analysts and journalists. Beyond that, good investors walk Main Street to observe what common folks are saying, thinking, and doing.

What should you look for? Mainly market power and management excellence. Yes, you can have one without the other, but it's a tougher road. Companies with excellent management but poor market power will stay ordinary, while companies with poor management and excellent market power will always underperform.

Much of the rest of this chapter explores market power and management excellence and their lollapalooza effects on the value equation. Along the way, we examine a few other intangibles affecting asset productivity and capital structure components of ROE (return on investment), and we also make a stop to look at ownership.

Don't drive in dense fog

Lollapalooza is a good thing, but when a company seems to be all lollapalooza, look out! There's much to be said — especially for value investors — in understanding the business today and for the long term. When you can't figure out what the business is or where it will be in six months, how can you develop a sense of strategic financials and intrinsic value strong enough to commit capital?

Warren Buffett is famous for his avoidance of technology investments. Although Microsoft meets almost any definition of a powerful, profitable, growing franchise, Buffett says he can't see what's beyond five or ten years for the company. He simply considers technology outside his circle of competence and stays away, despite great respect for his good friend Bill Gates.

Although we think it *is* possible to find value in technology companies, that isn't really the point. The point is that value investing requires developing a solid understanding of the company and of the business to which you plan to commit capital. If you can't understand the business, understanding the intangibles and their effects on the financials will be hard.

Understanding an industry

It's usually a good idea to understand an industry before committing investment capital to a company within the industry. Understand banking before buying a bank, insurance before buying an insurance company, the auto industry before buying an auto company or supplier, and so forth. Yet, for the casual or nonprofessional investor, little concrete information is available on just how an industry is organized, who the players are, and how it's expected to perform in the near and long term. What do you do?

Acquiring industry information is sort of an art and varies by industry. Sure, if you're willing to pay the price, you can access Standard & Poor's, Moody's, and professional market research services, for example, International Data Group (IDG) for the information technology business. But without paying hundreds, or thousands, a year, how can you develop industry fluency? Here are a few tips:

✔ Read the newspaper and the newswires. If you follow an industry in the major financial papers, you'll find out what's reported regularly and where to find it. *The Wall Street Journal* has regular sales statistics on auto sales and a regular subsection on technology. Keep your eyes on the "Marketplace" section. Pick a couple of companies in the industry and watch the newswires (such as Yahoo! Finance). Releases and stories cover not only companies but also their markets and industries. Read, read, read.

✔ Check out brokerage reports. You may not trust everything put forth by analysts, but they usually do a decent job assessing industries and their players. Much of this information originates from the big paid-for services mentioned earlier. Brokerage houses choose industries to cover and provide fairly frequent updates. The trick is to get these reports without being an account holder (if you *are*, all the better). Visit broker offices, find a friend, and so forth. Some reports are also available through online broker research pages. For example, Credit Suisse First Boston (CSFB) and U.S. Trust research reports are available through Charles Schwab.

✔ Check out Value Line. Although we try to stick to recommending free sources of advice for nonprofessional investors, we frequently mention Value Line (which you must subscribe to if your local library doesn't carry it) as the deserving exception. Value Line does an industry synopsis in each weekly report. The problem is, there's no telling what industry it will review when.

Still, archives fill the gap, and as long-term investors, you may find that overly frequent updates are too much "noise."

✔ Library. Depending on the fiscal health of your local government, your library might offer help. Many libraries carry Moody's, Standard & Poor's, and other research services, but check publication dates before digging in.

✔ Government agencies. Agencies and departments such as the Department of Commerce and Federal Trade Commission can provide important industry studies and barometers. Finding the really relevant stuff can be challenging but handy.

✔ Find a friend — a friend in the business, that is. An insider's view can be valuable, but watch for distortions. Many insiders focus on "trees" and lose view of the forest. Still, as a barometer of industry health and as a resource to find out about an industry's structure (channel structure, supply chain, competition), an informative friend can be a good friend indeed.

✔ Stop, look and listen. More about this later, but it pays to make your own observations about what's selling and what isn't selling, emergent and dying trends. It would hardly require detailed research to discover whether SUVs are replacing large four-door sedans in the auto market.

Value investors are resourceful types, and we're confident that you'll find a way to get the important industry information that you need.

A company whose business is creating products that "leverage the capabilities of fibre channel technology to better manage the growth of mission-critical data by overcoming the limitations of the traditional small computer system interface (SCSI), which is a captive storage architecture" is probably outside, way outside, the circle of competence for most people. When in doubt, keep it simple and stick to hamburgers and Cokes.

Market Power

Market power is all about *advantage*. Market power is strength in franchise, brand, customer base, supply chain power, or other competence that gives the company an advantage, or an edge, in the marketplace. Advantage drives *and protects* the first component of ROE: profitability.

Companies with no market power are controlled by the industry they're in. They're vulnerable to the whims of their competitors and anyone who chooses to enter their market. As a result, achieving growth is difficult; in theory, they can grow no faster than the industry as a whole. And improving profitability is even more difficult. Profits attract competitors and aggressive pricing, which eliminates the profits. Companies producing undifferentiated or commodity products can succeed if excellent management creates leading cost structures, customer base, and reputation, but advantage is hard to maintain.

The franchise factor

A franchise is probably the most valuable asset a business can have. And we're not talking about the franchise you can buy from a restaurant or convenience store chain allowing you to sell merchandise or services under someone else's logo. We use *franchise* to refer to an established, sustainable, powerful position in a market.

Understanding the franchise advantage

Why should you care about franchises? Because they produce profits — sustainable and growing profits — over a long period of time. Coca-Cola is the classic case of the franchise, a situation in which the power of the brand and the reputation of the company have created a near-unassailable fortress around the production and sale of flavored sugar water. Franchises, according to Buffett, sell something people want for which there's no close substitute. Franchises beget market power, and market power begets pricing and supply chain power, and pricing and supply chain power beget profits.

Building a "moat"

Franchises also create barriers to entry. If you can grill burgers, you can set up a hamburger stand, but can you set up a McDonald's? Would anyone come? Warren Buffett uses the metaphor "creating a moat" to describe franchise power that keeps competitors away — and keeps the business and its fundamentals moving in the right direction.

What determines the width and depth of a "moat"? For this discussion, we identify five factors that can define market advantage:

- **Brand:** The company or product moniker with so much behind it.

- **Market share and leadership:** Presence in the marketplace and the 600-pound gorillaship that has the others following — or attacking — the business.

- **Customer base:** Would customers climb walls to buy the product?

- **Special competencies:** Assets or knowledge in place. Got a big power plant in Northern California?

- **Supply-chain power:** Can the business dictate terms with its suppliers or its sales channel?

The brand centerpiece

The marketing profession makes its by living evaluating and developing the "four Ps" — product, price, promotion, and place (physical distribution) — of a company's product or product line. Marketers continuously tinker with the right mix of these inputs towards building market presence, product volume, and market share.

You can't possibly know all that goes into achieving the right marketing mix. Heck, the marketeers themselves don't know how well a given mix or strategy works. But you can pick up on one external manifestation of the marketing machine that creates enduring value: the brand.

No brand is created overnight (although it got close in the dot-com craze, when, of all things, going public was considered a brand-building strategy!). Brands are built over time through a combination of good products and good presentation of those products to the marketplace.

What goes into a brand

Textbooks are written on brand dynamics, brand psychology, the brand name and how many letters it should have, and even brand colors. We won't go too deep, but we do identify a few key factors that you can recognize:

- **Image:** One of the most important attributes of a brand, brand *image* is how the public perceives the brand in the marketplace. Product quality is part of a brand image, but it goes beyond physical quality into association with ideas and images from the real world. People tend to associate Wrangler with rugged Western jeans, Banana Republic with adventure clothing, and Harley-Davidson with rugged individualism. Image branding and marketing can be very powerful and sustainable, but the landscape is littered with the carcasses of quality and image failures. Anyone want to buy a set of Firestone tires?

✔ **Familiarity:** It ain't glamorous, and we can't really tell about quality. But we buy Tide and Cheer anyway. Could it be the advertising? The packaging? The fact it's available everywhere? Familiarity creates mindshare, and drives repeat, or *habitual* purchase, and creates barriers for entry. Most value investors place a high value on habitual repeat purchase.

✔ **Reputation:** This one may be a composite of the first two but deserves its own mention. Reputation builds slowly over time and provides a powerful umbrella giving storm shelter when other things go wrong. But it must be nurtured and handled with care. A defining case study is Procter & Gamble's handling of its Rely tampons and their link to toxic shock syndrome; this case provided the model for companies to come forth and admit mistakes. Denial prolongs the battle, and while maybe providing short-term financial wins, has long-term negative consequences. When considering companies to invest in, look for businesses that manage their mistakes well.

The last word on brand

Brand is a complex and fascinating part of a company's identity, and it can tell a lot about a company's value. It's up to you to decide how valuable the brand is in the marketplace both today and in the future. Does the brand support stronger pricing? Does it foster repeat purchase? Is the brand extendable into new markets or into other products (as in Nike golf balls or Titleist clothing)? Does it define the market (as in Coke or Kleenex)? It all becomes part of the value appraisal, perhaps without involving a single number.

Even with the use of expensive market research, assessing and assigning a value to a brand in the marketplace is very difficult. Individual investors don't have expensive market research at their disposal, and so must rely on keen observations and judgment to assess the value of a brand, sometimes known as brand *equity*. Later in this chapter, we present a checklist you can use assess each of the components — image, familiarity, and reputation — and then decide overall if brand equity is an advantage, a disadvantage, or a "neutral" for the business.

Market share and leadership

Have you heard the term "600-pound gorilla" used to describe certain industry players? For example, maybe you've heard of Cisco being called the 600-pound gorilla of the networking industry or of someone referring to Home Depot as the 600-pound gorilla of the retail home improvement industry. A 600-pound gorilla is considered a leader in its industry.

Market leadership is closely tied to brand as a powerful marketing and pricing tool. Market leadership means that a company defines the market, sets the pace in price and product, and (usually) is tied to a strong brand. And market leadership often leads to cost advantages through buying power and economies of scale.

And certainly a company with monopoly power will have an advantage.

But market leadership is a two-edged sword. Although it can translate to pricing and purchasing power, being number one also makes your business a prime target of numbers two, three, and so forth. So a market leader must devote a lot of energy to staying that way and must avoid the trap of resting on laurels and maintaining position through arrogance. The pre-Gerstner IBM and the General Motors of the 1960s are examples of situations that serve as reminders that market leadership isn't always a good thing — nor is it permanent.

So we look for two items in the assessment: (1) to what degree does the business possess market share and leadership and (2) does it do the right things and have the right attitude to maintain its market position and grow it? If a company is continually struggling to maintain a five or ten percent share in the market — or worse yet, losing share —, that's a negative.

Customer base

A strong and loyal customer base is an important intangible asset. Why? A company with a loyal customer base can depend on repeat sales and spends less money acquiring new customers. Profitability increases through lower marketing costs and repeat sales driven other than by price. Customer base "nirvana" occurs when customers repeat-buy the product regardless of price and evangelize the product and company to others.

A business treating a customer base as an asset is more successful than one that treats it as a liability. The company that "gets it" carefully manages and *cultivates* its customer base. Such a company learns about its customers, listens to them, talks to them, and nurtures loyalty and referrals. Successful companies build a mutually beneficial relationship with their companies. Companies that don't "get it" treat their customers as a cost center and must continually pay to acquire new customers and reacquire old ones. Good examples of companies that "get it" are Apple and Harley-Davidson. Harley has done a particularly good job of capitalizing on its customer base.

How do you tell? You can't always tell unless you're a direct customer of the company. Still, word of mouth and the tone and manner of public communications can provide a lot of information. And don't be fooled just because a company has a loyalty or points program. Such programs don't always mean that a company is listening, nor do they always differentiate (anyone out there a member of an airline program?), but they're a step in the right direction. Managing loyalty and the customer asset takes on different forms depending on the industry. A company selling $2 products through a retail grocer takes a different approach than one selling plane tickets or automobiles.

Score for strong, loyal customer base and business strategies that employ the customer base as an asset and capitalize on it. Don't forget that this applies to business-to-business companies, not only to consumer businesses.

Special competencies

Does the business you're evaluating have a distinctive competence? Does it just happen to control the operating system of the PC, so that its applications will work better than everyone else's? Does it have a Coke formula and 75 years of ingrained brand history recognized by 80 percent of the world's population? Does it have a "razors-and-blades" business model — a product and a series of repurchased consumable products that make it work — guaranteeing a revenue and profit stream (for example, Gillette, Hewlett-Packard, and Lexmark)? Does it have deep enough pockets to write insurance policies where no others can? Or does it have some other kind of infrastructure, business model, or technology that's difficult to duplicate? Score a "plus" if this is the case.

The supply chain

Indeed, if investors examine market power influence on pricing and sales, they still tend to overlook factors influencing a company's cost structure today and in the future. Wanna buy airline stock? Keep in mind dependence on oil for fuel, well-organized labor, scarce aircraft in a two-supplier market, and tight, government-controlled availability of airport facilities. Are airlines in control of their cost picture? Clearly not. Although other factors may not be so grim, airlines have seldom been considered value investments.

On the other hand, companies can exert considerable influence and control over their suppliers. Sears certainly influences, if not controls, Whirlpool. Auto companies have traditionally exerted a great deal of influence over their suppliers. Being the 600-pound gorilla in any industry usually means power on the supply side, for every supplier wants such a lucrative customer deal.

When we talk about "supply chain," we usually are referring *up* the chain toward suppliers of business resources. A broader definition looks down the chain into sales and distribution channels. If a company has sustainable control or influence over its distribution partners — a sizable portion of their business and a good relationship — that's a good thing. A business that continually has to fight or pay for shelf space is at a disadvantage. So when evaluating the business, look at distribution channels and their influence on stability, sustainable and growable sales, and stable costs. A company that can *economically* sell directly to its customers may have an advantage.

Think about the resources needed to sustain and grow the business, and try to picture whether the company is likely to be in a better or worse position five or ten years down the road. Give the company a "plus" for supplier power, and give another "plus" if a company has channel power.

All about Management

Market power can deliver huge intangible benefits to a business and business results. Less visible in the marketplace but just as important is another intangible pillar: company management. Like market power, we're talking a qualitative, sensory assessment, not drawn from formulas, tools, and specific resources.

We examine four attributes of management excellence: competence, candor, independence, and customer focus. You get a chance to evaluate your company's managers, much as (for those of you working for someone else) your own performance might be evaluated by others.

For those who've been around the block in the job or investment world, management excellence may seem to be an insufferable oxymoron. Yet, Warren Buffett views management as an X-factor that can make all the difference, and he feels he can judge a lot about a company from a short meeting with its senior management.

Evaluating management excellence can be tricky. You don't sit or work with these managers on a daily basis; in fact, much of what they do is deliberately kept secret. Yet, a sensitive antenna can pick up a lot over a period of time. But if you learn about a company in the morning and want to invest that afternoon, appraising management can be pretty difficult.

Solid information about a company's management is usually hard to find except what you see in the press. Yahoo! Finance provides links to the bios and executive compensation of management, but these do little to help you assess performance. Read the paper and watch corporate communications and press releases to catch the buzz about a company's management.

The following sections describe the management excellence factors.

Competence

Does management have the right vision, make the right decisions, and offer good reasons for those decisions? Sure, anyone can talk up a good future for a business, but does it stand on its own two feet? Does management make sound investments in existing businesses? In new businesses? Or does it grope for growth, itching for acquisitions because it believes that it needs to be doing something? Does it understand — and control — expenses? Does it make changes when changes should be made, being neither too eager nor too reluctant to make them? Does it make reasonable projections about growth and earnings? We could go on and on, but suffice it to say that good management understands the business, has a realistic view of it, has a solid rationale behind strategies and decisions, and employs resources wisely within it.

Candor

Ever notice that more is heard from many managers when things are going well than when they aren't? Value investors like managers who communicate quickly and honestly about business issues and problems — and without undue spin. These managers disclose as much data as they can about their businesses, including information about sector performance, unit productivity, and key strategies and investments. According to Buffett, managers who confess mistakes publicly are "more likely to correct them." Honesty is the best policy.

Along with candor, a little of the right attitude goes a long way. Arrogant managers, who hide problems, think they can solve them all, or, worse yet, think they are invincible and have no problems are bound for trouble.

Independence

Good management teams think and act independently. They think and act for the long-term health of the business and resist the temptation to pour energy and resources into achieving this quarter's results. Buffett calls this approach "avoiding the institutional imperative, " which means turning aside the short-term pressures of Wall Street, its analysts, and institutional investors to do what's right for the business long term. They have a vision, a mission, and a plan and follow them, avoiding distractions. And leadership plays a big part. Unlikely to follow the lead of others, they play to win and to *beat* the competition, not just to keep up with it.

Customer focus

A management team focused on customers is more likely to succeed than one focused on its internal issues and on competitors. Does the company know its customers? Who they are and their needs? Do communications and advertisements stress how company products benefit customers? Does management spend time with customers? Do communications talk about customers and customer "wins," or are they focused on the glories and challenges of the business itself?

Ownership

By looking at a company's ownership, particularly those who own the largest pieces of the business, you can discover something of the attractiveness of the business to others — and to its own management. Pure and experienced value investors may shun this information, preferring to rely on their own appraisal rather than follow the lead of others. But as you develop your personal expertise and style, it may be valuable to look at who else owns the company.

Management as owners

Management ownership reflects management commitment. Close to management ownership is insider ownership: owners with access to internal company information — *usually* management.

You can use Yahoo! Finance to look at what it refers to as "Insider and 5%+ Owners"; that is, the percentage of outstanding shares owned by insiders and large shareholders (registering with the SEC as holding 5 percent or more of the company).

Insider buys and sells can tell something, but we think that this indicator is overrated. Executives routinely sell options and shares as part of their compensation package, so it's easy to read too much into this activity. Exceptionally large sales, at peak or trough prices, *may* signal something.

Institutions as owners

Yahoo! Finance shows the top ten institutional shareholders — usually large banks, pension funds, or trusts. The larger the holdings, and the more blue chip the names, the better. You can also see whether institutions have been *buying*, but realize that this data may be outdated.

Mutual funds as owners

Yahoo! Finance also shows the top ten largest mutual fund holders. Look for who, how much, and what kind of fund. If the top ten funds all are value funds, that may be a good sign.

Assets and Capital Structure

We need to cover a few quick intangibles worth a look as influencers and leading indicators of asset productivity and capital structure.

Asset productivity

There are two key intangibles: cost structure and channel structure.

Cost structure

Cost structure sounds like it belongs with "profitability" and not "asset productivity," and in a sense, it does. But we put it here because it's a lot about assets and especially about the fixed infrastructure of the business.

Cost structure has to do with the cost of doing business and the flexibility and adaptability of the infrastructure driving that cost. A company with a high cost structure (meaning that it has big investments in property, plant, or equipment or is located in a high-cost area) is more vulnerable to downturns and reduced capacity utilization. Further, earnings quality, subject to discretionary depreciation and amortization policies, becomes more dubious.

Tuned to the right channel?

We cover channel structure earlier, under market power. The issue was the balance of power between the company and its channels — who dictates to whom — and what effect that had on profits. Here we look at channel structure slightly differently: How does channel structure affect asset utilization? A business required to carry high receivables, finance a lot of inventory, and build a lot of infrastructure to support its channel strategy is at an asset-productivity disadvantage. Many dot-coms forgot this. They "disintermediated" retail outlets (the bricks and mortar) but took on a lot of infrastructure costs in computer equipment and software, proving to be more expensive and perishable than expected. On the other hand, Dell Computer has done a masterful job of improving asset productivity by shifting its asset burdens back to its suppliers (and you wouldn't want shares of any of *those* businesses).

Operating leverage

Operating leverage is a topic best left for finance textbooks and those wanting a heavier financial assessment, but the basic concept is still useful. *Operating leverage* reflects the degree to which a business is built on fixed versus current assets. A steel mill or railroad is heavily steeped in fixed assets, while a retailer or publisher has relatively few fixed assets.

High fixed assets are a two-edged sword. When a business is operating at full capacity (or greater), unit costs decline. But when a business is operating at less than full capacity (either because of business cycles, industry trends, or (shudder!) overbuilt capacity), fixed costs still need to be paid, and asset utilization drops. Your goal — based on what you read, see, and feel — is to decide whether the business is committed to the right asset levels and can operate at capacity. Starbucks can furnish an example: Although store space is relatively less consuming than a steel mill, one has to evaluate the possibility of overbuilding stores. What would happen if business declined because of competition, or if people stopped drinking coffee? Like everything else, it's a judgment call.

Capital offenses?

The main issues we address towards defining successful capital structure were covered as part of the discussion of capital requirements and leverage in Chapter 13. The intangible list is light, and for this exercise includes only the debt ratings of outside agencies. Company debt securities — bonds, debentures, and other forms of credit — are routinely rated for safety by major credit agencies, principally Standard & Poor's and Moody's, for U.S. securities anyway.

We would take a quick look at debt ratings (the higher the better) and the direction of these ratings. Watch for changes such as announcements of credit watches and negative positions by the agencies.

Debt ratings and their explanations are found on the Web sites for Standard & Poor's and Moody's, but you have to register to get access. Of similar value is Value Line's "Financial Strength" assessment, located in the bottom-right corner of the Investment Survey sheet.

Walking the Streets

We can't close this chapter until we mention the concept of walking Main Street and keeping your eyes and ears peeled to what's going on in your little corner of the world. Peter Lynch advocated this strategy long ago — buy what you know and buy what you see is going well. If the line at Starbucks is persistently out the door, all your home-based-business friends are considering Starbucks as their office, and you deeply believe Starbucks has replaced the corner tavern as the place to fritter away idle time and money, those factors together should work positively for the company. The trick is in extrapolating that impression! Make a point of visiting Starbucks when you travel, too, so you can see how well the idea works in other places.

It's Lollapalooza Time

We spoke of an intangibles checklist at the beginning of this chapter, and here it is. Figure 14-1 shows an intangibles checklist. You can use this separately or together with the strategic financials checklist in Chapter 13 to get a good grasp of business performance, business potential, and overall company value.

Figure 14-1:
Strategic
intangibles
checklist.

VALUE APPRAISAL CHECKLIST	Strategic Intangibles		Enter: "+" if positive, "-" if negative, "0" if neutral, "blank" if not evaluated
Company:			

First Tier Metrics	Intangibles	Supporting Criteria	Number	Trend	Comparison	Total	Comments
PROFITABILITY Net Profit / Sales %	**MARKET POWER**						
	Brand	Image Familiarity Reputation					
	Market Share and Leadership						
	Customer Assets	Customer value recognized? Customer value realized?					
	Special Competencies						
	Supply Chain Control	Control input costs? Control channel?					
	MANAGEMENT EFFECTIVENESS	Competence Candor Independence Customer focus					
	OWNERSHIP	Management as owners Institutions as owners Mutual funds as owners					
PRODUCTIVITY Sales/Assets	**ASSET PRODUCTIVITY**	Cost structure Channel structure					
CAPITAL STRUCTURE Assets/Equity	**CREDIT RATING**						
	"STREET WALK"						
SUMMARY							

The IBM Example

Figure 14-2 shows checklist as you might use it for IBM, which is a pretty positive story with elements favoring strong future financials. As a gesture of realism, we didn't fill everything out. This is a long checklist, and it probably isn't necessary to complete it all.

VALUE APPRAISAL CHECKLIST — Strategic Intangibles

Company: IBM

Enter:
"+" if positive
"-" if negative
"0" if neutral
"blank" if not evaluated

First Tier Metrics	Intangibles	Supporting Criteria	Number	Trend	Comparison	Total	Comments
PROFITABILITY Net Profit / Sales %	**MARKET POWER**		+	+	+	+	large and solid
	Brand		+	+	+	+	one of world's best
		Image	+	+	+	+	service, service, service
		Familiarity	+	0	+	+	one of most familiar, around the world
		Reputation	+	+	+	+	one of best, around the world
	Market Share and Leadership		+	0	+	+	strong, especially international
	Customer Assets		0	0	+	+/0	sometimes arrogant, but aware
		Customer value recognized?	+	0	+	+	ads call out customer successes
		Customer value realized?	0	0	+	+/0	hard to tell
	Special Competencies		+	0	+	+	resources, labs
	Supply Chain Control		0	+	0	0/+	not rated
		Control input costs?					
		Control channel?	0	+	0	0/+	taking greater charge by selling direct
	MANAGEMENT EFFECTIVENESS		+	+/0	+	+	very good last 10 years but Gerstner leaving
		Competence	+	+	+	+	solid focus and delivery on ROE, share buybacks
		Candor	0/-	0	0	0	never an IBM strong poing
		Independence	+/0	+/0	+/0	+/0	can be short term focused, bureaucratic
		Customer focus	0/+	0/+	+	0/+	getting a little better
	OWNERSHIP						not evaluated
		Management as owners					
		Institutions as owners					
		Mutual funds as owners					
PRODUCTIVITY Sales/Assets	**ASSET PRODUCTIVITY**		0	0	0	0	not a huge advantage, maybe a disadvantage
		Cost structure	0/-	0/-	-	0/-	high fixed costs, employee costs
		Channel structure	+/0	+	+	+	good distributors, strong sales force, good direct channel
CAPITAL STRUCTURE Assets/Equity	**CREDIT RATING**		+	+	+	+	always one of best
	"STREET WALK"		+	+	+	+	re-established their great name
SUMMARY			+	+	+	+	market power and management overcome other weaknesses, moving in right direction

Figure 14-2: Strategic intangibles checklist for IBM.

TECHNICAL STUFF

Sultans of SWOT

As an alternative approach to defining intangibles, some business and marketing analysts employ a tool arising from the marketing consulting world: the *SWOT* analysis. SWOT stands for strengths, weaknesses, opportunities, and threats. The process consists of evaluating the four attributes for the company being examined. Consultants specialize in creating four-box grids to categorize almost anything in the business world, and SWOT provides a perfect example.

The following figure shows how one might be filled out for IBM:

Compared with the intangibles framework presented in this chapter, this analysis is more subjective. There is no scoring system, and attributes aren't tied directly to ROE components. Still, it provides an easy, practical framework, a "viable alternative," as the consultants say.

S *trengths*	**W** *eaknesses*
• Brand and brand name • Financial strength • Tradition • Product line breadth • Solid consulting practice • Strong channel relationships • Loyal customer base • Overseas strengh	• Bureaucracy • Slow to change • high cost structure
O *pportunities*	**T** *hreats*
• Build services business • Leverage service business to develop product sales • Leverage "total e-business" solution platform	• More nimble competitors • Continued erosion of mainframe business • Overhiring , excessive infrastructure and cost

Chapter 15

Warren's Way

· ·

In This Chapter

▶ Following the Buffett approach to business value and investing

▶ Understanding Buffett's business, management, financial, and market tenets

· ·

The market, like the Lord, helps those who help themselves. But unlike the Lord, the market does not forgive those who know not what they do.

—Warren Buffett

*W*ant to do the impossible? Try writing a book on value investing without mentioning Warren Buffett It would be easier to write a book about American history without mentioning Thomas Jefferson or a book about the physics of relativity without mentioning Albert Einstein. Although this is not a book about Buffett *per se*, we wouldn't want to write a book on value investing without capitalizing on his vast insight, experience, and clairvoyance (not to mention his humor) to help explain it.

This book is designed to help you understand value investing and to develop your own effective value investing style. We present and use Mr. Buffett's example as an art teacher would use Rembrandt, Picasso, or Monet to help you develop your own painting style. You don't necessarily have to copy or duplicate the Buffett style; but you should try to learn from it.

In Chapters 11 through 14, we describe a system for appraising intrinsic values, financials, and intangibles of a business. Formulas, ratios, and checklists delivered a rather lengthy, in-depth analysis. Does Mr. Buffett do all of this analyzing? Yeah, pretty much. As we explain in this chapter, our principles are aligned with his. But Buffett's experience, judgment, and preferences reduce the complex to a relatively simple 12-point formula, now presented as a sort of *For Dummies* guide within a *For Dummies* guide. But the material in Chapters 11 through 14 shouldn't be ignored or forgotten — because it contributes to understanding the principles behind Warren's Way.

Robert Hagstrom, Senior VP at Legg Mason (a value-oriented mutual fund group) is the author of *The Warren Buffett Way, The Warren Buffett Portfolio,* and *The Essential Buffett* (all published by John Wiley and Sons). Hagstrom has done a good job of identifying and explaining the Twelve Tenets of the Warren Buffett Way. In this chapter, we follow Mr. Hagstrom's Twelve Tenets framework.

The Buffett Wisdom

Describing Mr. Buffett's wisdom, mindset, and approach to life in full would be an ambitious project indeed, and beyond our scope. (Many others have attempted it, and the best we've found is the 1,100-page *Of Permanent Value* by Andy Kilpatrick, published by McGraw-Hill.) A few basic paradigms form a background canvas onto which the more specific tenets of Warren's Way are painted.

Summing up Warren's Way in one sentence, it could read (quoting Hagstrom): ". . . [H]e looks for companies he understands — businesses that have favorable long-term prospects, are operated by honest and competent people, and importantly, are available at attractive prices."

Here are some additional "basics" of Warren's Way:

✔ **Buying shares is equivalent to buying the business.** You must have the same rigor, the same approach, and the same discipline.

✔ **A value investor is a business analyst, not a market or security analyst.** The focus is on the business, not the stock or stock price.

✔ **A business valuation is complete and holistic.** It encompasses financials, intangibles, and price.

✔ **The market values stocks correctly much of the time, but not all the time.** Over- and undervaluation exist *somewhere* in the markets at all times. The trick is finding it.

✔ **Long term is the only term.** "Our favorite holding period is forever," says Buffett. Further, Buffett rails against short-term trading as a waste of money and, worse, a distraction away from what's really important in a business and towards short-term investor satisfaction.

✔ **Always think future value and opportunity cost.** The power of compounding is one of the sacred tenets of investing. And an investment must be considered against all of its alternatives.

Tenets, Anyone?

From Hagstrom's analysis, the Buffett approach contains 12 major tenets grouped into 4 categories:

- ✔ **Business Tenets** are a high-level view of the business itself, including its markets and marketing strategy.
- ✔ **Management Tenets** are qualities desired in senior management.
- ✔ **Financial tenets** are a deeper view of the financials and financial strategy.
- ✔ **Market tenets** relate the value of the business to the price of the stock (in contrast to *marketing attributes* and *market power,* described in Chapter 14).

Within each category there are 2 to 4 tenets, adding up to the total of 12. Here's the list, again from Robert Hagstrom's analysis:

- ✔ **Business Tenets:**
  - Is the business simple and understandable?
  - Does the business have a consistent operating history?
  - Does the business have favorable long-term prospects?
- ✔ **Management Tenets:**
  - Is management rational?
  - Is management candid with its shareholders?
  - Does management resist the institutional imperative?
- ✔ **Financial Tenets:**
  - Focus on return on equity (ROE), not earnings per share.
  - Calculate owner earnings.
  - Look for companies with high profit margins.
  - For every dollar retained, make sure the company has created at least one dollar of market value.
- ✔ **Market Tenets:**
  - What is the value of the business?
  - Can the business be purchased at a significant discount to its value?

Could this become *your* golden checklist? Maybe so. In what follows, we take a closer look.

Business tenets

Business tenets really represent a 30,000-foot overview of the business itself, including its markets, market position, and strategy.

A simple and understandable business

According to Buffett, an investor can't consistently achieve success without understanding the underlying business. Anything else is pure luck, an in-and-out trip to the Wall Street casino. If you can't understand the business or the industry, you're looking for trouble.

This is where the *circle of competence* concept comes in. Buffett steadfastly sticks to businesses he understands — and understands well enough to *predict*. His old adage is that "risk comes from not knowing what you're doing." The more you understand the business, its driving forces, and the numbers, the less likely you are as an investor to make mistakes. And that is another key part of the Buffett Way: Avoid big mistakes. Big mistakes hurt portfolio performance, and worse, they derail the compounding gravy train (see Chapter 4). Buffett avoids technology shares for this reason. Even for tech companies with apparent enduring value, such as Microsoft, he simply can't predict where they're going five or ten years down the road. Changing technology, changing markets, competitors, regulation — you name it — all get in the way of judging and predicting sustained performance.

Interestingly, Buffett recently declared that, if utility regulation went away, he would become a utility investor. Certainly, utility companies fit every other characteristic of a value business: market power (no pun intended), locked in, steady growth, strong cash flow, and an understandable business. Yet the vast Berkshire Hathaway portfolio only has dabbled in one utility stock: Iowa-based Mid American Energy. Now we know why: Because of regulation, the company can't control its future, and the investor can't predict it.

Buffett would tell us not to take on and solve complex business valuation problems, but to *avoid* them. He would recommend that we do ordinary things exceptionally well in business valuation and don't look for challenges. In other words, keep it simple and avoid complexity.

Consistent operating history

Related to avoiding complexity, Buffett would tell us to stay away from companies going through fundamental strategic or operational shifts, and to avoid turnaround situations (although some may appear to be great values). In his words: "Turnarounds seldom turn," "severe change and exceptional returns usually don't mix," and "energy can be more profitably expended by purchasing good businesses at reasonable prices, rather than difficult businesses at 'cheaper' prices." So stick to companies that produce the same products — and the same or improving results — through the years. Would anyone like a Coke?

Favorable long term prospects

The first part of this tenet is to look for companies with valuable, sustainable franchises — and to avoid the bulk of the rest of the business world locked up in commodity businesses (in his view, everything becomes a commodity business sooner or later, unless you're Microsoft). For more discussion of franchise and what it means, see Chapter 14.

The key to franchises is the ability to control — and raise — prices, without necessarily losing market share. Lasting market power is key. Businesses without franchise compete only on price and/or expensive advertising. Adding in the competition, there is little prospect for profits, profit growth, and high ROE. In fact, the only downside for businesses *with* a franchise is that they form glaring targets for others who want to challenge it. Companies like Coke and Procter & Gamble spend billions of dollars and lots of energy preserving their franchises.

Management tenets

Bottom line: Buffett looks for managers who think and act like owners of the company. Do they behave as though it were their *own* business? People who spend their own money make better decisions than those who spend the money of others.

Management should be rational

It seems obvious that management should be rational, doesn't it? Yet, it isn't always the case.

The rational manager has a sound, clear, long-term vision for the business, and executes consistently toward it. Furthermore, in Buffett's eyes, management must make good decisions about allocating capital. An effective management can overcome external pressure and internal politics to invest in (allocate capital to)what really makes sense for the business and for its return on equity (ROE).

Too often, managers invest in old ideas despite below-average returns. They believe hopeless situations will turn around. They believe toughness and sheer determination can pull it off. And they have a hard time admitting they're wrong and that the world has changed. Sound familiar? Corporate history is littered with the casualties.

Further, managers feeling an itch with the status quo — or responding to external pressure — will become overactive. Start this business, exit that business, change brands, fill the shelves with new products even though they cannibalize existing ones, look for an acquisition. Somehow, they feel the need to do something, anything. It often turns out to be anything but good for the business. Was New Coke a result of management itch, poor judgment, or a carefully concocted marketing ploy? Most believe it to be a mistake, but was it really the act of a rational management looking to revitalize and confirm the old brand? We think it was.

And in Buffett's view, if management can't find projects or investments with adequate returns, they should return the returns to the shareholders in the form of dividends. As dividends set continuing expectations and receive unfavorable tax treatment, the alternative is share repurchases, a Buffett favorite. According to Buffett, when management buys shares in the market, they regard the owners' best interests over a need to unnecessarily expand corporate structure.

To tell the truth: Candor

As a concept, this one's also pretty obvious, but wow, consider the failures! How many of us have seen management reports that sweep all the bad stuff under the rug and promise all will be great — just wait 'til next year! How many have seen management crow when things are going good. They're always quoted in the paper, always headlining the trade show, doing their own TV commercials, and so on. Then when things turn south, they're nowhere to be found. And it gets worse when they start spending more time monkeying with financial statements and reporting than they spend managing the business.

Buffett consistently seeks managers who can admit mistakes and then study and learn from those mistakes. A manager who spends 15 minutes talking about the successes and 2 hours discussing the failures is the right kind of manager. And a management team that shares detailed data about the business — segment performance, unit volumes, and so on — gets higher marks. Honesty is the best policy.

Resisting the institutional imperative

What is the *institutional imperative?* Good question. It is a combination of real-world factors that makes managers behave in less-than-rational ways. External influences are led by Wall Street and its analysts, fund managers, and large shareholders. Add internal organizational bureaucracy, legacy, the Peter Principle, and the tendency for subordinates to agreeably support management biases (all common organizational dynamics), and you get a powerful witches' brew of factors turning rational decision-making astray.

The result: Management teams engage in folly beyond our wildest dreams. Okay, outright folly isn't *always* the result, but tentative behavior and resistance to change often come up. Short-term focus creeps in: Gotta meet your numbers and do as well as competitors this quarter. Never mind the long term.

Managers don't want to lose credibility either outside or inside, so they often follow a failure path or put energy into the wrong things instead of managing for the future. The failure path can be doing nothing, or it can be reaching for unsound businesses or acquisitions in desperate attempts to meet institutional imperative despite unsound strategy. Was Ford's acquisition of Jaguar (and later Volvo) or the ill-fated Quaker Oats acquisition of Snapple driven by institutional imperative or sound business strategy? One wonders.

The right path is a path of *independence*. Independent managers give both sides of the story and resist the temptation to bow to external pressure. They do what's right for the business in the long term. If they meet with analysts at all, the meetings are short and devoid of fluff, and are more about long-term strategy and vision than prognosticating this quarter's results. Independently thinking managers don't let the analysts set their targets, and don't cast everything else aside to meet them.

The management assessment

Summary: Businesses managed with reason, honesty, and independence are destined to come out ahead.

But how do you, the investor, the outsider, learn enough about management? There's no hope of ever meeting them in person or knowing the detail of what they are up to. Much of that's hidden behind the corporate veil of secrecy. Thus, some investors and analysts take the path of measuring performance by the numbers, end of story. But this approach does little as a leading indicator of results. Buffett's recommendation: Read, read, read. Read annual reports, in sequence, to get a feel of how management perspectives and strategies change. Compare the statements of managers for different companies in the industry. Look closely at interviews, speeches, and professional presentations. Get a feel from the company's Web sites. Weigh it all, but don't overweigh it. Excellent management doesn't fix mediocre businesses. As Buffett put it, "A horse that can count to ten is a remarkable horse — not a remarkable mathematician." Don't forget context.

Financial tenets

For those of you who followed us through Chapters 11 through 14, Buffett's financial tenets will be familiar. The Buffett approach is a back-to-basics approach focused on earnings — real earnings — and the fundamental earnings productivity of the business. Not surprisingly, the focus is also on the longer haul, not year-to-year performance and comparisons.

It's ROE for me and thee

Return on equity (ROE) — the dollars earned per dollars invested by the owners — is the single most important financial yardstick for any business.

However, many companies focus instead on increased dollar earnings or earnings per share. But for Buffett and value investors, these events are less meaningful, particularly if ROE is actually declining. Because retained earnings (not paid out to shareholders) become part of equity, maintaining or increasing ROE is particularly challenging, requiring larger increases in earnings. The company that maintains or grows ROE is accomplishing something; the company that shows declining ROE may still be growing earnings while actually producing poorer returns for its owners.

Buffett rightly insists on purifying the ROE measure, removing the effects of investment gains and extraordinary items. Investment gains make ROE look better without any improvement in business fundamentals , while the effects of extraordinary items on both numerator and denominator should be understood.

Buffett is also cautious about using leverage to improve ROE (for more discussion, see Chapter 13). A good ROE *without* debt is better than one *with* debt. Although Buffett would err on the side of reducing or eliminating debt, he's not totally against borrowing where it makes business sense; that is where margin of safety is maintained and the borrowed money is put to productive use. If good ROE can *only* be achieved by carrying large amounts of debt, watch out.

Owner earnings

Buffett was hardly the first to recognize that earnings and earnings measures can be less than pure. For reasons explored in Chapters 6, 7, and 8 and especially Chapter 9, earnings may not tell the whole story.

Many analysts use cash flow as a more realistic indicator of business performance. But cash flow can have its limitations as well, particularly when large irregular capital expenditures fall outside the analyst's time horizon. No matter how you look at it, business performance must include funds required to build and sustain infrastructure, whether accounted for on a *cash basis* (lump sum disbursements) or *depreciation* (periodic recovery). So Buffett uses cash flow, but he goes further to include capital expenditures and changes in working capital. This is the only logical course, especially when taking a long-term perspective. To Buffett, short-term cash flows devoid of capital requirements "are frequently used by marketers of business and securities in attempts to justify the unjustifiable and thereby sell what should be unsaleable." We couldn't have said it any better.

So the tenet boils down to this: Use *owner earnings* (net income plus depreciation, depletion, and amortization) — less capital expenditures and working capital infusions — to fairly evaluate business performance.

Behind the curtain: Profit margins

Behind every successful business is an operating machine producing healthy profit margins. Gross margin and net operating margin (after expenses) are important. Gross margins indicate market power and potential. Both gross and net margins reflect control of costs and expenses. Effective margins and effective cost controls are not discrete events but rather a self-evident way of life for successful businesses and their management teams. Managers who rely on one-time write-offs to control costs are not managing expenses and margins effectively on a day-to-day basis. Look for consistently healthy, growing profit margins and low overhead costs.

A dollar for a dollar

This tenet drifts a bit from pure company internals to bring in market valuation. Buffett looks for companies for whom every dollar in retained earnings should result in a dollar of increased book value, and a dollar of increased book value should achieve a dollar increment in stock price. Although subject to the whims of Mr. Market, in the long term, stock prices should appreciate as business value appreciates. If this isn't happening, something is wrong either with the numbers or the economic prospects of the business itself.

Market tenets

Up to this point, this chapter concentrates on the value of the business itself. Share price — and whether to buy into the business — have hardly entered the discussion. Market tenets concern rational decisions about price and value, and whether it's time to buy a company.

Determine the value of a business

We beat this to a pulp in Chapters 11 through 14, so we won't go into a detailed treatise on intrinsic and strategic value. But it's apparent that the intrinsic value principle described in Chapter 12 (a business is worth what the owners can take out of it) is the centerpiece of Buffett's business valuation approach.

Buffett will look at total future owner earnings and insist on an understandable, predictable pattern (a circle of competence). These earnings, or *coupons,* are discounted back to the present to arrive at a fair figure to compare to price and alternative investments. And what about the discount rate? Buffett usually uses the higher of a current risk-free bond rate or 10 percent, and instead of adding risk premium to the discount rate, he requires a lower price to provide a margin of safety. Buffett's approach, although principally sound, avoids getting stuck on the finer (but never precise) ramifications of risk and discount rates. "Risk comes in not knowing what you're doing" and "I put a heavy weight on certainty" are timeless Buffettisms that apply.

Swing at good pitches only

The fitting last tenet is the notion of buying only at attractive prices. The preceding eleven tenets may indicate *business* success, but they won't insure *investment* success. Investment success means finding a *business* bound for success, and buying it at a *price* bound for success.

So the essential strategy is to "find companies with above average returns, and buy their stock when it is priced below its intrinsic value." The margin of safety thus provided creates a lot of upside leverage for the owner; at the same time, it mitigates the risk of declining value and magnifies the expected return (business growth plus return to core intrinsic value).

And don't forget the *quality* variable. It may not be realistic to expect a business with really wonderful prospects to show up for sale at a big discount to value. Although the original Buffett approach (and the Graham approach before that) was to find good companies at a deep discount, the more modern value approach (brought to Buffett in part by Charlie Munger) is to pay up for quality where it makes sense, even to multiples of book value.

A corollary principle (and one of the hardest lessons for the investor) is *patience*. Metaphorically, it is the notion of "swinging only at strikes" and better yet, swinging at strikes *you like*. The true value investor can pass up a lot of investment opportunities, even many that fall within the zone. The idea is to wait for one that looks really good, then swing hard. Too many investors pull the trigger too quickly and foul off pitches outside the zone or in the wrong place in the zone. Wait for the investment down the middle, with truly excellent business prospects at a truly great price relative to value. Be patient.

Chapter 16

Shopping for Value: Deciding When the Price Is Right

> *The higher the price, the lower the rate-of-return potential. It's that simple.*
>
> —Timothy Vick, *How to Pick Stocks Like Warren Buffett*

You tried it on and it fits. You like it and it looks good on you. Now, on to the next issue: the price tag. Look at the number. Does the price make sense? Compared to benefits and value received? Seems kind of high. You ponder. Maybe it doesn't fit as well as you thought, and it isn't quite your color anyway. Or perhaps you checked the price *first*. It looked like a good deal. Now let's try it on. A bargain-hunter's paradise.

Regardless of the exact approach, sooner or later, *price* enters the value equation. An attractive price or price-to-something ratio may have led you to the stock in the first place. And it is the inevitable final check we'll make when deciding to buy or sell, even the very moment the order is launched.

If you've read this book from the beginning, up to now, focus has been on business and company value. Now it's the price tag, the market price as set by the investing public. In this chapter, we examine the price tag, and help you establish your system for deciding if the price is right.

The Inside-Out Approach to Buying

Why haven't we explored price yet? You bargain hunters (which most value investors are) probably expected the price discussion to start in Chapter 2. What gives?

Impulse buying not allowed

This book takes an inside-out approach. That is, we look at the merchandise in detail before considering a buying decision. It's the way most people look (or should look) at buying a big-ticket item such as a car, a house, or a college education. And is a securities investment a big decision? You bet. For the avid Buffettonian, a stock purchase is a *life* decision.

So that's why we've led the tour through business valuation, in some detail, before discussing price. If the value investor has a good sense for the *value* of a company (intrinsic value, ROE and drivers, and intangibles), a conscious and deliberate buying decision can be made after price is known.

But it still isn't a formula

Even with all the analysis, we regret to inform you that buying decisions are still not black-and-white formula answers. Intrinsic value of $22, ROE of 25 percent, good management, sustainable margins, growth, familiar brand, price of $18. Should you buy? It's still a gray area.

A lot is going your way in this example. The chances of going wrong aren't huge. But before pulling the trigger, you must first think about risk and uncertainty (the downside) and you must think about the alternatives. A $22 stock for $18 may be better than a $50 stock for $30. And in a risky environment, neither may be as good as a 6 percent bond. Just like a swimsuit on a store rack is evaluated against other swimsuits, as well as its own price, so it must be for a business purchase — or really a capital allocation — decision.

Moving outside

"Inside" business appraisal was largely based on profit, growth, and growth drivers in many layers of detail — solid and improving business fundamentals. As we head out into the real world of markets and prices, the focus shifts to putting the right price tag on the fundamentals. More to the point, we're deciding if the current price tag makes sense.

What did the market miss?

The value investor seeks one of two scenarios:

✔ Scenario 1: The market underestimates strong and improving fundamentals.

✔ Scenario 2: Fundamentals are not improving, but they're better than the market thinks. This is the turnaround situation, or what Buffett calls "one-puff" investments: finding a business, like a cigar, that has one good puff of investor payback left. Also included are *asset plays*. Asset plays are situations in which the business itself may be difficult, but the underlying assets, including cash, natural resources, real estate, and patents, have value beyond the current stock price.

Riskier and harder to assess, Scenario 2 is often best left for the professional investor. Turnarounds often don't turn around, and precise asset appraisal is difficult. Value investors specializing in Scenario 2 investments often look to unlock value by *acquisition*. Predicting and valuing turnarounds, asset plays, and acquisitions is challenging. The hard part is figuring out how and when the value will be unlocked. For this discussion, we'll stay closer to Scenario 1: attaching price to strong and improving fundamentals.

All in the P/E Family

By far, the most popular valuation tool is the Price to Earnings, or P/E ratio. It's in every newspaper, and it pops up at every cocktail party investing discussion. And yes, P/E will furnish a cornerstone for *our* pricing discussion. P/E, once well understood, is one of the major ways that investors make sense of the price tag. In this chapter, we explore P/E and its components and drivers, what it really tells us, and how to deploy it to price a business.

The P/E ratio is the main thread that attaches price to value: *P* is price and *E* is earnings — the fundamental end product of the business. Through *E* and growth projections, P/E connects price with the intrinsic and strategic valuation presented in Chapters 11 through 14. We explore this connection as this chapter progresses. We'll also explore related valuation measures: Price to Book (P/B) and Price to Sales (P/S).

There is no formula for applying P/E. "If it's 17 you buy and if it's 25 you sell" doesn't work. A deeper understanding of the P/E and underlying fundamentals is required. The following sections provide some of that depth.

The many faces of P/E

P/E is the ratio of the stock price to annual earnings for a company. Seems like P/E should just be P/E, end of story, right? A simple snapshot comparison of price and earnings. Price is pretty clear: today's price. But how does one define today's earnings, since earnings aren't a snapshot item but represent instead activity for a 12-month period? *Which* 12-month period? The one just finished, the one upcoming, a combination? Actual performance or an extrapolation of the most recently completed quarter? Indeed, P/E is influenced by the period used to identify earnings, and some important lessons can be learned by looking at different P/E figures. Also important to recognize: Different data sources calculate P/E differently, so watch out!

To illustrate the point, we'll share different cuts of P/E and P/E-related measures from *The Value Line Investment Survey*. Figures are found at the top and in the body of each company's Investment Survey page.

- **P/E** in Value Line is calculated by dividing recent stock price by the total of the last six months' actual earnings plus the next six months' estimated earnings. This is a realistic way to do it. Many publications take the most recent 12 months' actual, which is okay but a little conservative. It can also overweight one-time events up to a year ago.

- **Trailing P/E** is price divided by the last 12 months' actual earnings, often found in the newspaper. Value Line shows their current P/E next to the trailing P/E. Comparing current and trailing P/Es is interesting: A current P/E less than trailing P/E says price may not have caught up with projections. Or- there is risk and a wait-and-see attitude about the projection.

- **Median P/E** is the median statistical P/E figure exhibited by that company over the past ten years. A current P/E below the median shows possible underpricing or changes in business fundamentals. If the current P/E is greater than median, the stock may be overpriced. Be careful to factor in interest rates. If interest rates are decreasing, then norm P/Es will tend to increase.

- **Relative P/E** is a look at a stock's P/E versus the aggregate Value Line universe of 1,700 stocks they follow. Comparison can tell you if a stock flies higher or lower than the market. To a great degree, that is a function of growth (we'll get to that) but also may indicate over- or underpriced situations.

- **Average Annual P/E** tracks *average* price for the year (as opposed to recent price) divided by actual 12-month earnings for the year. Whereas median P/E sums up the last ten years into a single figure, Average Annual P/E is shown for the span of Value Line coverage: 15 years on the sheets. This figure is good for analyzing trends such as P/E and market behavior over time.

- **Average Annual Relative P/E** normalizes the Average Annual P/E cited above against the Value Line universe. So if P/E is rising at the same pace as market P/E (change in interest rates, irrational exuberance, or whatever), this ratio stays constant. If this ratio increases, that suggests that growth prospects are better, or at least viewed that way in the market. If this ratio decreases, the company is being looked at less favorably.

If you have Value Line, we suggest becoming familiar with these figures. If you don't have Value Line, make sure you understand where your P/E data comes from and what it represents. Generally you will only get the 12-month trailing P/E, and possibly a more "current" variation.

And don't forget, analysis often goes beyond P/E, beyond price to *earnings*. Many analysts and sophisticated investors prefer to look at price as it compares to cash flow or *free* cash flow — as truer indicators of business performance. You won't find these figures in the newspaper, and while Value Line provides many of the ingredients, you won't find calculated figures there, either.

Earnings yield

What is P/E? It is the ratio of share price to earnings. But there's more information than meets the eye. First, P/E tells how many years it would take to recoup an investment, with earnings staying the same. A P/E of 17 means that with flat earnings, it would take 17 years to recover your investment. A P/E of 40 means 40 years. That's a long time, and should tell you that something else is at work to support a high P/E: Competent investors don't wait 40 years just to get their money back! That *something* is either growth potential or understated current earnings.

But a greater revelation occurs when we turn the ratio upside down. The inverse ratio *(earnings yield)* tells the annual percentage return implied by the P/E. It is simply 1/(P/E). If P/E is 10, than 1/(P/E) is 0.1 or 10 percent. If P/E is 40 then 1/(P/E) is 0.025 or 2.5 percent. This figure is the equivalent yield the investor would use to compare this earnings stream to, suppose, a bond. A bond returning $5 on a face value of $100 yields 5 percent. A stock returning $5 in earnings on $100 invested (stock price) could also be said to yield 5 percent, and would have a P/E ratio of, you guessed it, 20 ($100 ÷ $5).

Earnings yield makes more sense to trained investors. Earnings yield can be used to compare to other investments including, but not exclusively, bonds and fixed income investments. P/E is just a number, earnings yield is a rate of return comparable across all investment forms.

Table 16-1 is one of the simpler math tables you'll see in value investing, but it illustrates the wide range of investment yields implied by different P/E ratios.

Table 16-1	Converting P/E to Earnings Yield
P/E	*Earnings Yield*
1	100.0 percent
5	20.0 percent
8	12.5 percent
10	10.0 percent
12	8.3 percent
15	6.7 percent
20	5.0 percent
30	3.3 percent
40	2.5 percent
50	2.0 percent
60	1.7 percent
75	1.3 percent
100	1.0 percent

P/E and Interest Rates

Once earnings yield is understood, it becomes easier to comprehend market-driven P/E fluctuations over time. When rates are low, P/E's tend to be higher. The reason: *equivalent* yield. Much has been made of the recent rise in P/E's to over 30 for the S&P 500 (1998–2000) and the subsequent decline to "only" 22 or so. But some (not all) of this is due to lower interest rates. If 10-year Treasuries (the best barometer for a risk-free rate of return) are just barely over 5%, the *equivalent* earnings yield — *with no growth prospects* — converted to P/E, is about 20. Growth prospects would justify a higher P/E. So while the "market" P/E of 22 still seems high (in the early 90's it was only 15), it can be partially explained by the low interest rate environment. Conversely, when interest rates rise (1994, 2000), earnings yield must rise. Consequently, P/E's fall and stock prices head south.

Lesson 2: P/E and Growth

We wish we could tell you that looking at price, P/E, and earnings yield was all there is to it. Find an earnings yield of 6 percent (P/E of 17), beat the bond, and move on. But you're buying equities, not bonds, right? Because you want to participate in company growth and success. And why do you want to do that? Because, simply, you want to leave that static bond yield in the dust — if not today, sometime in the near future. So to do that, you assume some risk that earnings won't happen, but basically you're hanging your hat on growth and a stock price that keeps up with it.

Buy a bond for $100, receive $5 per year for 10, 20, 30 years, never look back. Buy a stock for $100, earnings per share of $5 for 10, 20, or 30 years with no change? Should have bought the bond. Why? Less risk.

But suppose the $5 earnings coupon grows at 10 percent per year. What happens at the end of year 10? Get out the compounding formula. Five bucks times (1+10 percent) to the tenth power is $12.97. If the price were to stay the same, your $100 investment would be returning $12.97 in year 10, which is almost 13 percent earnings yield, or an implied P/E of 7.7 at today's price. Table 16-2 shows future earnings yields realized in the case of a bond with no growth versus a stock with a 10 percent earnings growth.

Table 16-2	Earnings Yield: Bond versus Growth Stock
Bond	*Stock*
Coupon/earnings yield	5 percent
Investment	$100
Year 1 return	$5
Earnings growth	0 percent
Year 10 return	$5
Earnings Yield (EY) year 1	5 percent
Earnings Yield (EY) year 10	5 percent

So you can see that assessing growth is a major factor in analyzing a stock price through P/E. What is the earnings yield today, what will it be in the future, and how does it get into the equation?

PEG is a tool, not the answer

PEG should be used as a guideline and an investing tool, but be careful to avoid overdependence on this quick, easy-to-calculate, and easy-to-understand figure when making long-term investment decisions. The denominator in PEG is the earnings growth rate, and the careful value investor looks closely at growth assumptions and supporting business fundamentals. PEG can be used as a selection or screening tool to identify stocks for deeper analysis, and also works at the end of the appraisal process to determine if price is in line with (or is lower than) corresponding growth prospects. But it, by itself, isn't the answer.

A PEG in a poke

As a sharp reader, you may be recognizing familiar themes. As we discuss in Chapter 12, intrinsic value is built on future returns as cash flows and particularly the growth of those cash flows. We'll get back to intrinsic value shortly. In the meantime, you may have heard about the PEG ratio — *price/earnings to growth* — briefly introduced in Chapter 10. PEG relates, or *normalizes*, the P/E to the growth rate. With PEG, apparently high P/E ratios are supported by look-ahead growth. PEG thus becomes a better tool to compare stocks with different P/Es and different underlying growth assumptions.

By itself, it's hard to tell whether a P/E is good or bad. A stock with a P/E of 30 may be a better deal than another stock with a P/E of 15. Why? Because of growth. A stock of a no-growth company with a P/E of 15 will never achieve an earnings yield beyond 7.5 percent (1/15). Meanwhile the company with a P/E of 30, with a growth rate of 20 percent, eventually achieves an earnings yield greater than 20 percent. The analysis is similar to what is shown in Table 16-2.

Enter the practice of *normalizing* P/E by the growth rate. To do that, we divide all P/Es by the company's growth rate to create a ratio known as (Price/Earnings)/Growth, or PEG for short. *G* is the growth rate, expressed as a whole number (that is, the percentage times 100). So a company with a P/E of 30 and a growth rate of 20 percent has a PEG of 1.5.

So now we have a standard for comparison. Company A with a P/E of 18 and a growth rate of 12 percent has the same PEG as Company B with a P/E of 30 and a growth rate of 20 percent. Are the two P/Es the same? 30 versus 18? Clearly not — until we identify the underlying growth fundamentals, apply PEG, and find out they are indeed priced equally.

Table 16-3 extends Table 16-2 to show the relationship between future earnings yield, P/E, and PEG. Watch what happens to PEG and future earnings yields as growth assumptions rise. Low PEG ratios (less than 2) correspond to high future earnings yields.

Table 16-3	Earnings Growth, Earnings Yield, and PEG				
Bond	Stock 1	Stock 2	Stock 3	Stock 4	Stock 5
Coupon/ Earnings Yield	5 percent	5 percent	5 percent	5 percent	5 percent
Investment	$100	$100	$100	$100	$100
Year 1 return	$5	$5	$5	$5	$5
Earnings growth	0 percent	5 percent	10 percent	15 percent	20 percent
Year 10 return	$5	$8.14	$12.97	$20.23	$30.96
EY (year 1)	5 percent	5 percent	5 percent	5 percent	5 percent
EY (year 10)	5 percent	8.1 percent	13 percent	20.2 percent	31 percent
Year 1 P/E	N/A	20	20	20	20
Year 1 PEG	N/A	4	2	1.3	1

You can see that the PEG = 2 scenario corresponds to a future earnings yield of 13 percent. A PEG of 1.3 correlates to 20 percent, and a PEG of 1 correlates to a future earnings yield of 31 percent on today's investment price. If PEG goes up to 4, on the other hand, future earnings yield is only 8.1 percent.

So what is a "good" PEG ratio? It all depends on the implied future rate of return you're looking for, which depends on investment objectives, risk tolerance, and current risk-free (bond) interest rates. A PEG of 2.7 or less implies a future earnings yield of 10 percent or more. Anything over 2.7, implying a future earnings yield of less than 10 percent, is probably less return at more risk than most investors desire. PEG of 1 or less is great (but hard to find), a PEG between 1 and 2 is good, between 2 and 3 is marginal, anything over 3 should probably be avoided.

Hurdle rates and the 15 percent rule

This lesson may sound complicated, like something from the latest economics textbook. But it actually comes straight from the Buffett school of stock selection. The goal: Determine if a stock's price can feasibly grow at a minimum annual compounded rate, or *hurdle rate*. If it can, it may be considered for purchase; if it can't, it's rejected.

Not surprisingly, the analysis examines current stock price, earnings growth, and potential future stock price based on that growth. If the growth-supported future stock price can appreciate at a compounded annual growth rate (CAGR) meeting or exceeding the hurdle rate, it is in buy territory. If appreciation potential is short of the required price growth hurdle, the stock is rejected. *Either the current stock price is too high or the projected growth is too weak to meet the growth hurdle.* Figure 16-1 shows an example of a stock price that is too high to continue growing at the "hurdle" growth rate, given current earnings growth projections.

Price Growth Analysis - Coca-Cola						
15% Hurdle (Warren Buffett Rule)						
Current price	$ 47.00			all data from Value Line		
Current P/E	29.2					
Median P/E	31					
Base earnings	$ 1.48					
Earnings growth rate	9.5%					
Required hurdle	15%					
Year	EPS	15% growth price	15% price growth P/E	Future price, median P/E	Investment can return hurdle rate?	
1	$ 1.62					
2	$ 1.77					
3	$ 1.94					
4	$ 2.13					
5	$ 2.33					
6	$ 2.55					
7	$ 2.79					
8	$ 3.06					
9	$ 3.35					
10	$ 3.67	$ 190.14	51.8	$ 113.70	NO	
Implied compounded growth rate:			9.2%			

Figure 16-1: Coca Cola's price growth analysis for the 15 percent hurdle.

What's going on here? Starting out, Coke has a current stock price of $47 and current (2000) earnings of $1.62 per share. P/E is a rather large 29.2, PEG is a rather large 3.07 (29.2/9.5 based on Value Line projected growth). Caution flags are flying.

But the analysis continues to project a Year 10 EPS of $3.67 (standard compounding at 9.5 percent). Now, the fundamental question: given these assumptions, can the stock price grow at 15 percent compounded annually?

Moving along (and looking at Year 10), we first calculate what the stock price would be *if it did* grow at 15 percent annually. Again, the compounding formula: 15 percent at 10 years gives a stock price of $190.14 from today's base of $47. The implied P/E at 10 years would be 51.8 ($190.14/3.67). The caution flags turn into warning flags.

The final test is to project what the stock price is *most likely* to be in ten years. In this analysis, we use the *median P/E* from Value Line — the average P/E over the last ten years — to project forward what the P/E might be ten years from now. Median P/E is used to factor out price swings, interest rate fluctuations, and so on. That figure for Coke is 31. Projecting ten-year price is easy: 31 × 3.67, or $113.70. That is the price Coke can reasonably sell for based on experienced median P/E and forward projected earnings.

This "reasonable" price is far less than the required 15 percent hurdle price of $190.14, so you would not buy Coke based on this requirement. *Projected earnings growth won't support a 15% compounded return on the stock price, because the current price is already too high.* (We suspect indeed that Mr. Buffett would today consider Coke overpriced and unable to meet his investing objectives, but such was clearly not the case in 1988–1989).

As a technicality (a minor one for most stocks), the investor must account for dividends as part of the total return when comparing price appreciation to the hurdle price objective. So if Coke pays a dividend of 68 cents per share, over ten years a total of $6.80 would find its way into the investor's pocket, to add to the $113.70 estimated price, to reach $120.50 total value realized by the investor. It is more accurate to compare this figure to the $190.14 hurdle, though it doesn't make any difference in the final decision for Coke. Don't forget the possibility of dividend growth. In fact, for most stocks, the dividend won't greatly influence the analysis, but don't forget it's there.

Before rejecting Coke altogether, you must consider whether the 9.5 percent growth rate is really right. If sales, profitability and/or productivity are in for major improvement, Coke could still be a good buy. Don't forget the fundamentals underlying earnings and earnings growth.

Deconstructing P/E

You may have seen published figures for Price-to-Sales (P/S) and Price-to-Book (P/B) ratios. These ratios can help clarify the current price of a stock and the context for that price. But do they relate to earnings, already established as the primary driver of company value and stock price growth? If you take a closer look, the answer is "yes."

If we take apart P/E (or more accurately its inverse Earnings-to-Price or *earnings yield [EY]*), we can build two equations breaking earnings yield into its components.

Deconstruction #1: Price, sales, net profit

The first deconstruction looks at price, sales, and profits:

$$\text{Earnings/Price (EY)} = \text{Earnings/Sales} \times \text{Sales/Price}$$

Yes, yet another equation. But a closer look reveals familiar territory. Earnings/sales translates to *net profit margin,* which is a key measure of success. Sales/Price is the inverse of the more common P/S ratio. So the equation could be restated as:

$$\text{Price/Earnings (P/E)} = (1/\text{Profit Margin}) \times \text{Price/Sales (P/S)}$$

Twisting this around in our already overworked brains, we see that a given EY (or P/E) is driven by profit margins and the ratio of price to sales. *A high P/S ratio may be justified by a high profit margin, because the resulting EY will be favorable.* But if a company has a high P/S and a *low* profit margin, the resulting earnings yield would be low, and the resulting investment would be suspect.

A bunch of P/S

If Company A has a P/S ratio of 4 and Company B has a P/S ratio of 1, most investors would jump at the chance to buy Company B. Invest a dollar for a dollar of sales, and the profit margin will take care of the rest. Future growth is gravy. Many small businesses are bought and sold on this basis. But what if profit margins are chronically thin? The resulting earnings will suffer, and the price won't be justified, which is why investors shouldn't look at P/S in a vacuum.

P/S ratios below 2 are generally considered attractive. But it depends on the profit margin. Some companies in basic industries or thin-margined retail are actually well below 1. Ford has a P/S ratio of only 0.23, but a net profit margin of only 3.3 percent. When P/S creeps up to 3, investors become skeptical. Four or greater, and look out — unless profit margins and/or growth potential are exceptional.

A price, sales, and profit " map"

P/S nirvana could be a situation where a company had a relatively low P/S *and* high profit margins. Looking at a variety of stocks, relatively few companies have *both* a P/S of less than 3 *and* a net profit margin greater than 10 percent. Looking through from earnings to sales to price, such companies would be in a "sweet spot." The stock price is relatively low compared to both sales and profitability. Companies "close" to the sweet spot may have a low P/S but also low margins, or high margins but high price relative to sales generation.

Sky high

Amazingly, in the recent bull run, P/S ratios went into orbit. Cisco at one point sported a P/S ratio of 30 ($82 on $2.65 sales per share). With a P/S ratio of 30, net profit margin would have to be 100 percent just to get "down" to a P/E of 30 or earnings yield of 3.3 percent! High profit margins and high growth would be expected to be sure, but the business would have to grow an awful lot to justify those kinds of valuations.

Figure 16-2 relates P/S and margins to help guide price decisions.

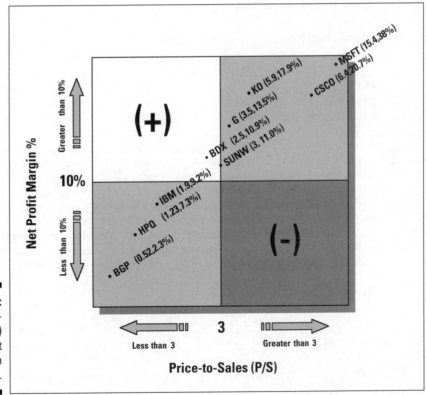

Figure 16-2:
Price-to-Sales (P/S) and Profit Margin Map.

In Figure 16-2, selected stocks are mapped by P/S and Profit Margin. Stocks in the upper-left quadrant would be "sweet-spot" stocks, sporting both low P/S and high profit margins. Out of 25 stocks we looked at, only Becton, Dickenson & Co (BDK), a medical supplier, fell into this quadrant with a P/S of 2.5 and a net profit margin of 10.9 percent. Using this analysis, we could say that BDK is reasonably priced, if not a good value. BDK has a good, fundamentally balanced chance of achieving healthy and sustained earnings yield. Net profit trends, drivers, and sales trends would have to be examined before confirming this outlook.

Figure 1621 shows stocks close to the sweet spot, but not quite there. Normally these are in better shape than companies farther away. By this standard, IBM and Gillette (G) are close, and if profitability trends (IBM) and sales trends (G) are favorable, they will soon enter the "sweet" quadrant. Conversely, if we could get Microsoft (MSFT) closer to a P/S of 3 from its current lofty 15.4, either by reducing stock price or dramatically increasing sales, it might start to look like a good buy.

Again, like most other tools, P/S deconstruction shouldn't be overused or overly depended upon, but it's a good way to check if price is in balance with sales and earnings potential.

Deconstruction #2: Price, book value, ROE

Earnings yield can be examined through another path: book value and profit return on book value, which is more widely known as return on equity, or ROE. A company with a high ROE is initially a good purchase candidate unless the price is out of line with the underlying equity. Enter the third "cousin" of P/E: the Price-to-Book or P/B ratio.

When buying a share of stock, ideally you would want to receive a dollar of owner's equity for each dollar invested. However, such is rarely the case. Accounting practices distort the true equity value of companies, and a dollar-for-dollar approach would omit growth and growth potential from consideration. So typically, most companies sell at a multiple to book value. Companies selling below book value are hard to find and may indicate overvalued assets or other forms of financial distress. The classic Graham value investing school called for buying companies selling at less than book value or working capital, but "clean" opportunities seldom come forward today.

The equation:

Earnings Yield (EY) = Earnings/Equity (ROE) × Equity/Price (1/(P/B))

Or

Price/Earnings (P/E) = 1/ROE × Price-to-Book (P/B)

So again, a combination of healthy ROE and reasonable P/B indicates value. Because of the wide range of accounting practices, hard and fast rules are less reliable, but companies with an ROE of greater than 20 percent and a P/B of 5 or less achieving earnings yield with a balanced approach.

In Chapters 13 and 14, we devoted a lot to deconstructing ROE and understanding drivers and leading indicators. If a company has a good ROE story, present and future, and a relatively low P/B today, the investor may be in "value" territory.

Again, the law of large numbers and competition can rear its ugly head at the least opportune moments. Very high P/B ratios might be sustained by very high ROEs, but very high ROEs themselves are hard to sustain (see Chapter 13).

Lesson 4: Recognizing value and un-value

This lesson summarizes how to use P/E and its "family" of measures to recognize value and un-value in stocks and stock prices.

Value

First, find sound and improving business fundamentals — improving ROE drivers and intangibles. Then:

> Earnings yield > bond yield (now or soon)
>
> PEG 2 or less (earnings yield with growth)
>
> Stock price growth potential exceeds hurdle rate (15 percent, 10 years)
>
> P/S < 3 and profit margin > 10 percent (good fundamentals at reasonable price)
>
> P/B < 5 and ROE > 15 percent (good fundamentals at reasonable price)

With good fundamentals, intangibles, and reasonable pricing determined by the preceding (the more factors comply, the better) we're probably on the right price-for-value track.

Look out for "large numbers"

When a share price valuation is built on high P/S ratios and very high profit margins, watch out for the "law of large numbers" and competition. The law of large numbers says that, sooner or later, things move toward averages or norms. The P/S ratio, and thus stock price, might be vulnerable to downside surprises if the margins prove unsustainable. Microsoft supports its price and high P/S ratio (15.4) with exceptionally high margins. That may be okay for market-dominant Microsoft, but other "mortal" companies might be walking the edge of a cliff. Companies with very low P/S ratios and low margins might sustain price valuation with high sales or sales growth, but watch out for sales downturns. Retailers, especially glamorous "concept" retailers, often walk the edge of the sales downturn "cliff." As in golf, away from the edges and toward the middle is the best bet.

Un-value

Earnings yield < bond yield with low growth prospects

PEG > 3, high P/E and/or low growth

Stock price growth falls short of hurdle rate (15 percent)

P/S > 3 with low margins

P/B > 5 with low ROE

Making the Buy Decision

Earlier in this chapter, we explained the use of P/E as one of the main tools to relate price to company value. P/E, especially with its family of measures, is a great set of tools. But we devote a lot of space in Chapters 12 through 15 to calculating intrinsic and strategic value, and these only *sort of* came into the P/E equation through earnings. Did we leave out the major tenets of value investing while starting down the aisle towards committing to buy a business? Is there some mistake?

Not really. (But would we admit it if there were?) All pieces of that in-depth appraisal create a better understanding of the business, a better understanding of the fundamentals upon which earnings and future owner returns are based. They help shape the earnings estimate — and the investors' confidence in the estimates.

But it's worth raising a few more principles to consider in the buying decision. In the following sections, we cover those principles, and then revisit the checklist one more time, in a simplified format, to finish building the appraisal process.

From P/E to P/I

Ten-plus pages of detailed price assessment using P/E, earnings yield, P/B, P/S, and hardly a word about intrinsic value? After 20-plus pages about it in Chapter 12? After repeated Graham and Buffett quotes about how cash returns and intrinsic value define the value of a business? Explanation, please.

The explanation is simple. If you went to the trouble to calculate intrinsic value, and you feel good about the answer, by all means, use it. The formula is really simple: If price is greater than intrinsic value, the stock is overpriced; if it's less than intrinsic value, it is underpriced (for you math heads, that's buy if P/I (Price to Intrinsic Value) is less than 1 and sell if P/I is greater than 1).

So are you casting aside P/E by using P/I instead? No. P/E and especially PEG look at the same things: earnings and growth. Intrinsic value looks at earnings growth in more detail, with varying growth rates. Intrinsic value also looks explicitly at the current interest rate climate and risk through the cost of capital, where P/E and PEG look at it only indirectly by earnings yield comparisons.

So really, P/E and its family are really closely related to P/I, and due to the complexity of intrinsic value and the fact that we've never seen a P/I ratio in the paper or other popular financial resources, it's good to know both approaches. Both the principles and the calculation provide valuable insight.

What about that "strategic" stuff?

Strategic financials and intangibles, covered in depth in Chapters 13 and 14, mainly contribute to understanding the business and supporting the growth projections used in the pricing models. They can be especially important in determining upside or downside. If today's growth rate for Coca-Cola is projected at 9.5 percent, you can, by your own absorption of strategic financials and intangibles, decide if this makes sense, and which alternative scenarios you want to emphasize. Value investors should never lose sight of leading indicators, and never be reluctant to reevaluate a company if they change.

Buy low, improve your chances

We cover this one a bit in Chapter 4. Simply, this buy rule follows two concepts:

- ✔ Provide a margin of safety.
- ✔ Allow for proportionally better returns on dollars invested.

Probably the second most common investing mistake (after throwing good money after bad) is finding and buying a great company (with growth, intrinsic value, supporting fundamentals, and intangibles all there) but paying too much for it. Paying too much simultaneously creates downside vulnerability and limits upside potential.

Don't be afraid to take a few pitches. You don't have to swing at every pitch, and the next one might be better.

Part IV
Becoming a
Value Investor

The 5th Wave   By Rich Tennant

"All right, ready everyone! We've got some clown out here who looks interested."

In this part . . .

*W*e offer information on setting goals and developing your own value investing style. We provide some commentary on how to figure out what works best for you. Because value investment choices go far beyond common stock, we present chapters describing mutual funds, bonds and convertible securities, real estate and real estate investment trusts, and other specialty investments.

Chapter 17

Shopping for Value: A Practical Approach

> *Once you're able to tell the story of a stock to your family, your friends, or the dog, and so that even a child could understand it, then you have a proper grasp of the situation.*
>
> —Peter Lynch, *One Up on Wall Street*

*I*n this chapter, we try to distill the knowledge and background presented earlier in this book into a workable, practical approach for everyday use. Sort of a *Reader's Digest* version of value investing, if that helps. We add a little flavor by describing nontraditional or special situations that may find their way onto your value-investing dinner plate from time to time.

As a Reminder . . .

Like gift giving, in value investing it's really the *thought* that counts. Or more precisely, it's the thought *process,* that is, the way of thinking about your investments, that's important. Analysis only serves to support the thinking.

Throughout this book, we share many analytical building blocks and approaches to appraising company value and many ways to decide if the price paid for that value is right. But we also repeatedly make the point that no single method works all the time, and if one *did,* the whole thing wouldn't work anyway because everyone would make the same findings and buy the same companies — and values would no longer be values. Every article, every book, every value investor has a unique application of the value investing thought process.

The thought process is the intellectual process — the *philosophy* — that the value investor internalizes. The tools are there to help, and different tools will help more at different times. If you strive to understand the business value underlying the price before you buy, investing history will be on your side. As you get good at understanding value and price, your investment decisions and performance will only improve.

In the real, practical world of value investing, value comes in all forms. There is so much detail on any given company (much of which you can't know) that it often isn't realistic to become a walking encyclopedia on a company or its fundamentals. And formulas and ratios, although they work and can help, hardly can deliver absolute answers. Usually, taking a few shortcuts makes sense, reserving the deepest analysis to the most critical, difficult, and largest investing decisions.

Further, you need to be practical with your time. You can't spend days on each company. You can't analyze all companies in the investing universe. In this chapter, we outline a simplified, practical approach to help the new value investor get started, and to help experienced value investors improve their game. You'll undoubtedly find yourself adding plays to your value investing game book as you gain experience.

Situations, Special and Otherwise

As a value investor, you'll find that value comes wrapped in all kinds of packages. The mainstream case we lay out in detail is the growth case, where solid and improving business fundamentals point to solid business growth down the road, and where the market has undervalued that growth. That's arguably the most clear-cut, least risky, and easiest-to-understand scenario. But other situations do present themselves, and although they may take weeks of professional-level analysis to understand, they can be interesting. And in a few cases, they may be as easily justified by your own observations, common sense, and gut feel as by the numbers.

Throughout most of this book, we try to train you as a do-it-yourselfer. But in many of the special situations, do-it-yourself may not suffice. Some of these value drivers can be well hidden and subjective — like a company's breakup value. They often turn into value not through normal business results but by being unlocked through acquisitions and restructurings. For these situations it makes sense to rely a bit more on industry professionals and analysts, who have access to key, paid-for data and a lot of historical precedent. They can also pick up the phone and call the company itself or others who might have interest in the assets. Smart value investors know when to — and when not to — rely on the work of others.

In the following sections, we provide a quick tour of the "situational" landscape.

Growth at a Reasonable Price (GARP)

GARP is the mainstream scenario of reasonable market valuation — or undervaluation — of growth potential. Many brokers and industry professionals use the "GARP" acronym to refer this investing scenario and strategy.

Without reviewing the analysis here, suffice it to say that solid and improving fundamentals and supporting intangibles are key. As part of the assessment the value investor must ask how realistic are the growth projections, particularly over time, and whether the company takes a balanced approach to the business and fundamentals. Or are we betting on an extreme but temporary success in short-term margins, market share, revenue, or profit? The *G* in GARP must be sustainable, not a short-term blip or shift in business models.

Fire sale

Occasionally companies experience deep price declines due to actual or anticipated news or announcements. These declines can get out of hand, as more and more bad spin circulates in the market and investors (and institutions) head for seemingly safer waters. The decline is either a one-shot affair or a longer, momentum-driven decline.

Getting creamed

The one-day hit was recently exhibited by Oakley (an eyewear company), when its largest retailer cut orders in favor of their parent company's own products. Oakley stock declined from just above $17 to about $11 in one day, wiping out a third of its market value. Other examples are too numerous to mention, but anytime a stock loses a quarter, a third, or half of its value in one day, it might be worth a glance. Just keep in mind that the reasons for these slaughters are sometimes justified, and the road to recovery may be difficult. There may be more trouble than meets the eye. At the same time, a value investor may find bargains among such distressed inventory.

Smoke and mirrors

Some apparent asset plays can be a mirage. Find a company selling at a low price-to-book, look at assets, and notice that per-share assets are higher than the share price. Is it a good buy? Depends on the quality and liquidity of the assets on the books. Large manufacturers and other capital-intensive companies often have overvalued assets on the books. If the assets are largely based on buildings, equipment, and intangibles, watch out, but if they are cash, securities, marketable natural resources, land, and the like, there may be an asset-play opportunity. If there is a large cash hoard, make sure the company is cash-flow positive or nearly so. You don't want this cash to disappear as "cash burn."

Misreading the tea leaves

Longer declines are illustrated by nearly the entire telecom and fiber optics sector: long, slow persistent declines driven by ever-increasing negative sentiment. The reasons are fairly obvious considering the history of telecom deregulation, the Internet boom, over-ordering, excess capacity, excess expectations, and subsequent bust. But still, most market players were focused on the short-term write-offs, layoffs, and lack of visibility; few looked at the long-term prospects for these businesses. These bust cycles happen all the time. Some are company-specific, others are inherent in their industry. Widespread negative sentiment can produce very attractive buying opportunities.

Blown, or overblown?

The trick for the value investor is to decide whether the situation is overblown, and whether it really is a buying opportunity. Assessing the strength of the core business is essential. If the franchise and long-term growth potential is intact, the situation may present a good opportunity. If Oakley can easily find another channel or set up its own, no harm, no foul. If a fiber optics maker can make the necessary business adjustments to preserve cash and some profit, retain customers, and position itself for better times, the current price could be oversold. These are tricky situations but offer good potential to careful value investors. Warren Buffett has frequently feasted on such overreactions, as he did with *The Washington Post*.

Asset play

We start this book describing AGAP: Assets and Growth at a Price. "AGAP" steps a bit beyond "GARP" to include another element: assets.

Although in the mainstream case, assets are in place only as resources upon which to build business growth and thus aren't valued separately, there will be cases in which the assets themselves create the value. In other words, the company owns them, but they aren't involved — or aren't completely involved — in producing the company's revenue and profit stream. Or they could be used more effectively somewhere else, or they simply aren't valued correctly on the books. The point is, their actual value exceeds reported value in the business as it is currently defined.

Actual value exceeding reported value usually in one of two forms: undervalued assets on the books and breakup values that exceed current business value.

Undervalued assets

Both physical and intangible assets can be undervalued, sometimes significantly. Frequently this occurs for non-depreciable assets that have been held for a long time, such as land. Land is often carried on the books at purchase value, which is almost always less than current market value, especially if held for a long time.

The classic example is railroads, which hold millions of acres originally granted for free when they were built. Some of this land is used in the business, but a great majority isn't, especially for western roads. Something like 1 percent of all land in California is owned by just a couple of railroad firms. Similar situations occur in oil and other natural resource businesses.

Intellectual property can also be undervalued (although in many cases, especially with acquisitions, it is *over*valued, watch out!). Patents and other unique, homegrown know-how can have significant value, although corporate history is littered with companies (Xerox, Bell Labs [Lucent], IBM) that failed to capitalize on the wealth potential.

The key to undervalued asset plays is whether the assets are really that valuable, and what the strategy is for unlocking that value. Railroads until recently have done little to try to realize the value of their land assets. (Now, we're starting to see rail yards converted to downtown plazas, but sometimes at great expense for environmental cleanups).

Look for companies with millions of acres or barrels on the books, examine current market prices, decide for yourself if there's an opportunity. Then look for evidence that the company itself recognizes the opportunity. Union Pacific Corporation (a railroad parent company) for years not only looked to sell its rail-adjacent land, but to target potential customer companies who would build facilities along its lines and ship by rail. They had a whole real estate subsidiary set up around this idea. It was a good strategy, but so far, it's a drop in the bucket compared to potential.

When the sum of the parts exceeds the whole

Big, stagnant, set-in-their-ways companies sometimes offer hidden opportunities. If they were to break into parts, each part would be free to focus on its core opportunities. Improved focus and reduced corporate bureaucracy can work wonders towards rekindling growth, satisfying customers, and building successful new brands. The classic example is AT&T, whose breakup created billions in new business value (despite the fact that the breakup was far from voluntary).

The key is to identify these companies, then try to visualize what they may look like as individual parts, as individual businesses. It isn't always a successful strategy, because new overhead must be created to run each business, and synergies are lost. We doubt that a breakup of General Motors, whose dealer network and common parts platforms would be lost, would work.

It makes more sense where multiple, unrelated, or poorly related businesses exist under one corporate umbrella. If the customers are different, technologies are different, or business models are different, separation sometimes leads to value. Hewlett-Packard and Agilent Technologies (one selling technology end products and the other selling "things that make things work" to other technology companies) made a logical break, but overhead issues have so far hampered success.

Markets tend to undervalue huge conglomerates. It is hard to appreciate and understand the value of each component in detail, so the investing and analysis public tend to discount what they don't understand.

So put all this together, and you may look at a General Electric or Procter & Gamble and wonder if there is more value than meets the stock pages. Listen to rumors, picture the transition, look for clues that management may be thinking along the same lines (a few small divestitures may be an experiment). This is an area where professional analysts can provide good information on which companies are "in play" and what their breakup value may be.

Growth kickers

From time to time, relatively steady companies come up with small subsidiary businesses, sometimes related and sometimes not, that can perk up business growth. Telecom companies got into the cell phone business and 3M is sticking with the Post-It boom. 3Com acquired a little project known as the Palm Pilot in a merger with modem-maker US Robotics. Twenty years ago, the growthless Southern Pacific Railroad started using its right-of-way for telecommunications lines in a business that eventually became Sprint.

These kickers can kindle growth, rekindle growth, and provide good, saleable assets downstream. They may be like finding chunks of chicken in a bowl of soup — not there in every spoonful and maybe not there at all. But when a big company crows about a small new product or business development in its portfolio within its ranks, keep your eyes open.

Turning the ship around

Many companies go through restructurings, downsizing, and spinning off businesses deemed not vital to the core business. There is usually a "back-to-basics" and "focus" theme to these events, and they usually occur after extended periods of poor business results. Auto companies (particularly Chrysler) went through this years ago, and Lucent Technologies is going through it now.

Do turnarounds work? According to Buffett and many other professionals, generally not. A few do, and when they do, there's usually a big impact on shareholder value (witness again Chrysler). Determining worthy value investments in these situations is difficult. Probably the best approach is to try to place a value on the core remaining business with new resources generated by the asset sale. Again here, the work of professionals shouldn't be ignored.

Riding the cyclical

Generally, cyclical companies shouldn't be confused with value investments. Growth, although apparent in the short term, usually isn't sustainable. Investors are getting wiser and aren't as likely to bid up prices in good times, nor bid them way down in bad times, so this form of market timing doesn't work as well.

But occasionally companies caught in the cyclical pool come up with strategies to climb out of it, and move more steadily up and to the right. International expansion can reduce cyclical effects. Manufacturing companies diversify into more recession-proof financial services (which make more money as poor business conditions beget lower interest rates). General Electric has figured this out, and Ford has tried. Other smaller companies may have more effective cycle-beating strategies, because it's hard to keep such big ships as Ford and GE from turning when the wind shifts. If a company seems cheap and has something new in its portfolio to avoid cyclical price and earnings behavior, it might be worth a look.

Finally, Let's Get Practical

In full recognition of the fact that you probably aren't a professional investor, and you probably don't have time to drag your line on the analytic bottoms of the investing lake, we want to present a practical, simplified model for picking out value investments.

The goal is to boil the selection process down to something that could be handled in twenty minutes or less per company. Now for sure, we wouldn't expect a commitment of $10 million to a company based on this analysis, but it provides grounds for making small investments or pursuing further research. At the end of the drill, you should, as Peter Lynch hypothesizes, tell the story of a stock to family, friends, and favorite pets. And most of all, to be able to understand, *yourself,* why you like or don't like a business as an investment.

Steps along the way

The major steps are

- ✔ **Selection:** Using the screening tools, work the 5000-stock universe down to 10, 20, maybe 50 to look at more closely. Pick a few and dig deeper.

- ✔ **Understanding the industry:** This step is optional if you're already familiar, but understand industry dynamics, trends, industry players, and how your selected company fits in its industry.

- ✔ **Appraisal:** We've furnished a simplified checklist covering financials, intangibles, and valuation in one page to help develop and summarize the story.

After you make the decision to invest, downstream steps are to track the story and decide if and when to sell. As you may have picked up, these two elements can be drawn out over a very long time.

Step 1: Selection

The first step is selection. Screening tools exist in many places to enter singular or multiple criteria to narrow the search. Of course, this isn't the *only* way to find out about good stocks. Good selections can come from your own experiences or from the barstool next to you. So long as the appraisal step is performed, it really doesn't matter how it gets into the top of the funnel.

With experience you'll develop a screening path that best meets your investing tastes and objectives. Good screening packages are available in Yahoo! Finance, Charles Schwab (repackaged from Standard & Poor's), Quicken, Microsoft Money, and most other online and software-based investment services and tools. Some are better than others, allowing more factors and combinations of factors to be supplied. There are canned value screens already set up in some services; these typically do a fair job.

The old computer axiom "garbage in, garbage out" applies to stock screeners. Extraordinary events in the numbers can cause a company to have a distorted growth rate, ROE, P/E ratio and so forth. In part, that's why the screen, by itself, doesn't work.

Step 2: Get into in the industry

This step is optional: If you are already familiar with the industry, its players, and recent news and trends, it probably isn't necessary. But if you enter this process through a stock screen, chances are you'll come up with something like the Aztar Corporation — not exactly a household name — and will have to find out what industry it is in and learn a bit about it.

The first best place to go in starting the investigation of a screened candidate are the Yahoo! Finance quote and profile pages. The quote page provides, of course, the stock quote, and if you want, charts to observe past stock price performance. Don't stop too long here, because value investing isn't about price trends. But you can get an idea of what's happening with the company in comparison to the overall market, and you can see whether there is a possible fire sale situation. More importantly, there is a list of recent newswire items; from these news stories a picture of the company and the industry can be started.

The profile page then gives a synopsis of the company's business and financials, its sector and industry (under "Competitors"). The more detailed "Statistics at a glance" further develops the financial picture.

As we discuss in Chapter 14, there are many sources for intangibles, some straightforward, some harder to find. A cruise through *The Wall Street Journal, Business Week,* or any related trade magazine can build industry knowledge. Online versions are especially useful with their search capability.

Look for . . .

- ✔ What industry the company is in (and if it doesn't fit one neatly, as in "Starbucks" and "restaurants," make a note of that).

- ✔ General industry trends (buggy whips are bad, telecom has turned bad, oil and the defense sector might be good).

- ✔ The role of your company in the industry (dominant player, number two and trying harder, vanquished and retrenching, and so forth). Look at market share and changes in market share.

- ✔ Industry characteristics that may affect financial appraisal. This one's harder, it's hard to know from publicly available material that, for instance, booksellers can return most all inventory for 100 percent cash, reducing inventory risk and making otherwise large inventory balances not look so bad. If you have the time (and it probably takes more than ten minutes), it's worth talking to someone in the business.

Throughout the book we've taken a cautionary approach to professional investment analysts and their work. But most of the industry reports they put together — based on professionally available information, industry contacts, and years of tracking the industry — are good and well written. These industry reports are worth looking at to understand an industry and its players. There are a lot of ways to get at these reports — some for free and some for a signup or a fee. If you have a broker (online or full service) start there.

Step 3: Appraise and praise

We won't drag you, kicking and screaming, through the entire investment appraisal process *again*. Instead, we'll furnish a one-page checklist (see Figure 17-1), derived from the more detailed versions presented in Chapters 13 and 14.

Figure 17-1:
Value
investing
appraisal,
short form.

Short form value appraisal *Attach supporting data if necessary*	**Company** [ ]
	Date [ ] **Price** [ ]
SITUATION ☐ Growth: strong and improving fundamentals ☐ Asset Play ☐ Price Fall	☐ Restructure/Turnaround ☐ Other special situation [ ]

	Grade	**Factors**	**Assessment**
FINANCIALS	[ ]	•ROE steady or rising, above 20% •Net Profit % improving, above 10% •Gross margins improving •Asset and unit productivity improving •Cash generator, producer not consumer of capital •Reasonable debt load •Repurchasing shares •Consistent performance •Better than competition and industry	

INTANGIBLES	[ ]	•Market power strong and growing
		  --brand, market share, customer
		  loyalty
		  --positioned for long term growth
		•Strong, effective, management
		  --pursuing shareholder interests
		•Favorable 'SWOT' analysis	

VALUATION	[ ]	•Price < Intrinsic value •Favorable P/E / earnings yield •Earnings yield at or near bond yield •PEG < 2 •P/S < 3 •P/B < 5 •can meet 15% hurdle	
OVERALL	[ ]	**DECISION** ☐ Buy ☐ Look to buy at or below [ ] ☐ Move on	

We think that most of the information you should consider or fill in on this form is available in three or four places:

- ✔ "Financials" information is best derived from Value Line or the annual report. Yahoo! Finance can fill in. Value Line is probably the fastest.

- ✔ "Intangibles" is from your own experience, reading, news stories, and what you see and hear on the street. But if it's late at night and everything's closed, your friends in the industry have all gone to bed and so forth, a trip through the company's Web site or the online financial press can tell a lot.

✔ "Valuation" is straightforward and the easiest information to find on Value Line. Though it might turn a 20-minute appraisal into a 30-minute one, a conservative intrinsic value run on Quicken.com (www.quicken.com) can be time well spent.

Making the grade

Each appraisal "category" has a grade box next to it. Earlier, on the detailed value appraisal forms of Chapters 13 and 14, we suggested a "+/-/0" rating scheme. You can grade these categories as you wish, however. as these category grades are a composite of many different factors, we've more often used the schoolhouse standard: A/B/C/D/F.

Try to capture as many factors as possible in the assessment and write them down (under "assessment"). It's interesting to file these away, then look at them again six months to years down the road to see what happened and whether your original appraisal made sense.

What's your scenario?

Uncertainty is a constant "given" in any business. The economy can and does change. Industries change, and the role and success of individual businesses within an industry can change, sometimes very quickly. And as we've pointed out many times, the data and tools used to construct appraisals don't yield absolute answers. So a good appraisal strategy includes at least some attention to best-, worst-, and average-case scenarios. You may wish to "run the numbers" assuming the best and worst of sales, margins, expenses, intangibles, and so forth. If you don't want to do the numbers, it's at least a good idea to think through best and worst cases. At minimum, ask yourself *what if* things don't quite turn out right, what's the downside?

If it looks good, there might be something better

Chess players are taught early on to keep looking for moves, even after they spot a good one, because a better one might be out there.

From this point on, the decision is yours. If a stock comes through this appraisal looking good, it's worth "running" a few more from your search. In our experience, it's also a good idea to run a competitor or two, just to confirm your selection is best.

It Ain't Over Till It's Over

We often wonder out loud what baseball sage Yogi Berra would say about value investing. Really, it's so common sense and practical that his philosophy would likely fit right in.

What do we mean, "It ain't over till it's over"? Supposedly, a value stock was to be acquired and kept for a long time, even a *lifetime*. True, but especially in today's world of change, business fortunes can turn on a dime, either as a result of macroeconomic and industry factors, or micro problems that escaped your initial read and surfaced during ownership. Lucent Technologies is a poster child for both happening at once (not that Lucent was ever particularly a value stock at a P/E of 60, a P/S of 5, and a basketful of acquisitions under its belt, but it did have the growth and the story).

The point is that you have to keep up with your investments, even after purchase. If you were fortunate enough to do a good job up front, nighttime sleep should come easy. Stability and consistency are good things to have. But no longer is it possible to buy a company and stuff the stock certificate into your mattress. Even Buffett sells shares, and sells them every year.

The best way to keep track is to use many of the same tools used to make the investment decision in the first place. Watch the financials and intangibles through Yahoo! Finance, quarterly Value Line updates, and of course, the newspaper. Repeating the "short-form" appraisal every now and then doesn't hurt either.

And now, the hardest part. You thought "marrying" the stock was difficult, full of unknowns and subjective assessments? Try the *divorce*! In investing, selling can be one of the hardest things to do. Investors get emotionally vested in their decisions, and hanging on becomes more a matter of hope — and desire to be right "after all" — than a rational, conscious decision based on a company's merit. What we can say for sure is that true value investors don't think this way. Value investors watch their businesses perform just as a good manager would, and when they stop performing, they get out. It's really one of the great attributes of stock investing: Investors don't get the headaches that managers and small business owners get. When things turn, or when a better opportunity arises, they can just sell and move on. The upshot: Keep track the company's story, and be ready to reappraise and move on if the new appraisal comes up short.

Chapter 18

Is the Feeling Mutual?

In This Chapter

▶ Understanding the role of mutual funds in value investing

▶ Reviewing mutual fund terminology

▶ Finding out where to get mutual fund information

▶ Identifying the pros and cons of using mutual funds

▶ Introducing closed-end funds

▶ Finding value in value funds

Although the selection and ownership of individual stocks certainly provides more fodder for chats around the water cooler, mutual funds are the backbone of many investors' portfolios. According to the Investment Company Institute, an association of investment managers, nearly half of all American households hold at least one mutual fund. Fidelity, Vanguard, and Putnam have all become household names. Pick up a financial magazine or turn on the tube and you're certain to find yet another fund portfolio manager who has gained celebrity status.

But value investing is a do-it-yourself enterprise, right? Learn about businesses, appraise them, and buy when the price is right. Value investors are taught to do their own analysis to find a few good companies that they plan to hang onto for the long term. So where do funds fit into the value investing picture?

The truth is, certain funds invest just as a value investor would individually. There aren't many (although their numbers are increasing with the re-emerging popularity of value), but they do exist. And if you can employ a fund manager and a staff to do exactly what you would do, with all the expensive professional information right at hand, well, why not? Berkshire Hathaway shareholders have done it for years, so why shouldn't you?

But don't be fooled. Each fund is distinct, and they all come with particular nuances with which the informed investor should become familiar. Even an experienced investor could get overwhelmed with the over 8,000 mutual funds in the U.S. With so many to choose from, how does a value investor find just the right one? In this chapter, we explore open-end and closed-end mutual funds and their role in value investing as an alternative to selecting individual stocks. In Chapter 19, we explore REITs and convertible securities as other popular value investing alternatives.

Why Mutual Funds?

To be honest, if you're an experienced investor with time on your hands and all the right information and tools at your fingertips, you may not need mutual funds. But if you're just starting out, don't have time, or need to build out a portfolio, they may make sense.

Mutual funds have solid benefits to offer investors large and small. Selecting stocks can be a daunting chore for busy people. Although you may choose to be knowledgeable about your investments, you may not have the time or inclination to be actively involved in reading detailed financial information and selecting stocks. In this case, mutual funds are a natural and simple choice. Even if you want to make your own selection of stock, mutual funds may serve a great purpose in your portfolio.

One popular strategy for getting started in value investing is to use all the tools and skills that you pick up in this book to get started picking stocks on a small scale. Then select a good core value-oriented mutual fund (we discuss fund selection a little later) to put to work the remaining bulk of your investment dollars. Practice makes perfect. As you gain confidence with your stock selection skills, you can move more dollars into individual equities and allocate fewer dollars to funds.

Mutual funds can also be a great tool to round out a stock portfolio. You may not feel comfortable choosing foreign stocks, small company stocks, or stocks in some other specialty area. Take advantage of professional money managers to get exposure in these areas.

Whether or not you're a do-it-yourselfer, funds have their place.

A Mutual Fund Short Course

We don't cover all the details and nuances of mutual funds and how they work in this book. That's best left for other books, such as *Mutual Funds For Dummies,* 3rd Edition, by Eric Tyson (Hungry Minds, Inc.), or the many and varied mutual fund Web sites. In the following sections, we offer a brief overview.

What is a mutual fund?

Borrowing the wisdom of Forrest Gump, mutual funds are like a box of chocolates. Mutual funds are the box; the stocks, bonds, cash, fees, and so on are the surprises inside. When you purchase a mutual fund, you buy a share in the ownership of all the chocolates inside the box. A share in the ownership entitles you to have a little piece of every one of those chocolates in the box (whether you like nuts and cordials or not).

A mutual fund is an investment company set up specifically for the purpose of, you guessed it, investing. By the rules of investment companies, which are in place to avoid double taxation, investors buy shares of a portfolio, and at least 90 percent of the returns from that portfolio must be distributed to shareholders.

To borrow more wisdom from Forrest Gump, you never know what you're gonna get. We explore this more later, but suffice it to say that the investor puts a lot of faith in the portfolio manager when selecting a fund. Even when it sounds like a value fund, you can't be sure until you've broken it open and given it a good look. Sometimes even then, you get fooled when you bite in and find out it only *looked* like the one you wanted. Mutual funds can be tricky and investing in them isn't simple. Although you can't see or influence individual portfolio decisions made by the fund manager, it's worth appraising each fund as a business, so look at the management and its objectives, strategies, and measurable results. Fund investing may not require as much diligence or business understanding as stock investing (after all, you're paying someone else to do the detail work), but it does require some homework.

Open end, closed end, which end is up?

Don't get too hung up on the difference between closed-end and open-end funds. Open-end funds are the "normal" mutual funds seen quoted every day in the paper. There is no exchange trading of the shares; open-end fund shares aren't bought and sold among individuals but rather between individuals and the fund company. Individuals send in money, which immediately becomes part of the fund and is converted into new shares owned by the investor. Each share represents that investor's proportionate share of the net asset value of that fund. If the investor sells or redeems shares, those shares go away and the investor is sent a check for his proportionate share of the fund's net assets.

Not sure whether it is an open-end fund or a closed-end fund? Look at the symbol: All open-end mutual fund symbols are made up of five letters. Closed-end funds trade on exchanges and therefore have a three or four letter symbol. Furthermore, open-end mutual funds are usually listed in the Mutual Fund section of newspaper stock listings, whereas closed-end funds are found in the exchange listings according to where they trade or in a separate Closed-End Fund listing.

Closed-end funds trade on exchanges and their prices aren't directly linked to the underlying value of assets held in the fund. There are many more open-end funds than closed-end funds, and investors will find a much greater variety of fund and fund companies to work with in the open-end part of the spectrum. But closed-end funds can provide a unique opportunity for value investors: share prices often trade at a *discount* to underlying portfolio value.

Pricing

When you invest in a mutual fund, you actually buy shares of the fund itself. These shares represent a proportional claim of ownership to the underlying security (stock, bond, and so on). The mutual fund share price is the Net Asset Value (NAV). The NAV is determined by taking the total assets in the fund and subtracting out any liabilities and the expenses charged on the fund, then dividing by the number of shares outstanding.

NAV = [Assets – (Liabilities + Expenses)] ÷ number of shares outstanding

where "assets" represent the combined current values of all securities held in the portfolio

The NAV fluctuates each day according to the market price movements of the underlying securities held by the fund, but does not change based on additional investments in the fund.

For example, you send a check for $1,000 to Hot Performance Financial, a popular mutual fund family, along with an application to buy the Soaring Price Value Fund. The current selling price is $13 per share. Therefore, you purchase 76.92 shares ($1,000 ÷ $13), assuming no sales charge. When you buy into the Soaring Price Value Fund, the total assets of the fund rise by the amount invested (in our example, $1,000). Similarly, the number of shares outstanding is increased by the number of shares issued to you. Mathematically, these figures cancel out one another, so the NAV doesn't change when you come in. Although the number of shares increases, the assets in the fund increase proportionally by the amount of your investment. But when the price of underlying securities changes, the value of your shares changes.

There is no limit to the number of shares that a fund will issue. Closed-end funds have a fixed number of issuable shares. Open-end funds must stand ready to buy back shares from investors every day.

No load off our minds

The fund *load* is another ubiquitous topic in newspapers, magazines, and radio talk shows. Not to be confused with the trucking industry term, *load* in this case represents the sales charge for buying the fund. It has nothing to do with fund value or the quality of the fund's investments or investment practice.

Whenever you buy a mutual fund from someone (broker, planner, advisor), a sales commission is involved somewhere. The question is, who picks it up and when? With load funds, the investor pays a sales charge, usually 4 to 6 percent of the initial investment for equity funds. This type of load is a front-end load, which is normally deducted from the value of the investment — it's not an additional charge. Sometimes sales charges are *backloaded* onto the sale, rather than the purchase, of the fund shares. These loads diminish the longer you hold the fund, typically disappearing after six or eight years. With no-load funds, the sales charge isn't collected directly from the shareholder, but instead is taken out of the returns — and net asset value — of the fund over time. In any case, the person offering the fund for sale gets paid for the advice they've offered. With load funds, performance may appear higher, as sales charges have already been paid up front instead of being deducted from portfolio profits.

So should you purchase load or no-load mutual funds? Without this question, many a talk show host would have run out of things to talk about years ago. The answer, particularly for value investors, is to look beyond the sales charge. Value investors should look at the product: the fund, the fund company, the management, and the performance. If the product is right, buy the fund. Particularly in the long run, the difference between load and no-load funds goes away: One way or another, the fees are paid.

What types of funds are available?

The task of sorting through the 8,000 mutual funds offered by over 100 mutual fund companies would surely be a daunting one without the use of classification systems developed in the industry.

There are literally dozens of types of mutual funds, ranging from the most aggressive small company speculative funds all the way to stable, doughty, short-term bond funds. Bond, stock, international, U.S., growth, income, hedge, option, convertibles, tax-free bond, high-yield bond, government bond, and on and on — not to mention *combinations* of all the above, and of course, value funds.

Style in a box

Morningstar Investment Services, the flagship of fund information packagers for individual and professional investors alike, puts out one of the better and more widely used stock fund classification systems. In their words, "To help investors cut through the confusion and profusion of fund categories, Morningstar has designed the Style Box, a visual tool for better understanding a fund's true investment strategy." There are style boxes for U.S. equities, international equities, and fixed income investments. We focus on the U.S. equity style box (see Figure 18-1). The U.S. equity style box is a good place to start to identify value funds.

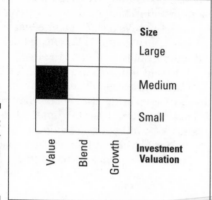

Figure 18-1:
Morningstar
Stock Fund
Equity style
box.

As you can see in Figure 18-1, the style box is a simple grid (we probably could have thought of it ourselves). But it's a unique and powerful tool to classify funds. For the value investor, it's a great place to get started moving in the right direction. In the following sections, we take the style box apart into its two dimensions.

Small, medium, and large

Size refers to market capitalization (*market cap,* for you buzzworders). Market cap is total capitalization, which in turn is current share price times the number of shares outstanding. The three sizes are:

- ✓ **Small, or small cap:** Companies with market cap less than $1 billion
- ✓ **Medium, or midcap:** Companies between $1 billion and $5 billion
- ✓ **Large, or large cap:** Companies worth more than $5 billion

Caf, decaf, and half-caf

In the Morningstar style box, size definitions are pretty easy to grasp; investment valuation is where it gets more interesting. Many investors and financial writers simply equate *value* with *conservative.* Any investment that is safe, with steady income or returns, and that doesn't fluctuate much is sometimes called a *value stock.* Don't let this confuse you. *Value* really refers more to "reasonably priced" or "underpriced" and can represent assets that are stable, growing, or even declining in value.

Although Morningstar puts forth a grid that seemingly implies that value can't include growth, a closer look at the definitions reveals that the Morningstar folks are on the right track, and although not perfect, the system is useful to at least initially filter out a majority of funds. It is based on examining average P/E and price-to-book ratios of their holdings *relative* to the market (in this case, the S&P 500):

✔ **Value funds** contain stocks that, on average, have a low combined P/E and P/B ratio relative to the S&P 500. Want a number? To be a value fund, the combined relative ratios of P/E and P/B must be less than 1.75. Thus, a fund containing stocks that, on average, have a P/B equal to the S&P 500 must have a an average P/E only three quarters, or 0.75 times the S&P 500 P/E to qualify. (Note that if either average P/B or P/E is much greater than 1 times the S&P 500, the fund isn't likely to qualify as a value fund because relative ratios are unlikely to be very small and can't be negative). In mid-2001, the stocks in the S&P 500 have an average P/E of about 23, and P/B averages of about 6. So a fund with an average P/E of 23 and an average P/B of 4.5 would just make it as a value fund.

✔ **Blend funds** fall in between 1.75 and 2.25.

✔ **Growth funds** have a combined relative average P/E and P/B greater than 2.25.

For a more complete discussion of the Morningstar Style Box, see www. morningstar.com/glossary/InvestmentStyle.htm.

The Morningstar Style Box can help you identify and select value-oriented mutual funds. But inside this rather quantitative classification can lurk many different interpretations of the value philosophy and strategy. To get closer to where a fund is really coming from, it's a good idea to look at the fund's stated objective, especially its strategy or approach. Most importantly, you need to look at a list of current holdings.

An example of a philosophically "aligned" fund is the Legg Mason Value Trust (www.leggmason.com), who states as its approach: "Follows a value discipline by purchasing large-capitalization stocks at large discounts to the assessment of their intrinsic value." A scan of the stocks held by the fund reveals that it hits the value investing nail right on the head. Check the Statement of Additional Information (published at least yearly by every fund) and individual fund Web sites for clear statements on strategy and approach.

Information, Please

As with information about individual companies and stocks, many fine Web sites and information services are designed around providing mutual fund information. Most of the major financial Web sites and brokerages contain a mutual fund section or fund center.

A variety of information is available, ranging from simple data to greater levels of value-added analysis and recommendations. And as with stocks, the cost ranges from free, to requiring an account or registration, to modest consumer-level fee ranges, all the way to professional services costing thousands a year. If you work with a full-service brokerage firm (Merrill Lynch, Paine Webber, and so on) and frequently even with a mini-serve broker such as Charles Schwab, you gain access to this professional information through the broker.

A morning star

Of the major Web sites providing diversified financial data — a group that includes CBS Marketwatch (cbs.marketwatch.com), Zacks (www.zacks.com), and Yahoo! Finance (quote.yahoo.com) — only one has its roots in the mutual fund world: Morningstar. Morningstar Investment Services is a bellwether mutual fund information service and portal.

Morningstar (www.morningstar.com) provides several data services, some for free, some for a modest fee ($11.95/month or $99/year), and it also offers advanced professional services that are unavailable outside the professional investment community. Morningstar developed many of the original fund rating and classification systems (including the style box mentioned above). The summaries and research reports it issues still form the standard for mutual fund analysis and reporting.

Fund selectors

Just as there are for stocks, fund screeners and selectors are available on most mutual fund financial Web sites. Morningstar has a Toolbox with Fund Selector, Quickrank, and Compare tools — all useful to narrow down the funds meeting your investment goals and objectives from the thousands that are available. Select by style, size, and investment strategy. Then run through the selected list and look at the category ranking and style for each fund, and you're well on your way to selecting the proper fund. Selectors go deeper than performance to provide management characteristics of the fund, such as fees and expenses, sales charges (load/no load), management tenure, and other important noninvestment criteria.

The Inside Scoop on the Upside and Downside

It's time to stick a toe into the great debate about mutual funds and what's good and bad about them. There has been a lot of press on this over the years. Mutual funds offer distinct advantages and disadvantages, and don't work for every investor. Part of the author team of this book comes from the mutual fund industry and is deeply familiar with the debate. This section presents a balanced view to help you determine if funds are right for you.

Mutual funds aren't as exciting or as fun as stocks. But, to be sure, investing is not a sport, nor for most of us, is it entertainment. If excitement is what you're after, skydiving or snake charming may be a better bet. Investing is about making money and it isn't meant to be anything else. Most well run mutual funds are boring. Solid, boring, consistent: These words describe (and are even flattering to) mutual funds, especially value funds. There is hardly any point in picking up the paper more than once a month or so if you have mutual funds, and if your cash is stuffed away in a good value fund, you can probably check the paper less frequently than that.

Most investing and personal finance experts cite four main areas of benefit for mutual fund investing:

✔ Expertise

✔ Diversification

✔ Convenience

✔ Lower cost of entry

Point, counterpoint

In the following sections, we explore the benefits of mutual funds. We also, explain the downside that accompanies each benefit, a downside that may or may not be of concern to you.

Expertise: Professional money managers

Professional management can be a big help — it's good to have experienced, trained pros with time to spend on your side. But knowing whether they're really working for you can be difficult.

Pro: Let the pros do it

Selecting stocks and managing a portfolio can take a lot of time, knowledge, and hard work. It is a full time job. Mutual funds are managed by skilled professionals who track economic, corporate, and market events, trends, rumors, and data that most of us don't have time to plow through every day. Moreover, fund managers often have coveted access to company management teams who can provide insight and information that regular folks like us simply don't receive. Analysts and portfolio managers make a career of poring over the quarterly and annual reports that we would find better use for as sleep aids.

Mutual fund families manage billions of dollars. As in many other areas of life, money provides access. Although analysts and portfolio managers cannot trade on insider information, they are often privy to more timely and complete information than the average investor. For mutual fund managers to attend management conferences in person or hold one-on-one meetings with senior company management is not at all uncommon.

Professional managers also have the advantage of objectivity. Making dispassionate decisions is easier for them because the money being managed isn't their own. They look at overall performance and usually avoid getting emotionally attached to any one stock.

Con: No control

When you choose a mutual fund, you put your faith in the management and give up the power to choose which stocks are bought and sold and when. This can result in owning stocks that you don't necessarily want to own.

Many managers have a tendency to drift in their style toward whatever area is currently performing. Given that managers are normally paid a percentage of the assets under their care, you can be sure that they pay very close attention to performance. The better a fund's performance, the more likely it will be to attract new assets. More assets mean a larger paycheck to the fund manager. Chasing performance can often be so enticing that a manager drifts away from his stated style. Style shift can be detected through Morningstar style history, portfolio changes, churn, changes in stated objectives, and even changes in managers.

A shift in strategy can be difficult to detect, but it's worth keeping an eye out for. The last thing you want to find your large-cap value manager buying is small-cap growth stocks!

Con: Fees and expenses

You can't have experts managing your money without forking over some dough. As with all services, management of a mutual fund portfolio is performed at a cost. In fact, management cost can chew up 2 percent or more of the return of an actively managed portfolio, which means that in order to achieve a 5 percent return for you, the fund has to achieve a 7 percent return! (For more on the long term effects of a 2 percent cut in investing returns, see Chapter 4.) Still, the management fees for value funds tend to be a bit lower, because they are less active. But the fee is still worth checking out before you invest. Less than 1.5 percent or even 1 percent is good. But remember, like everything else in life, you get what you pay for. If you want Bill Miller (Legg Mason) or Bill Nygren (Oakmark) on your side, you may have to pay up for quality.

Diversification: Soup, not just beans

Some diversification is good, but too much can work against you.

Pro: Less volatility

Mutual funds offer investors instant diversification. Every dollar invested in a mutual fund gets spread among a number of different securities. Lower risk is the primary benefit. A variety of stocks in a fund portfolio can insulate the portfolio from the effects of negative individual stocks.

Con: Enough is enough

In the same way that diversifying a portfolio limits the detrimental effect of any one stock, too many stocks can eliminate the upside effect of a home run. Many funds are over-diversified, holding 100 or more stocks. A fund manager with a good strategy, solid research, and a portfolio of a manageable size shouldn't dilute his performance with too many stocks. Studies show little benefit in diversifying a portfolio much beyond 20 stocks. We like a manager, especially in the value arena, to build a thorough understanding of relatively few businesses and be able to follow them closely. That's hard to do with a fund that owns 100 companies.

Convenience

When you don't have the time to put into stock selection and monitoring or just don't feel the itch to pick your own stocks, mutual funds can be a saving grace. Professional customer service, quick buys and sells, and no-cost switching between funds can more than offset the cost of professional management.

Pro: Convenience of purchase and sale

Mutual funds continually issue new shares and stand ready to repurchase outstanding shares when an investor wants to redeem. Investors don't have to worry about what the market thinks or how the market would price their mutual fund shares. Shares are priced at market close each day, so anyone wanting to redeem his shares will receive the current NAV for any shares he wants to sell, regardless of quantity. Large block trades are as easily accomplished as small $100 transactions — no waiting, no market movement.

Pro: Customer service

Fund management handles all transactions, collection of gains and income, and other administrative duties. Investors receive clean, simple statements of income, gains, and tax information. Most fund companies employ helpful professionals to answer questions and track down information on demand for investors. Shareholder services can be helpful on April 13 when you just can't for the life of you find a lost statement to determine your cost basis and your taxes are due in 48 hours. Convenience is a much overlooked benefit of fund investing.

Tax talk

A major downside of mutual funds is taxation. Mutual funds are required to pay out nearly all their net income each year. Depending on the type of fund, the payments can be doled out on a regular basis throughout the year or all at once at year end. Whether they choose to take the capital gain in cash or reinvest it back into the fund to purchase more shares, those investors who own the fund on the record date receive all capital gains and dividends as ordinary income and are therefore responsible for any taxes that occur as a consequence.

Capital gains occur when the portfolio manager sells a stock for profit. Because all gains must be paid out each year, this profit is passed proportionally to each shareholder, who in turn is responsible to pay tax on the gain. When owning individual stocks, investors can time the sale of stock so as to minimize tax consequences. When owning a mutual fund, the timing on all buys and sells is under the control of the portfolio manager, who knows nothing of your tax situation.

The danger is in buying a fund that has a lot of capital gains built into it, then having to shoulder the tax on that gain yourself. Suppose the portfolio manager buys 100 shares of a stock for $30 per share (a $3,000 total investment) in January. In March, you purchase shares of his fund. On that day, the 100 shares bought back in January are now worth $65 each ($6,500). Because the NAV, or share price of the fund, reflects this higher stock price in the portfolio, you pay a higher price for the fund because of the increase in the price of the stock. The very next day, on March 13, the fund manager decides to sell the stock at $65. The $35 capital gain is all yours to pay tax on, even though you realized none of it since you bought in late. At

year end, you'll get an unexpected surprise in the form of a capital gain to report.

The biggest capital gain surprises can come from older, established funds that made great investments long ago, such as Microsoft for $3, for example. Funds that trade frequently, scoring high on turnover, also create capital gain exposure, more and sooner. High turnover can signify tax inefficiency, as well as bring value focus into question. Predicting these tax pitfalls can be tough unless you want to examine the cost basis of every investment and try to predict timing of the sale.

The most convenient method for checking the potential capital gains exposure of a fund is, again, the Internet. Morningstar.com provides detailed profiles on thousands of funds for free. Enter the mutual fund symbol on the Quicktakes Report section and click on View Additional Performance Information just below the annual returns section. The last section is a rough tax analysis of the fund you are researching. In this section, Morningstar also provides a pre-tax and an after-tax return for the fund to demonstrate the impact of taxes on your portfolio performance.

Another tool you can use to take a bigger picture look at mutual fund tax effects is PersonalFund.com. Under the basic fund profile, you can find out exactly what your fund paid in capital gains last year. Also, if you can get through the nonsense about the obese jockey, this Web site will break down the exact dollar amount you paid to own the fund based on the fund's expenses and your investment, including the tax bill personalized to your income tax bracket.

Pro: Fund switch

Most fund families allow investors to switch from one fund in a family to another, without cost. Compared to switching individual stocks in a brokerage account, this latitude can create big savings. For longer term value investors, this advantage can be useful as investment needs change over time.

Pro: Ease of entry for small investors

You can start investing in many mutual funds with a small initial investment. Automatic monthly investments — as well as dollar cost averaging — are easy to do and are virtually free. Some fund families will take as little as $50 per month; that $50 may otherwise be enough to buy only one share of a favorite stock.

Introducing Closed-End Funds

Closed-end funds are investment companies that are similar to the open-end funds we describe in the bulk of this chapter. But unlike open-end funds, closed-end funds trade on exchanges and have valuation characteristics like a stock: The price may be, and usually is, different than the value of the underlying assets.

Closed-end funds have actually been in existence as an investing vehicle much longer than their open-end counterparts. They differ from open-end funds (normally called *mutual funds*) mostly in capital structure. Closed-end funds are investment companies whose shares are listed on a stock exchange or are traded in the over-the-counter market. Shares are traded between investors, not between an investor and the fund company. Like other publicly traded securities, the market price of closed-end fund shares fluctuates and is determined by supply and demand in the marketplace.

Because of the popularity of open-end funds, closed-end funds have become somewhat of a background player in the fund business. Because they are not major players and their prices are relatively stable, closed-end funds are not listed daily by most financial publications although they are listed at certain times. The best place to get a listing is the Monday edition of *The Wall Street Journal*. You can also try the Saturday *New York Times* or the Wednesday *Barron's*. There are several hundred funds listed. Price, net asset value (NAV), and discounts or premiums are all reported.

The price of a closed-end fund is tied to the market value of the underlying securities. But it doesn't match NAV exactly. There is no process to peg the price to the NAV daily. Instead, the price is set by the market, based on supply and demand for the shares of the fund. In a sense, a closed-end fund is a security within a security — a basket of fluctuating stocks trading inside a traded stock *shell*. Closed-end funds provide investors with two ways to make and two ways to lose money:

✔ The underlying value of the securities portfolio changes.

✔ The market's *assessment* of the value of the portfolio changes, which usually creates a *discount* or *premium* to portfolio value in the price of closed-end fund shares.

Are discounts common?

Most closed-end funds sell at a discount. A recent sampling showed that more than two-thirds of equity funds trade at a discount, and over 90 percent of international equity funds trade at a discount. Many discounts are modest (5 to 10 percent), but many are 30 percent or more.

Why a discount?

There is much research and speculation about why discounts are common, but for our purposes, the debate isn't nearly as important as understanding a few of the most common reasons. When selecting a closed-end fund, investors must determine the reason the fund is trading at a discount and whether the discount is significant enough to be attractive. A discount may be justified by uncertainty, popularity, or perceptions of the fund and the underlying asset base. All three factors can work to cause a fund based on securities in Russia or Turkey, for example, to sell at a discount. Likewise, during the heyday of the Asian Tigers, many Asian country–based funds sold at a premium. The reason? Popularity and the *perception* of future growth and gains.

Kinds of closed-end funds

There are many types of closed-end funds. *The Wall Street Journal* lists closed-end funds under fourteen different headings. The prominent categories for value investors include world-equity funds, specialized-equity funds and convertible-security funds, as well as several forms of fixed income or bond funds. Under the category of world-equity funds, you find the famous country funds, which are good vehicles to introduce international diversification into a portfolio. However, note that there are no value funds, per se.

Information, please

From an information perspective, closed-end funds are treated more like traded stocks (which they are) than open-end mutual funds. But because they are a specialized, less commonly used, and less understood vehicle, you won't find as much information in typical stock information sources.

Still, *Standard & Poor's, Value Line,* and others cover closed-end funds. And closed-end funds are equity securities, subject to the reporting requirements of any stock. So prospectuses, as well as annual and periodic reports, are all available. Most funds also offer phone support and access to information on their Web sites.

The Value Line Investment Survey does cover a few closed-end funds in its 1,700-stock universe and quarterly reporting. Value Line does a good job of customizing its reporting around the special characteristics of closed-end funds.

Using closed-end funds

Just as with open-end funds, closed-end funds can be used to build out a portfolio or add specific components that the portfolio needs, such as international exposure. Patient value investors seek not only a good price (meaning a good discount), but also a fund with solid long-term potential. Many pros use closed-end funds, including Warren Buffett. In 1972, Source Capital was trading at nearly a 50 percent discount to NAV. Buffett purchased almost 20 percent of the outstanding shares. Though the fund experienced many price movements in the interim, Buffett hung in there for five years before selling. His estimated profit topped $15.7 million.

Using and Choosing Value Funds

So you've decided that you want to start investing in mutual funds, either as your primary market vehicle or as a complement to your current investing practice. How do you choose the right fund? What are the critical things to consider?

Appraise your own needs

Do you want to hand over the management of your portfolio to a professional? Would you like to tackle some of your investments on your own and enlist help on the more eclectic areas? Do you want to focus on a few stocks for 50 percent of your investments, and then use funds to build out your portfolio? Maybe you can figure out large-cap companies because their products and intangibles are visible, while you use funds to build out the small-cap portion of your portfolio?

Before getting started, mapping your investment strategy is a good thing to do. Establish what niche mutual funds in general, and value funds in particular, will play.

Style

When you have an idea what you're looking for, it's time to plow through the 8,000 or more mutual funds that are out there to find the ones that are suitable for you.

Given the subject at hand and the fact that you are still reading, we're pretty sure you are looking for a value fund. Size matters, and a mix of large-, medium-, and small-cap funds makes sense for a well-rounded portfolio (although you may want to mix individual stocks into each of these size buckets). Size diversity will reduce the volatility of your total portfolio. The theory goes that when large companies aren't performing, small or middle-sized companies will and vice versa. International will buoy you up in years when the domestic markets are underperforming, and so on.

Even if you choose to select individual stocks for your portfolio, funds may be helpful to you to gain exposure to middle- or small-sized companies that are somewhat tougher to research on your own. If you choose to research different asset classes, make sure to compare the funds you are considering to their own peer group. Interestingly, a common rule holds that midcap funds will provide you about 70 to 80 percent of the performance of a small-cap fund with only about half of the volatility.

Risk

Life is full of risks — crossing the street, falling in love, bungee jumping. Value investors, as a rule, avoid risk and like to hide behind the familiar margin of safety. The trick is determining the amount of risk you find acceptable. Review the volatility and market correlation measures we discussed in "Statistics, More Statistics" earlier in this chapter. Don't forget to look at risk compared to peer groups. And make sure the risk level in the fund is congruent with your investing objectives.

Performance and cost

Every mutual fund prospectus in America includes some version of the phrase "past performance is not necessarily an indication of how it will perform in the future." There are few things that you can be completely certain about when you invest. Take advantage of those you can count on. In trying to decide among all the choices, disregard the colorful advice shouting up from the magazines at the supermarket checkout stand: "The 10 Best Funds to buy now!" Countless investors have lost big buying the best performing fund of *last* year. Your goal is to find the one that will perform well this or next year. Who cares how much money the investors who owned it last year made? You didn't own it then!

At least the rules were recently changed about how mutual fund companies report performance. For years, they could show percentage returns calculated almost as they pleased. Naturally this led to use of arithmetic mean return rates, especially as returns rocketed in the late '90s (A 50 percent loss followed by a 100 percent gain results in a 25 percent gain by arithmetic mean and a 0 percent gain by geometric mean). Return rates looked extraordinarily enticing. You couldn't pick up a financial page without finding ads from two or three funds trumpeting 40 or 50 percent gains. Now, the more realistic and conservative geometric mean is used. You can now compare mutual fund gains to any other gain, even a gain received as normal compounded bank interest.

Myriad studies have shown that past *outperformance* by funds is not a solid predictor of solid performance in the future. However, past *underperformance* caused by high fees and poor tax efficiency generally does persist. The authors at PersonalFund.com state it bluntly but accurately: In short, the familiar disclaimer that "Past performance cannot guarantee future results" should really read, "Past performance is *largely useless* in predicting future results."

Training Wheels

Still confused about how to use mutual funds? Clearly, the mainline benefits of offloading stock selection, getting professional help and expertise, adding convenience, and creating diversification are important. You can start out as a value investor using value funds as your main vehicle.

A popular strategy for starting out in value investing is to pick a few individual value stocks on your own, using the tools and skills that you can find in earlier chapters of this book. You can select a value fund to put your remaining investment dollars to work. Here, too, practice makes perfect! As you gain confidence and feel more certain about your stock selection skills, you can move more dollars into individual equities and allocate fewer dollars to funds.

Mutual funds can also be a great tool to round out a stock portfolio. You may not feel comfortable choosing small company or foreign stocks or stocks in some other specialty area. Take advantage of professional money managers to get exposure in these areas.

Chapter 19

Out of Stock: Special Value Investing Vehicles

In This Chapter

▶ Putting real estate to work for you through REITs

▶ Understanding and using convertible bonds

For as long as investing has existed as a concept, people and their companies have dreamed up different investment vehicles to meet the needs of the investing public and the companies raising capital from sale of securities. Many types of investments and investment vehicles exist outside the mainstream choices of equities or equity mutual funds, many of which can be interesting to the value investor.

In this chapter, we present two of the more specialized and lesser-used investments we think you'll want to know about. Because of their specialized use, the information we provide here will give you a level of familiarity, but not expertise. Before you use these vehicles on your own, we recommend that you do more research. Many investors, particularly of value orientation, may consider real estate as a viable alternative to equity investments. We agree, but we also think that direct real estate investing is an art and a science in and of itself — and outside the scope of this book. The investment world has provided Real Estate Investment Trusts (REITs), which are securities representing baskets of real estate and in many ways whetting the appetite of the value investor. Then we explore convertible bonds (and preferred stocks) as a hybrid, best-of-both-worlds way to tap into both income and growth potential.

The Ground We Stand On: Real Estate

"They ain't making any more of it." How many times have you heard that phrase to refer to land and real estate, usually from smug real estate investors or real estate agents? Land would seem like a value investment. It's certainly long term, and the long-term price direction is clearly upward.

Fundamentals are there: increased demand, fixed supply. Should you consider land as a value investment? And if so, how? Value Line doesn't publish summaries on the five-acre parcel down the street; nor does anyone else that we know of.

So in the manner of mutual funds, enter in yet another investment vehicle to acquire something bigger than you can own individually — this time, Real Estate Investment Trusts (REITs).

REITs: What and why

In Chapter 18, we cover the advantages of mutual funds for diversifying risk, lowering costs, and the benefits of professional management. Because such an arrangement works well for stocks and bonds, shouldn't the same principle apply to other classes of assets? Well, in short, it does. A simple way to think of a Real Estate Investment Trust is as a closed end fund that owns real estate instead of stocks or bonds. REITs pool investor money to in order to allow average individual investors to invest in a portfolio of commercial or residential real estate properties. Let's face it: Unless you're Donald Trump or were married to him, it is unlikely that you'll ever own a 25-story building in New York City, a 100-unit apartment building in San Francisco, or a shopping mall in Dallas. REITs allow you to do just that. By buying shares in a REIT, you take proportional ownership in the real estate ventures that the trust owns — anything from penitentiaries to car dealerships or high-end residences.

REITs have qualities that make them very attractive to the value investor. Just like the closed end funds we discuss in Chapter 18, REITs are available on the NYSE, AMEX, and NASDAQ exchanges and trade at either a discount or premium to their NAV. There are about 180 listed REITS on the NYSE, 30 on the AMEX, and 15 or so on NASDAQ. REITs often trade at a discount, and as we've seen, discounts to NAV can offer diligent value investors the ability to buy a dollar's worth of assets for much less than a dollar.

REITs give small investors the ability to take advantage of real estate markets and cycles in concentrated geographic areas (such as San Diego or Baltimore), specific types of real estate (such as office buildings or residential developments), or broader national real estate trends (such as residences and suburban office space throughout the country).

Value investors may find REITs interesting for their ability to diversify an otherwise concentrated portfolio while hedging inevitable bearish cycles in stocks. REITs tend to move in random correlation to the stock market. Although the tech stocks were booming through most of 1999, REITs made an embarrassingly poor comparative showing. However in the 2001 bear market, REIT's have done fairly well and have emerged as an acceptable, if not wildly popular, investing alternative.

REITs have growth potential proportionate to the real estate market, and are a safe harbor for hedging stock market downturns. Real estate prices are more stable and money tends to go into real estate when it comes out of stocks. REITs are also an effective hedge against inflation, as real estate prices and rents tend to rise during inflationary periods. Average dividends are high, and although gains are managed with a long-term perspective, capital gains can be healthy, too. Overall returns have averaged 12.48 percent over the last 20 years through July 2001 according to the National Association of Real Estate Investment Trusts (NAREIT). In short, REITs are a long-term hard asset investment with a solid fixed current income stream.

Kinds of REITs

There are three primary types of REITs:

- ✔ **Equity REITs** own and operate property. An equity REIT must develop its properties with the intent to operate the real estate as opposed to selling it for a profit. The income earned by an equity REIT is from rent on the properties it owns. This is the most popular type of REIT.

- ✔ **Mortgage REITs** invest in, you guessed it, mortgages. Mortgage REITs can either lend money directly to buyers and owners of real estate or hold loans and other mortgage-backed securities. These REITs derive income from the interest on mortgages paid to the REIT or indirectly through the interest paid on the underlying loans.

- ✔ **Hybrid REITs** are those that actively own and operate real estate and make loans or invest in mortgage-backed securities. These REITs earn profits from the rent associated with ownership or from the interest associated with financing ownership or development of real estate through the mortgages they issue or hold.

REITs often have primary focus, such as a geographic location or a certain type of property. For example, one REIT may invest only in a certain geographic location but hold a number of different types of properties: apartments, warehouses, urban offices. Another may invest only in suburban office complexes but hold property all over the U.S. Investors in a REIT must understand exactly what they will own and where they will own it before they purchase a REIT.

Information, please

Unlike most stocks and mutual funds the REIT world is a quiet, clandestine world known well to the few who participate but largely a mystery to everyone else. REITs are perceived as boring, and for many years, as market underperformers. But as we've already learned, such is the lake from which many value "fish" are caught! But how do you find out where they are?

REITs are common stocks, so many of the common stock research tools can be used to find out about them. Find a ticker symbol, and you can get a quote and profile from Yahoo! Finance. They are covered as common stocks in Value Line. Even with these information sources, getting to exactly which properties are owned, what the rent and occupancy rate is, and whether the parking lot needs paving is difficult. Just like stocks, you have to place a little faith in these asset specifics, and the fundamentals, trends, and intangibles such as location (you knew that word would come up!) and management track record need to be followed.

NAREIT is a trade group portal providing a good summary of what REITs are and how to invest in them. We recommend this site (www.nareit.com) as a first stop to find out more, and to get a list of available and traded REITs.

Advantages of REITs

Value investors seeking to achieve above average returns must understand the advantages and disadvantages of REITs.

- ✔ **Access:** By pooling investor funds, REITs allow individuals to participate in an area of investment from which they would otherwise be blocked.

- ✔ **Professional management:** With REITs, individual investors receive the expertise and proven track record of real estate investment professionals.

- ✔ **Liquidity:** Unlike investments in private real estate deals, an investment in a REIT allows an investor the instant liquidity offered by major exchanges, such as the NYSE. According to REITNet, an industry source of REIT information on the Web, over 300 publicly traded REITs are operating in the U.S. with an average daily dollar volume that has more than quadrupled since 1998 to $260 million.

- ✔ **Tax advantage:** Unlike an equity interest in a corporation, profits from REITs are passed-through to the shareholder and only taxed once. Moreover, REIT shareholders do not have to comply with burdensome state filing requirements that the limited partnerships did.

- ✔ **Selection:** The wide variety of REIT offerings can provide investors the degree of focus or diversification desired. Some REITs diversify across geographic areas or types of real estate ventures while others are dedicated to areas as small as a single building in New York City.

- ✔ **Income stream:** Because REITs are required to distribute at least 95 percent of their annual earnings, they can offer a relatively stable and predictable income stream to investors. Because the percentage of their earnings that must be distributed each year is so high, REITs tend to be among those companies paying the highest dividends.

REITs and Returns

Funds From Operations (FFO) is an important measure of a REIT's operating performance. NAREIT defines FFO as net income (excluding gains or losses from sales of property or debt restructuring) with the depreciation of real estate added back. Most commercial real estate holds its value longer and more fully than other real equipment that a business might possess such as tools or vehicles. The depreciation that accounting assumes each year is often overstated. Current accounting processes may call for depreciation of a building (according to a certain formula) even though the REAL value of the building may have increased due to some outside force such as increased demand or low supply of vacancies in the area where the building is located. For this reason adding back the depreciation is a more clear way of measuring the operating profits of one REIT against another. When depreciation is added back, the trust clearly doesn't need such extensive cash flow to maintain and replace its physical assets. Remember, as we've said the physical assets may, in fact, be appreciating in value! Through accounting, FFO recaptures that cash flow and more completely demonstrates the REIT's annual performance.

Risks of investing in REITs

Although all of this sounds pretty enticing, an informed investor should understand that REITs have potential downsides:

✔ **Market risk:** The most obvious risk is the market for real estate. If a prolonged downward pressure mounts on the real estate sector, the value of a REIT can decrease despite even the most knowledgeable management and most lucrative projections.

✔ **Business risk:** Investors in REITs must take into account current and anticipated economic conditions for the property held within the trust in order to evaluate the current and future success of the endeavor. Conversely, even in a robust real estate market, a REIT will only be successful if the REIT's executive team can manage the REIT to profitability. Are the anticipated returns worth the risks involved to achieve it?

✔ **Interest rate risk:** Especially in the context of Mortgage REITs, a change in interest rates can have a huge impact on REITs. A portfolio of long-term fixed rates may be valuable in the face of declining rates but can spell disaster if the rest of the world is paying higher interest on borrowed money.

Investing in REITs

As value investors, our goal is to identify investments trading at valuations below their intrinsic value. Our objective then, is to identify REITs that have the most potential for significant appreciation relative to their risk. Because REITs are generally regarded as hedges or defensive investments, they are most likely to be overlooked during raging bull markets. Whenever the market is soaring, defensive plays such as REITs experience the least popularity.

In some ways, choosing a good REIT is like choosing any other value investment. An investor must analyze and compare a REIT's management quality, real and anticipated returns, yields, growth, reserves, and asset values. Many of the techniques that we cover in earlier chapters for common stock can be put to work here.

Value investors must always consider dividend yields and the P/E ratio. Look for P/E lower than the REIT average as an indicator of undervalue. For REITs, the average PE should be well below 20. Typical dividend yields over the long-term average 5 to 8 percent as compared to the typical 2 to 3 percent of the S&P. Couple this attractive yield with the fact that approximately one-quarter of it is considered return of capital and therefore nontaxable, the REIT can be a very attractive addition to a diversified income portfolio.

Price to Book is another measure that we cover in depth in other chapters. A REIT trading below its per share book value is essentially trading at a discount. And although we hold to the theory that bargains are always available in the market, there can be reasons for a discount besides incorrect market appraisal. REITs are not immune to asset quality problems, bad management and management decisions, declining markets, or poor expense management. Do the diligence.

Valuing a REIT

REITs are valued much as any other stock. You look at earnings, growth, fundamentals, and intangibles. What's different is the type and nature of the assets owned; that is, real property.

A good starting point is an examination of property portfolio. Because real estate is not traded regularly, the ability to ascertain values is limited to appraisals, replacement value and, for income-producing properties, discounted cash flow analysis. Appraisals are difficult to find. Looking at the properties and their location, and assessing commonly reported local real estate price trends, occupancy rates, and economic trends, and whether the book value of a property is sustainable, is probably best.

Investors should carefully examine *funds from operations* (FFO). FFO includes all income after operating expenses, but before depreciation and amortization. Growth in FFO typically comes from higher revenues, lower costs, and management's effective recognition of new business opportunities. REIT investors need to carefully read management reports to determine how dividends are being paid. REITs that demonstrate a growing FFO are generally more desirable, because this is a demonstration of an ability to raise rents and general continued economic viability. The best way for a REIT to grow revenue is to attain higher rates of building occupancy and continually increasing rents. As long as the supply and demand for new properties remains in balance and stable, market rents tend to rise as the economy expands, which is demonstrated by a growth in FFO. Beware of dividends that are being paid out of profit from the sale of property or from cash reserves; these payments are not sustainable.

Management is a key determinant in judging the quality of a REIT investment. These are the folks who will steer your ship. Be sure their experience and knowledge is up to the job. Read the prospectus or annual report carefully. Solid management will typically hold debt levels to 35 percent or less of the total capitalization of the trust. Some managers have long tenure and have weathered many storms. The lower the level of debt, the more conservative management tends to be. Conservative managers who invest their own dollars are a great asset to any REIT. Look for an ownership stake by management. The annual report or a 10k filing will clue you in to whether management holds any sizable positions.

If the REIT you choose is diversified with a number of different types of properties in different geographic regions, you will experience less volatility if an industry or locale experiences hard times. If you are more concentrated, be sure that the type of property or the geographic area continues to be economically viable into the foreseeable future. Occupancy rates for past and current years are available for most major and some smaller cities in the U.S. from commercial real estate Web sites. This information can help you determine whether your REIT has a bright or dim future in store.

Fortunately, listed REITs are reviewed by the major rating agencies, such as Standard & Poor's and Moody's. These sources of information can be very helpful in examining the operating results of particular REITs.

REIT appraisal is difficult, but there is another way! Many mutual fund families have funds built around REIT investments. REIT mutual funds are an easy way to get exposure to REITs without spending volumes of time researching the valuations of underlying holdings, vacancy rates, economic vibrancy, and so on. REITs are available through both closed- and open-end style funds. These can be researched just as any other fund.

A Shiny New Convertible (Bond)

Convertible securities — bonds and preferred stocks — are another interesting hybrid investment for the value investor. Brought about in part from a need to provide bond investors with a way to participate in the growth of the company, and the need of companies to reduce capital costs, convertible securities come to market and have been around for a while. Value investors can use convertibles as a way to produce safe income, and *in addition,* tap into the growth of successful businesses, often with a large discount to potential future value.

What are they?

A convertible bond has the same qualities as a straight bond (a fixed coupon and a set maturity date for return of principle) as well as an equity kicker or sweetener. Convertible preferred stock is senior to common stock in corporate liquidations, but for most other purposes it trades like a bond that pays regular dividends. The sweetener in the case of converts (as they are often called) is an enhancement that offers the investor an option to exchange the security for common stock. Naturally, there is no free lunch on Wall Street, but the conversion feature can be so attractive that the coupon is lower than prevailing bond yields. The conversion price is usually 15 to 25 percent higher than the common stock's current price at issuance, so if the stock price doesn't rise by that amount or more the investor has no reason to convert, and will sit back and collect the interest.

The investor must pay for the privilege of potential profit from the right to convert to common stock. If the stock price doesn't move in the investor's favor (that is, up), the investor loses only the difference between the amount of coupon available had he invested in a straight bond and the lower yielding amount paid by the convertible. The cost of the right to convert is that lower coupon. The issuer can pay you less in yield by offering this enhancement. As a tradeoff, the stock price may rise substantially and you'll profit from the strengthening of the stock price: Investors are basically betting on the upside of the stock price to juice up returns.

Convertibles, like other bonds, are typically issued in $1,000 increments. They are traded in bond markets, but not very actively. All convertibles are issued with documents that outline the *conversion ratio,* the number of common shares for which your bond can be converted; this is the number of shares of common stock the investor would receive in exchange for the bond if he chose to convert.

For example, a bond issued by Xerox may be convertible to 90 shares of Xerox convertible stock; thus the conversion ratio is 90. The *conversion value* is the current selling price of the underlying stock multiplied by the conversion ratio. Because the stock is currently trading at $10 per share, the current conversion value is $900 (90 shares at $10 each). This represents the current value of the bond if the conversion option were exercised and the shares of the common were immediately sold. Obviously, in this example the investor is better served holding the bond and collecting the coupon than converting. If the selling price of the stock moved to $18, the new conversion value would be $1,620 — a tidy $620 profit!

Obviously, the attractiveness of any convertible is directly correlated to the potential for gains on the common stock. Issuers know this and have taken advantage of the investor's craving for the upside potential of common stock by offering lower coupon to investors on convertibles. Here's an example to clarify this point: AOL is currently offering two 20-year bonds — a straight bond yielding 5.7 percent and a convertible yielding 4.5 percent. The possibility for capital gains on the underlying common stock of AOL may be enough to entice investors to accept 1.6 percent less in coupon. Assuming an investor does not convert during the first year he owns the bond, he has paid $12 for the privilege of owning the convertible. Instead of earning $57 in interest, he accepted $45 in hopes that the common stock price would rise.

The *investment value* of the bond is the price at which the security would trade if there were no conversion feature. This value is determined by the rating the bond receives from agencies such as Moody's or Standard & Poor's. The ratings agencies categorize the bond based relative to its peer group much the same way straight bonds are rated. The investment value is the price the bond would trade at if the company's stock declines to a price that makes the convertible feature of the bond worthless. Assuming the company is solvent and able to continue making debt payments, the bond will trade based on its yield alone, like every other bond.

Figure 19-1 shows the relationships between stock price, investment value, conversion value, and convertible price.

Information, please

Besides knowing how to comprehend conversion ratios and values easily in your head, the hardest part of convertible investing is finding out about the darned things in the first place. Bond listings are hard to find — major newspapers only publish small excerpts of bond trading activity, and converts are seldom traded very actively. You have to dig. And there is less available on the Internet than on just about any other type of investment we can name.

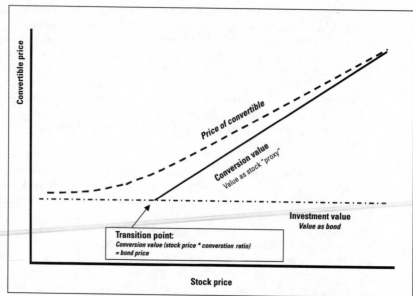

Figure 19-1:
Convertible
bond price
and price
factors.

Probably the best information source available for the average investor is the Value Line Convertibles Survey. This is a special subscription, separate from the Investment Survey. Trial subscriptions are commonly available for $65. The survey provides an excellent convertibles investing guide, lists of convertibles and their relevant statistics, and a ranking. The listing describes the security, but not the company, so you'll have to refer back to the Investment Survey for that.

You can find other convertible bond information on the Web, but it isn't easy, and we would judge the available resources as thin and inadequate compared to other investing resources we've found. Online brokerages have bond centers giving detailed information about credit ratings and yields, but little information (and no selection tools at the sites we checked) to isolate convertibles. There is one other site worth mentioning: ConvertBond.com (www.convertbond.com), a division of Morgan Stanley Dean Witter, Inc. The site is set up around convertibles and provides analysis and commentary, but it requires registration and a monthly subscription fee.

Even getting quotes is difficult. If you know a symbol and use a broker screen, you can get quotes. But finding out what's available in the first place may require a resource like Value Line.

Investing in convertibles

As value investors, we actively search for bargains provided by market ineffi-
ciencies. As we've seen from examples in past chapters, boring market sectors often fall out of favor in favor of sexier, high flyers. For value investors,
bonds in out-of-favor industries trading at or close to their investment value
can be a profitable opportunity. Buying bonds at their investment value can
significantly increase the bond yield and yield to maturity. Patient value
investors use convertibles as a proxy to buy and hold an underlying stock at
a low price waiting for the market to recognize its mistake. With convertibles,
value investors are literally being paid a coupon while they wait.

Convertibles give bond investors the potential for capital gains while avoiding
the risk of major declines experienced when owning common stock. Price
movements are cushioned by the bond's interest payment. Even when the
stock price is dropping fast, the coupon payment can entice investors to hang
in there. The price for the issuer's common stock tends to have the biggest
influence on the price of the convertible; if the stock price rises, the bond
price will also rise. Prices for convertible bonds behave like a stock when
their conversion value is above face value and like a bond when their conversion value is below face (refer to Figure 19-1). Unless deeply in the money, convertibles will be less volatile. An easy rule of thumb for investors to remember
is that convertibles will give you 60 to 70 percent of the performance on the
upside of the common stock with only 50 percent of the volatility.

Part V
The Part of Tens

The 5th Wave   By Rich Tennant

"In the interest of a future stock issuance, I highly recommend you _NOT_ use your family name as part of your corporate identity, Mr. Defunct."

In this part . . .

We present for your enjoyment some top-ten lists: ten characteristics of a good value stock, ten indications of an overvalued stock, and the ten habits of successful investors.

Chapter 20

Ten Signs of Value

> *The definition of a great company is one that will be great for 25 or 30 years.*
>
> —Warren Buffett

Finding value in a business is both art *and* science. Every investor combines art and science in his own way to develop his own set of value tenets to guide the investing process. But to help summarize, we draw ten core signs of value from material presented earlier in the book. Tangible signs are financial fundamentals leading directly to earnings and business growth, while intangible signs are leading indicators of good financial fundamentals. When all or most signs are present, the business is on the right track.

Tangible: Steady or Increasing Return on Equity (ROE)

ROE is the bottom-line return on equity capital invested. ROE is a composite measure, combining internal measures of profitability, productivity, and capital structure. For ROE to increase, at least one of these internal measures must be on the rise, and all three must be effectively managed to preserve the gain. As we explain in Chapter 13, when companies such as IBM improve all three component measures simultaneously, ROE growth can be dramatic.

As companies earn money, that money goes into retained earnings or is paid out to shareholders. Steady or increasing ROE is a sign of health, particularly for companies with a strategy to retain earnings. For those companies, increasing ROE is an especially challenging and worthy goal because the equity base, or denominator, consistently grows. A company steadily growing ROE is usually firing on all cylinders.

We like to see ROE greater than 15 percent and steady, or better yet, growing. We like a balanced approach, where profitability, productivity, and capital structure are all improving. And we like to see share repurchases to reduce the equity denominator, particularly when funded by excess cash generated by the business rather than external borrowing. Good ROE performance tells us that a lot of other things are going right, and is *prima facie* evidence of good management focused on the right things.

Tangible: Strong and Growing Profitability

Nothing grows a stock price like earnings. Earnings growth will do it every time, yet for some reason, investors like to invest without looking at a most important driver: profitability. Sales growth too can drive earnings growth, but sales growth sooner or later hits a wall. Investors forget that improving profitability is another path, besides sales growth, to achieve earnings growth. They also forget that *declining* profitability causes greater reliance on sales growth — a risky proposition.

Investors should look at total profitability and profitability trends. Like many other business fundamentals, profitability can be deconstructed into components: gross margin, operating expenses (particularly SG&A), operating margin, and net profit margin.

High gross margin is a sign of market power, and market power is a leading indicator of improving gross margins. Expense growth rates should run lower than sales growth rates. Otherwise, economies of scale are compromised. Look at profitability trends and comparisons to like industry players. Effective management and solid market positions lead to improved profitability, and improved profitability leads to improved earnings performance and stock price performance.

Tangible: Improving Productivity

Improving productivity is straightforward but often overlooked by casual investment approaches. Assets are resources employed by the company and contributed by shareholders to produce income. Is the company making good use of its assets? Is the company generating more sales and profits per unit or dollar of assets employed?

Look at both dollar and unit asset productivity. Find out the same store sales, sales per square foot, revenue per seat mile, revenue per employee, or sales per fixed asset or current asset dollar. Solid unit productivity numbers show strong markets and good management, while chronic declines and poor industry comparisons reflect the opposite, foretelling asset write-offs, increased capital requirements, and death by a thousand other cuts.

Tangible: Producer, Not Consumer, of Capital

If a company generates enough cash from its operations to pay down debt and buy back shares, that's a good thing. If the company generates insufficient cash to grow or even maintain the business, that's a bad thing. Look closely at the statement of cash flows (particularly over time)to find out whether the company produces excess cash and capital that can be employed elsewhere to grow company value or that can be returned to you as dividends or, even better, share buybacks. Focus on cash sourced from operations, used for business investments, and obtained from or returned to capital markets as financing.

Tangible: The Right Valuation Ratios

The market decouples price from the value of the business. As Warren Buffett says, price is what you pay, and value is what you get. If the markets were perfect, price and value would go hand in hand, but as we all know, markets aren't perfect.

Once you appraise the business value, look at price and use valuation ratios to connect the price to the business. The venerable P/E ratio is where most investors start, but it doesn't tell the whole story. Value investors look at present and future earnings yield (1 ÷ P/E). PEG — price earnings to growth — relates P/E to growth rates and tells you something about that earnings yield future. The relationships between price to sales (P/S), profit margins, price to book (P/B), and ROE are also important.

So a P/E of 25 or less is good given today's alternative earnings yields, but it doesn't mean that much without looking at the other numbers. We like to see a PEG of 2 or less, a P/S of 3 or less, and a P/B of 5 or less for growing companies and lower figures for steady or transitioning companies.

Intangible: A Franchise

Market power is tantamount to lasting earnings power, and a franchise (a market position that's difficult or impossible to duplicate) is the cornerstone of market power. An obvious, defensible franchise puts a company in a much better position to preserve and grow value. Franchises are a "moat" around the business. Companies that don't have a franchise are continuously vulnerable to competitive threats and must spend millions just to preserve the position they have.

Franchise drives improved current and future business results. Look for brand strength, product differentiation, intellectual property, international recognition, and channel position. If a company has something that another company can't reproduce regardless of resources, there is franchise value.

Intangible: Price Control

A company in control of its product prices probably possesses franchise power and is using it effectively. A company that markets its products and competes on virtues other than price has good market position. That company is more likely to preserve and grow future profit margins. If price is the central issue in every buyer's purchase decision, that's a problem. If a company must continually compete on price or mark down its merchandise or services to sell them, look for future trouble.

Watch a company in the marketplace, including its advertisements and overall approach to marketing. Ever see a Ford or Chrysler commercial that didn't have something about price (or financing rates)? Ever see an ad from BMW or Mercedes that *did?* Well, never say never, but the German carmakers are competing on product and franchise, while their American cousins must depend on price. Companies in control of their pricing are in much better position to deliver solid business results than companies that don't.

Intangible: Market Leadership

Market share is important in achieving price control and economies of scale in producing, marketing, and delivering products. A company with a large market share has an advantage, while those with small or declining market share must pay up just to catch up.

Look at the market position and share of a business and see whether it's a leader in its — or most of its — markets. Read industry reports from the trade press, financial press, and analysts. Then decide whether the company is there just because it got there first or whether it really has the products and franchise to stay there for the long term. If you decide that it's the latter, you're probably looking at value, but watch yourself when you go to market. You may be required to "pay up" for that value.

Intangible: Candid Management

Strong management and good leadership are often obvious just from a company's behavior. A company should achieve celebrity status in its industry and may even go beyond, such as GE did under CEO Jack Welch. The theory is that management that communicates with the press, with shareholders, and with its customers is probably doing a good job and has nothing to hide. The theory goes further to applaud management teams who do make mistakes and are able to admit them and correct them publicly. These management teams know what's going on and aren't afraid to deal with it, and they probably have the skills to do so.

Intangible: Customer Care

A company that appreciates the value of its customer base and capitalizes on that value is better positioned for long-term success. That company spends less to acquire new customers and has another "moat" to protect it from competition. Look for companies that know their customers and treat them as something more important than advertising targets. Look for situations of strong and unusual brand loyalty. Look for companies that manage customers as an asset to be valued, listened to, cared for, and retained — not a liability, where interactions and the costs of those interactions are the main focus. If a company is a faceless bureaucracy producing stupid products that customers don't want and if it has a reputation for poor service and response to customer issues, look out below.

Chapter 21

Ten Signs of Unvalue

> *Oftentimes, a little common sense will let you determine whether a stock is a screaming value or whether an outrageous price has robbed the stock of all future appeal.*
>
> —Timothy Vick, *How to Pick Stocks Like Warren Buffett*

Sometimes the best way to learn what something *is* is to observe what it is *not*. This chapter tells you what to avoid in your quest for value.

Tangible: Deteriorating Margins

Declining profit margins are usually a sign of trouble. Total earnings or earnings-per-share declines can happen in economic downturns when sales fall, but profit margins should remain relatively intact. Declining *gross* margins suggest declining market power, increased competition, product commoditization, deteriorating product mix, increased production cost structures, and a long list of other business evils. Declining *net* margins imply asset quality and efficiency problems and poor expense control.

Expenses, especially selling, general, and administrative (SG&A), should grow at less than the sales growth rate. When expense growth matches or, worse, exceeds sales growth, internal expense controls aren't working, and economies of scale are lost. Companies in start-up mode and larger companies with far-flung worldwide operations have particular difficulty here. If expenses grow because of a well-documented and communicated strategic initiative, such as a customer acquisition or retention campaign, that may be okay. But nameless, faceless, and growing expenses lead to trouble.

And if the company is losing money rather than reporting profits, there had better be a real good reason and clearly articulated evidence of a turnaround. Unless it's a minor and explainable blip on an otherwise good long-term track record, there is no place in a value portfolio for a money-losing business.

Tangible: Receivables or Inventory Growth Outpacing Sales

If accounts or notes receivable on the balance sheet grow faster than sales, a company is effectively lending money to its customers to buy its products. This is a very dangerous situation.

Excessive growth in either receivables or inventory as a percent of sales, especially if persistent, indicates loss of market and channel power. Company-made products aren't being bought on their merits but rather because of the terms (receivables) or availability (inventory). If inventory increases are caused by poor management and control, there is exposure to missed deliveries as the company tightens the inventory belt, resulting in too little of the *right* inventory. These indicators signify more trouble inside the company and in the marketplace, and they consistently lead to write-offs and loss of business when they become no longer sustainable.

Tangible: Poor Earnings Quality

If earnings appear to grow but you don't see matching growth in cash flows or book value, that's a sign that earnings are being generated on the back of accounting gimmicks. (Dividend payouts can also reduce cash flow and book value growth, so be sure to account for a high dividend payout.) With conservative accounting, cash flow should run consistently ahead of earnings with normal depreciation and amortization expenses.

Tangible: Inconsistent Results

Value investors like consistency and avoid surprises in top-line and bottom-line figures and everything in between. Companies prone to large write-offs raise questions about asset value and business decisions made over time. Good management teams react well to changes in market conditions and manage their businesses accordingly, while inattentive management teams let market conditions dictate their results — or worse. Look for steady margins, return on equity (ROE), asset productivity and valuations, expenses, and cash flows.

Tangible: Good Business, but Stock Is Too Expensive

Generalizing about these topics is hard, but price-to-earnings (P/E) ratio, PEG (price/earnings to growth), P/S (price to sales), and P/B (price to book) well in excess of market and industry averages spell trouble in making the numbers, as does overdependence on abnormal margins.

Look at P/E related to the market and the industry and look at earnings yield. Over 40 (2.5 percent earnings yield) is hard to justify in any case, and over 25 is hard to justify unless the growth story is there and intact. PEG greater than 3, P/S greater than 3, and P/B greater that 10 are signs of overcooked prices and raise questions of vulnerability and value.

Intangible: Acquisition Addiction

Acquisitions can be made for a variety of reasons, and many of them are valid. Plugging a product line gap or removing a key competitor from the market-place can justify an acquisition. But when a company makes acquisition after acquisition, seemingly just to grow the business (that is, keep the top line moving) beware.

Acquisitions are almost always difficult, consuming company focus and resources and causing at least some customer confusion. These short-term ramifications can usually be dealt with, but occasionally the resulting structure and culture clash can bring down otherwise viable businesses. When management is focused on making and digesting acquisitions, it's not focused on the core business, which can drift quickly towards out of control. And every acquisition adds a little more air to the goodwill balloon on the balance sheet, perhaps causing it eventually to pop.

Look at a company's acquisition history and see whether the company makes *good* acquisitions. Look at the resulting product line, market acceptance, and corporate culture. Also look at the history and growth of goodwill. If this makes you nervous, stay away.

Intangible: On the Discount Rack

A company continually discounting or incentivizing its products is clearly having trouble in the marketplace. Airfare wars, computer price wars, car wars, and the like are a bad sign. And although many of the companies involved hang the limited-time-only justification on such activities, they tend to be chronic. If a company appears to always depend on price gimmicks to grow — or worse, maintain — sales, look out. Has anyone paid the full $4.59 for a 12-pack of Coke lately?

Intangible: Losing Market Share

Some companies seem to continually beat their heads against the wall just to preserve market share, and sometimes, a very small market share to start with. Chronic market share erosion is disastrous. Companies lose economies of scale and pricing power and may have to resort to expensive campaigns just to stem the tide. And it doesn't do much for internal morale, let alone shareholder morale. Signs are everywhere: from what you see on the shelves to what you read in the press to what the companies (sometimes) tell you themselves.

As a general rule, avoid companies under siege in the marketplace.

Intangible: Can't Control Cost Structure

The inability to control the cost structure may sound the same as the deteriorating margins discussed earlier in this chapter, with emphasis on control and management of costs and expenses. But this one goes deeper — into the very cost structure of the business itself and the resources used to produce its products. Companies requiring tight resources over which they have little to no control are in a vulnerable position with little chance for above-average performance. Companies with expensive, frequently replaced, capital-intensive cost structures requiring continuous capital infusion also have bad field position with respect to value.

The classic case is the airline industry. Fuel, labor, airplanes, and airport slots make an airline work and together comprise perhaps 80 to 90 percent of an airline's cost structure. Yet, airlines have zero control over the price of any of these inputs. You know the oil story. Airlines are labor intensive and unionized, and their relationships with the unions have hardly been a strength. Airplanes are made by two companies and have long lead times with competition for the best models. And airport slots and air routes are controlled by governments. Need we say more?

Airlines thus have almost no influence or control over the inputs vital to their business, and they're subject to dips and wide swings in profitability when one or more factors go out of control. They can't easily adjust or control their business. And if they do find a way to be successful and achieve higher returns, one of these constituents will want a piece of the action. We're not saying that success is impossible (witness Southwest Airlines), but the odds are against it.

Intangible: Management in Hiding

It happens over and over. Management teams, once exuberant in talking up their successes, simply disappear when things start to go bad. Anyone seen much of Larry Ellison or Carly Fiorina or Jeff Bezos or Michael Armstrong lately? One could launch the argument that they're busy and focused on dealing with their business problems, but at the same time, one wonders. This is the opposite of management candor. Instead of publicly identifying and facing problems and articulating clear strategies for a return to success, they simply go into hiding. Now, you may not expect them to appear on CNBC every day to be considered candid, and you may not really care for celebrity managers. But if there's something important to say about the business, they should be around to say it.

And if they *do* come forth, it sounds like something you could have said yourself. "We've had a real tough quarter with this downturn blah, blah, blah . . . things are bad in Europe . . . blah, blah . . . and have limited visibility to the immediate future . . . blah, blah, blah . . . but we're expecting things to improve by the end of Q4." Managers who admit mistakes, discuss what parts of the business are hurting, explain the customer context, review specific financials, and articulate strategies to revitalize demand in certain businesses and exit others get a higher score with value investors.

Chapter 22

Ten Habits of Highly Successful Value Investors

All there is to investing is picking good stocks at good times and staying with them as long as they remain good companies.

—Warren Buffett

This chapter presents ten things to remember as you evolve your value investing style.

Do the Due Diligence

We're not talking about a dance, but as a value investor you must walk the walk — consistently, continuously, and with good form and focus. A value investor is rational and doesn't jump into an investment without knowing why. In business, you can't know everything, but you do need to examine the important stuff. Diligence continues beyond the purchase, keeping up with industry trends and company performance.

Think Independently and Trust Yourself

Be your own analyst. Do your own research and figure out what works for you. Don't listen to sales pitches, gossip, and hype. Be different and be proud to be different. The more different you are, the more you're likely to make in the market — in the long run. Think and act independently.

You've all heard this or that portfolio manager on CNBC espousing the virtues of his favorite stock. Few give solid fundamental reasons for their picks, and in many cases, they may actually be pumping positions they're already in to make a sale. Remember, portfolio managers, Wall Street firms, and brokers are in the business to make money. Remember who's who and what they're likely to want.

As a value investor, you should do your own research founded on real numbers emerging from the business. Chat rooms, TV, and industry and analyst forecasts are dangerous replacements for your own thinking.

Ignore the Market

Smart, well-equipped investors continually try to time the market. That approach been generally proven to be a waste of time. But more than that, buying a stock because of its price moves — particularly upward — is usually the *worst* reason to buy. Focus on the business and fundamentals and look at the market simply as a place to execute the transaction.

Always Think Long Term

This advice goes along with ignoring the market. A good business is a good business in the long term. Otherwise it isn't a good business. And never, ever forget the value of compounding and how negative performance negates its effects.

Remember That You're Buying a Business

Approach a stock purchase as though you were buying a company for yourself, even if you're buying only a millionth of it. Look at it as a business, not a stock. Think inside out. Become an expert on the company and the industry — understand the business. *Know how it makes its money.* Be able to explain the business, the industry, and your rationale for buying the stock, to a 10-year-old kid or any other bystander. By doing that, you'll get better at explaining it to yourself.

And don't forget that it's your own money. This applies to all investing, not just value investing. We're continually amazed at how people throw good, hard-earned money at almost anything, spending as little as a couple of minutes to analyze and execute an investment.

Always Buy "on Sale"

As a value investor, you want to own a good business, but value investing goes further than that. You want to own a good business *at an attractive price.* Sticking to this rule expands the potential return and creates the margin of safety or "moat" around your investment. When you buy at a favorable price, you create room for error and greater room for growth and tie up less capital. The excitement and satisfaction that you feel when getting a bargain in real life also applies to investing — with much greater long-term benefits.

Keep Emotion Out of It

A Southwest Airlines flight attendant once admonished passengers who were apparently taking too long to select a seat, "You aren't buying furniture, folks, just picking a place to park it for the next 50 minutes."

The wisdom shared is about avoiding emotional attachments to stocks and the businesses they represent. If you "LUV" Southwest Airlines, don't invest in it until you like the numbers. And if the numbers look good and you invest, but they start to look bad later, be able to recognize that. Value investors continuously look for the good and the bad and keep their rational wits about them as they decide to buy and keep their investments. The purpose of an investment is to achieve a greater financial goal and not to become a member of the family.

Don't hesitate to admit your mistakes. As we want our management teams to do, so must we do for ourselves. Value investors admit their mistakes and learn from them. They take the time to understand what changed (or was overlooked in the first place), and they move on. They have a rational "sell" model and aren't afraid to sell a business when underlying reasons to own it have changed or if the price is way out of line with value.

Invest to Meet Goals, Not to Earn Bragging Rights

Your investing should be aimed at one purpose: to earn money and build a secure long-term financial future. Other goals and objectives bring danger. Don't try to be better than everyone else, and bragging about your two-baggers at the water cooler is bad form and bad practice. Sound, consistent objectives, with a sustained, consistent approach for meeting them, work best. Be the tortoise, not the hare.

Swing Only at Good Pitches

If something looks good, wait. There may be something better. This is one of the harder pieces of advice to follow. You see a company you like, and it's selling at 75 percent of intrinsic value. Fundamentals look good, but there may be a question or two about intangibles. You have $20K in the bank from unloading those beaten-down tech stocks to realize this year's capital loss. Should you buy? It depends. If you pulled a screen of 20 companies, look at them all. Try a different screen. And if the ones you find are a good value today, chances are, if you're really playing for the longer term, they'll be a good value tomorrow and even a few days from now. Patience is a core virtue of the value investor.

Keep Your Antennae Up

Stop, look, and listen. Always be on the lookout for signs, large and small, of opportunity. Be equally aware of what's going on with companies you already own. Own Starbucks? Visit the place and have a latte once in a while. Own Ford? Rent one the next time you rent a car. Hilton Hotels? United Airlines? You get the picture. If you own a business that makes air compressors and tools but have no need for these tools yourself, ask someone who does, such as the next-door neighbor/contractor. And if you wish to hang out in the rail yard counting tank cars as Mr. Buffett once did, remember to stop, look, and listen there, too.

Index

• *B* •

• **C** •

margins, significance of, 333–334
market. *See also* stock
  attitude of Benjamin Graham toward, 33
  fluctuations, attitude toward, 10–11
  growth history analysis, 26–27
  growth rates, 27
  importance of, 340
  long-term growth rate, 25
  mutual fund performance, diversification and, 68
  P/E, growth and, 27–28
  REIT, risks, 317
  significance of, 24
  value stock growth in, 29
market cap funds (mutual funds), style box, 300
Market Guide (Multex), 164
market share
  business value and, 25
  defined
  discussion of, 242–243
  significance of, 336
market tenets (Warren Buffett), 256–257
market value, 12
maturity date, convertible bonds, 320
Median P/E
  defined, 266
  hurdle rate and, 273
Microsoft Money, screening tools, 290
momentum investing
  characteristics of, 15
  overview, 17
money
  appreciation over time, 50–51
  cash assets, 108
  compounding example, 53–55
  compounding formula, 51–53
  interest, 50
  rule of 72, 56–57
Morningstar Investment Services, 302
  capital gains information, 306
  fund selector, Web site, 302
  stock selector (stock screener), 85

  style box, 299
  Web site, 29
mortgage REITs, 315
Motley Fool
  Foolish Flow ratio, 168
  Web site, 79
Multex Investor Market Guide, ROE numbers and, 220
Multex Investor Web site, 85
mutual funds
  backloading, 299
  benefits, 296
  blend funds, 301
  capital gains, 306
  CBS Marketwatch Web site, 302
  closed-end, 297–298
  closed-end funds, 307–309
  commissions, 299
  control over, 304
  convenience of, 305
  customer service, 305
  discounts, 298
  diversification and, 305
  ease of entry, 307
  expenses, 304
  fees, 304
  front-end load, 299
  fund selectors, Web sites, 302
  growth funds, 301
  information gathering, 301–302
  load, 298–299
  Morningstar web site, 302
  NAV, 298
  open-end, 297–298
  overview, 297–299
  as owners, 248
  performance, assets and, 304
  performance, diversification and, 68
  price, 298
  professional management and, 303–304
  pros and cons, 302–307
  purchase convenience, 305

strategic profit formula, 214
testing first-tier components, 219
tiered fundamentals and, 218
un-value and, 278
value and, 277
Value Line, 220
variations, 174
role of company in industry, analysis and, 291
ROTC (return on total capital), compared to ROE, 216
rule FAS 123, 151
rule of 72, 56–57
rules, AGAP, 11

• S •

sales
  $20 billion wall, 67
  growth, significance of, 334
  income statements, 129
  mutual funds, 305
  P/E and, 274
sales per employee ratio, 168
sales per square foot ratio, 168
sales to asset ratio, ROE and, 224
scenarios, appraisal and, 293
screening tools
  analysis and, 290
  industry understanding and, 290–291
SEC 13F filings, 42
SEC (Securities and Exchange Commission), 92–93
  accounting practice watchdog activity, 156–157
  EDGAR Online, 82–83
  GAAP implementation and, 146
  Web site, 93
second-stage growth rates, 201
securities, convertible securities, 320–323
Security Analysis (Benjamin Graham), 15, 32–33

Security Analysis (David Dodd), 15
selection step in analysis, 290
SG&A (selling, general, and administrative) operating expenses
  overview, 132
  ROE and, 222
share price, book value and, 35
shareholder letters (Berkshire Hathaway), locating, 79
size, value funds, 310
small cap funds (mutual funds), style box, 300
smoke and mirrors, asset plays and, 286
soft assets, 34, 115–116
S&P 500 (Standard & Poor's 500 index)
  P/E activity, 27
  Price and Earnings over 50 years, 25–26
S&P Stock Screener, 84
specialized-equity funds, 308
speculation investing
  attitude of Benjamin Graham toward, 32
  characteristics of, 15
  overview, 19
spreadsheet models
  discounting calculations and, 63
  growth assumptions, 197–201
  intrinsic valuation, 195
statement of cash flows
  defined, 97
  information in, 77
statistical models, technical investing, 16
stock. *See also* market
  bargains, working capital and, 34
  blue chip, 17
  bond yield, relationship to, 36
  buying, reasons for, 9
  convertible securities, 320–323
  cyclical, 127
  diversification, wisdom of, 67–68
  earnings yield *versus* bonds, 269
  glamour, 17